Turbo C++ for Windows Inside & Out

Herbert Schildt

Turbo C++ for Windows Inside & Out

Osborne **McGraw-Hill**

Berkeley New York St. Louis San Francisco
Auckland Bogotá Hamburg London Madrid
Mexico City Milan Montreal New Delhi Panama City
Paris São Paulo Singapore Sydney
Tokyo Toronto

Osborne **McGraw-Hill**
2600 Tenth Street
Berkeley, California 94710
U.S.A.

For information on translations or book distributors outside of the U.S.A., please write to Osborne **McGraw-Hill** at the above address.

Turbo C++ for Windows Inside & Out

234567890 DOC 998765432

ISBN 0-07-881778-1

Publisher
Kenna S. Wood

Acquisitions Editor
Jeffrey M. Pepper

Associate Editor
Emily Rader

Technical Editor
Jeffrey Hsu

Project Editor
Laura Sackerman

Copy Editor
Dusty Bernard

Proofreading Coordinator
Wendy Goss

Proofreaders
Mick Arellano
Jeff Barash

Indexer
Valerie Robbins

Quality Control Specialist
Bob Myren

Computer Designer
Fred Lass

Illustrator
Susie C. Kim

Cover Designer
Mason Fong

Contents at a Glance

Part I

Part II

Contents

Part II

Introduction

Welcome to *Turbo C++ for Windows Inside & Out*. This book is a fast-start guide to both Turbo C++ programming and Windows programming using Borland's new ObjectWindows class library.

This book is divided into two parts:

Part I: The C++ Language

Part II: Windows Programming Using ObjectWindows

Part I teaches the Turbo C++ programming language. As you probably know, C++ is the extension of the C language that supports object-oriented programming. Turbo C++ supports the latest specification for both C—its base language—and C++. Because most programmers moving to C++ and to Windows programming already know C, this book concentrates on the C++ extensions. The advantage of this approach is that you don't need to wade through reams of material that you already know to find information about the new C++ features.

Important: This book assumes that you are a competent C programmer. If you don't know C, you must learn it before you can program in Turbo C++ or do Windows programming.

Once you know C++, you can proceed to Part II, which discusses Windows programming using Turbo C++ for Windows. Windows is a very complex programming environment. In fact, to fully describe all aspects of Windows requires several thousand pages of technical documentation. Therefore, it is far beyond the scope of this book to attempt to teach Windows programming in general. It is assumed that you have some minimal knowledge of Windows programming and access to Windows technical reference manuals. The purpose of this book is to introduce you to Borland's ObjectWindows class library.

ObjectWindows provides an alternative to Windows programming that greatly simplifies the task of creating Windows applications. If you have ever written a Windows application, you know how long and arduous a task it can be. Fortunately, using ObjectWindows, most of the details are masked from you and many of the tedious clerical details are performed automatically, behind the scenes.

Because ObjectWindows provides a convenient interface to the Windows programming environment, it, too, is quite large and complicated, requiring several hundred pages just to describe its features. This book does not try to describe its every feature and nuance. Instead, it provides a portal into ObjectWindows programming to help you get started quickly. In essence, this book is designed to help you get on the "fast track" to ObjectWindows programming.

Floppy Disk Offer

There are many useful and interesting functions, classes, and programs contained in this book. If you are like me, you would like to use them, but hate typing them into the computer. When I key in routines from a book it always seems that I type something wrong and spend hours trying to get the program to work. For this reason, I am offering the source code on floppy disk for all the functions and programs contained in this book, for $24.95. Just fill in the order blank on the next page and mail it, along with your payment, to the address shown. Or, if you're in a hurry, just call (217) 586-4021 (the number of my consulting office) and place your order by telephone. (VISA and MasterCard are accepted.)

Please send me _____ copies, at $24.95 each, of the programs in *Turbo C++ for Windows Inside & Out* on an IBM-compatible floppy disk.

Foreign orders only: Checks must be drawn on a U.S bank. Please add $5.00 for shipping and handling.

_____
Name

_____
Address

_____   _____   _____
City   State   ZIP

_____
Telephone number

Disk size (check one): 5 1/4" _____   3 1/2"_____

Method of payment: Check_____   VISA_____   MC_____

Credit card number: _____

Expiration date: _____

Signature: _____

Send to:

   Herbert Schildt
   398 County Road 2500 N
   Mahomet, IL 61853

or phone: (217) 586-4021
or FAX: (217) 586-4997

This offer subject to change or cancellation at any time.

Please allow 3 to 6 weeks for delivery. Osborne **McGraw-Hill** assumes NO responsibility for this offer. This is solely an offer of the author, Herbert Schildt, and not of Osborne **McGraw-Hill**.

PART

I

The C++ Language

*I*n Part I of this book you learn about C++'s object oriented extensions to the C language. Using Turbo C++ for Windows to create Windows programs requires that you have a firm understanding of C++. Specifically, you need to understand inheritance, overloading, and virtual functions.

C++ is essentially a superset of C, so everything you already know about C is applicable to C++. Many of the concepts embodied in C++ will be new, but don't worry; you are starting from a firm base.

Remember, this book assumes that you are an accomplished Turbo C programmer. If you are not, you must take some time to learn C, and specifically Turbo C. You cannot become a C++ programmer until you know C. Further, creating Windows applications is a challenging pursuit. It will be much easier for you if you are firmly grounded in C. (Windows programming is not for the novice programmer!)

The examples presented in Part I are not Windows applications. That is, they do not take advantage of the windowed environment and the special I/O functions that it requires. Instead, they use traditional TTY-based I/O functions. The reason for this is that you cannot write a Windows application using C++ until you know C++. However, you can use Turbo C++ for Windows to compile and run every program in this book without any trouble.

CHAPTER

An Overview of C++

*T*his chapter provides an overview of the central concepts embodied in C++. As you will see, the main features of C++ are highly interrelated, and a discussion of one often assumes prior knowledge of another. To help reduce this problem, this chapter introduces several features and techniques. Keep in mind that everything discussed here is examined in further detail in subsequent chapters.

Originally called "C with classes," C++ was developed by Bjarne Stroustrup at Bell Laboratories in Murray Hill, New Jersey, in 1980. Its name was changed in 1983 to C++. Since then it has undergone two major revisions—once in 1985 and again in 1989. The current version of C++ is 2.1, and it is this version that is implemented by Turbo C++ for Windows and discussed in this book. Turbo C++ for Windows was first released late in 1991.

As you will see, one of the motivating reasons for the development of C++ was to allow you, the programmer, to handle increasingly complex programs.

Although C++ can be applied to any type of programming task, it is ideally suited for creating Windows applications. One reason for this is that the Windows operating system is organized in an object oriented manner. In fact, in a very real way, a window *is* an object. Thus, Turbo C++ for Windows provides an optimal development environment for Windows applications.

Since C++ is an object oriented programming language and Windows is an object oriented operating system, it is important for you to understand the basic theory behind object oriented programming before learning any specifics about C++.

What Is Object Oriented Programming?

Object oriented programming (OOP for short) is a new way of approaching the job of programming. Approaches to programming have changed dramatically since the invention of the computer. The primary reason for this change is to accommodate the increasing complexity of programs. For example, when computers were first invented, programming was done by toggling in the binary machine instructions using the front panel. As long as programs were just a few hundred instructions long, this approach worked. As programs grew, assembly language was invented so a programmer could deal with larger, increasingly complex programs by using symbolic representations of the machine instructions. As programs continued to grow, high-level languages were introduced that gave the programmer more tools with which to handle complexity. The first widespread language was, of course, FORTRAN. While FORTRAN was a very impressive first step, it is hardly a language that encourages clear and easy-to-understand programs.

The 1960s gave birth to *structured programming.* This is the method encouraged by languages such as C and Pascal. Using structured languages, it was for the first time possible to write moderately complex programs fairly easily. However, once a project reaches a certain size, it gets uncontrollable. At some point, its complexity exceeds that which a programmer can manage even with structured programming.

Consider this: at each milestone in the development of programming, methods were created to allow the programmer to deal with increasingly greater complexity. Each step of the way, a new approach took the best elements of the previous methods and moved forward. Today, many projects are near or at the point where the structured approach no longer works. To solve this problem, object oriented programming was invented.

Object oriented programming has taken the best ideas of structured programming and combined them with several powerful new concepts that encourage you to look at the task of programming in a new light. Object oriented programming allows you to more easily decompose a problem into subgroups of related parts of the problem. Then, using the language, you can translate these subgroups into self-contained units called objects.

All object oriented programming languages have three things in common: objects, polymorphism, and inheritance. Let's take a look at these concepts now.

Objects

The single most important feature of an object oriented language is the object. Put simply, an *object* is a logical entity that contains data and code that manipulates that data. Within an object, some of the code and/or data may be private to the object and inaccessible by anything outside the object. Other code and/or data may be public and accessible by other parts of your program. By making sensitive items private, an object can prevent some other, unrelated part of the program from accidentally modifying or incorrectly using the items. The linkage of code and data in this way is referred to as *encapsulation.*

For all intents and purposes, an object is a variable of a user-defined type. It may seem strange at first to think of an object, which links both code and data, as a variable. However, in object oriented programming, this is precisely the case. When you define an object, you are implicitly creating a new data type.

Polymorphism

Object oriented programming languages support *polymorphism,* which essentially means that one name can be used for several related but slightly different purposes. Polymorphism allows one name to be used to specify a general class of action. However, depending upon what type of data is being dealt with, a specific instance of the general case is executed. For example, you might have a program that defines three different types of stacks. One stack might be used for integer values, one for floating-point values, and one for long integers. Because of polymorphism, you can create three sets of functions called **push()** and **pop()**, and the compiler will select the correct routine, depending upon what type of data the function is called with. In this example, the general concept is that of pushing and popping data onto and from a stack. The functions define the specific way this is done for each type of data.

The first object oriented programming languages were interpreters, so polymorphism was, of course, supported at run time. However, C++ is a compiled language. Therefore, in C++, both run-time and and compile-time polymorphism are supported.

Inheritance

Inheritance is the process by which one object can acquire the properties of another object. This is important because it supports the concept of classification. If you think about it, most knowledge is made manageable by hierarchical classifications. For example, a Red Delicious apple is part of the classification *apple,* which in turn is part of the *fruit* class, which is under the larger class *food.* Without the use of classifications, each object would have to explicitly define all of its characteristics. However, when you use classifications, an object need only define those qualities that make it unique within its class. It is the inheritance mechanism that makes it possible for one object to be a specific instance of a more general case.

A Few C++ Fundamentals

Since C++ is a superset of C, most C programs are implicitly C++ programs as well. (There are a few minor differences between ANSI C and C++ that will prevent a very few C programs from being compiled by a C++ compiler. These differences will be discussed in Chapter 7.) This means you can write C++ programs that look just like C programs. However, doing this is comparable to driving your car down the highway using second gear; you just aren't taking full advantage of its capabilities. Further, although C++ will allow you to write C-like programs, most C++ programmers use a style and certain features that are unique to C++. Because it is important to learn to write C++ programs that look like C++ programs, this section introduces a few of these features before moving on to the "meat" of C++.

Let's begin with an example. Examine this C++ program:

```
#include <iostream.h>
#include <stdio.h>

main()
{
  int i;
  char str[80];

  cout << "C++ is fun\n";  // this is a single-line comment
  /* you can still use C style comments, too */

  printf("You can use printf() if you like\n");
```

```
// input a number using >>
cout << "enter a number: ";
cin >> i;

// now, output a number using <<
cout << "your number is " << i << "\n";

// read a string
cout << "enter a string: ";
cin >> str;
// print it
cout << str;

return 0;
}
```

As you can see, this program looks quite different from the average C program. To begin, the header file IOSTREAM.H is included. This file is defined by C++ and is used to support C++-style I/O operations. (The header STDIO.H is included only to support the **printf()** function. It is not needed by the C++ I/O system.)

The next line that looks different is shown here:

```
cout << "C++ is fun\n";   // this is a single-line comment
```

This line introduces two new C++ features. First, the statement

```
cout << "C++ is fun\n";
```

causes **C++ is fun** to be displayed on the screen followed by a carriage return/linefeed combination. In C++, the << has an expanded role. It is still the left shift operator, but when it is used as shown in this example, it is also an output operator. The identifier **cout** is a stream that is, by default, linked to the screen and is similar to C's **stdout**. (Of course, like C, C++ supports I/O redirection, but for the sake of discussion, you can assume that **cout** refers to the screen.) The << operator causes whatever value is on its right side to be output to **cout**. You can use **cout** and the << operator to output any of the built-in data types plus strings of characters.

It is important to note that you can still use **printf()** (as the program illustrates) or any other of C's I/O functions. It is just that many programmers feel that using **cout <<** is more in the spirit of C++.

What follows the output expression is a C++ comment. In C++, comments are defined two ways. First, you can use a C-like comment, which works the same in C++ as it does in C. However, in C++, you can also define a *single-line comment* by using //. When you start a comment with //, whatever follows is ignored by the compiler until the end of the line is reached. In general, C++ programmers use C-like comments when a multiline comment is being created and use C++ single-line comments when only a single-line comment is needed.

Next, the program prompts the user for a number. The number is read from the keyboard using this statement:

```
cin >> i;
```

In C++, the >> operator still retains its right shift meaning. However, when used as shown, it also causes **i** to be given a value read from the stream **cin**, which is, by default, linked to the keyboard. (**cin** is similar to C's **stdin**.) In general, you can use **cin >>** to load a variable of any of the basic data types plus strings.

Although not illustrated by the program, you are free to use any of C's input functions, such as **scanf()**, instead of using **cin >>**. However, as stated, most programmers feel that **cin >>** is more in the spirit of C++.

The standard streams **cin** and **cout** are opened automatically when a C++ program begins execution. While you will not be using these streams when you write Windows applications, they will be used in this part of the book to help you learn C++. (As you may know, Windows I/O requires the use of special functions supplied by the Windows operating system.)

Another interesting line in the program is shown here:

```
cout << "your number is " << i << "\n";
```

As you can probably intuit, this causes the following phrase to be displayed (assuming **i** has the value 100):

```
your number is 100
```

followed by a carriage return/linefeed. In general, you can run together as many << output operations as you want.

The rest of the program demonstrates how you can read and write a string by using **cin >>** and **cout <<**. When reading a string in the manner shown in this program, input will stop when the first whitespace character is encountered. This is similar to the way that **scanf()** operates when inputting a string. (You will learn ways around this in later chapters.)

Running Non-Windows Applications

Traditionally, when you compile a non-Windows application that uses standard console I/O (such as **cout** or **cin** or calls to **printf()**), it will not coexist with the Windows environment. Instead, it will be given the entire screen and full control of the computer, preventing other Windows tasks from executing. The reason for this is obvious: the standard TTY-based I/O system knows nothing about a windowed environment. However, Turbo C++ for Windows includes a powerful new library called EasyWin that is automatically linked to any non-Windows program. This library automatically creates a default window for your program and allows it to run normally in a windowed environment. Just make sure you have selected Windows EXE from the Application menu under the Options main menu. Then, when you compile the examples in Part I of this book, you will be able to run them as is in a window created automatically for them.

 Note   When you compile this and other programs in Part I of this book, you will generate a warning message that simply states that no definition file is present. Definition files are used to create Windows applications and are not needed by the examples in Part I. Therefore, simply ignore the message.

Introducing C++ Classes

Now that you know some of the conventions and special features of C++, it is time to introduce its most important feature: the class. In C++, to create an object, you first must define its general form by using the keyword **class**. A *class* is syntactically similar to a structure. Let's begin with an example. This class defines a type called **queue** that is used to create a queue object.

```
#include <iostream.h>

// this creates the class queue
class queue {
   int q[100];
   int sloc, rloc;
public:
   void init();
   void qput(int i);
   int qget();
};
```

Let's look closely at this class declaration at this time.

A class may contain private as well as public parts. By default, all items defined in the class are private. For example, the variables **q**, **sloc**, and **rloc** are private. This means that they cannot be accessed by any function that is not a member of the class. This is one way that encapsulation is achieved—access to certain items of data can be tightly controlled by keeping them private. Although not shown in this example, you can also define private functions, which may only be called by other members of the class.

To make parts of a class public (that is, accessible to other parts of your program), you must declare them after the **public** keyword. All variables or functions defined after **public** are accessible by all other functions in the program. Essentially, the rest of your program accesses an object through its public functions and data. It should be mentioned at this time that although you can have public variables, philosophically you should try to limit or eliminate their use. Instead, you should make all data private and control access to it through public functions. One other point: notice that the **public** keyword is followed by a colon.

The functions **init()**, **qput()**, and **qget()** are called *member functions* because they are part of the class **queue**. Remember, a class forms a bond between code and data. Only those functions declared in the class have access to the private parts of that class.

Once you have defined a class, you can create an object of that type by using the class name. In fact, the class name becomes a new data type specifier. For example, the following creates an object called **intqueue** of type **queue**:

```
queue intqueue;
```

You may also create variables when the class is defined by putting their names after the closing curly brace, in exactly the same way as you do with a structure.

To review, in C++, the keyword **class** creates a new data type that may be used to create objects of that type. An object is a specific instance of a class.

The general form of a class declaration is

```
class class-name {
    private data and functions
public:
    public data and functions
} object-name-list;
```

Of course, the *object-name-list* may be empty.

Inside the declaration of **queue**, prototypes to the member functions were used. It is important to understand one point: in C++, when you need to tell the compiler about a function, you must use its full prototype form. (Actually, in C++, all functions must be prototyped. Prototypes are not optional.)

When it comes time to actually define a function that is a member of a class, you must tell the compiler which class the function belongs to by qualifying the name with the name of the class of which it is a member. For example, here is one way to code the **qput()** function:

```
void queue::qput(int i)
{
  if(sloc==100) {
    cout << "queue is full";
```

```
   return;
 }
 sloc++;
 q[sloc] = i;
}
```

The :: is called the *scope resolution operator*. It tells the compiler that this version of **qput()** belongs to the **queue** class or, put differently, that this **qput()** is in **queue**'s scope. As you will soon see, in C++, several different classes can use the same function names. The compiler knows which function belongs to which class because of the scope resolution operator and the class name. Because **qput()** is a member of the class **queue**, it may directly access the member variables **sloc** and **q**.

To call a member function from a part of your program that is not part of the class, you must use the object's name and the dot operator. For example, this calls **init()** for object **a**:

```
queue a, b;

a.init();
```

At this point it is very important to understand that **a** and **b** are two separate objects. This means, for example, that initializing **a** does not somehow cause **b** to also be initialized. The only relationship **a** has with **b** is that they are objects of the same type.

Each object of a class contains its own copies of the data included in the class. This means, for example, that **a**'s **sloc**, **rloc**, and **q** are completely separate from **b**'s copy of these variables.

Another important point to understand is that a member function can call another member function directly, without using the dot operator. It is only when a member function is called by code that does not belong to the class that the variable name and the dot operator must be used.

The program shown here puts together all the pieces and missing details and illustrates the **queue** class:

```
#include <iostream.h>
```

```
// this creates the class queue
class queue {
  int q[100];
  int sloc, rloc;
public:
  void init();
  void qput(int i);
  int qget();
};

void queue::init()
{
  rloc = sloc = 0;
}

void queue::qput(int i)
{
  if(sloc==100) {
    cout << "queue is full";
    return;
  }
  sloc++;
  q[sloc] = i;
}

int queue::qget()
{
  if(rloc == sloc) {
    cout << "queue underflow";
    return 0;
  }
  rloc++;
  return q[rloc];
}

main()
{
  queue a, b;  // create two queue objects

  a.init();
  b.init();
```

```
     a.qput(10);
     b.qput(19);

     a.qput(20);
     b.qput(1);

     cout << a.qget() << " ";
     cout << a.qget() << " ";
     cout << b.qget() << " ";
     cout << b.qget() << "\n";

     return 0;
}
```

This program displays

```
10 19 20 1
```

Remember that the private parts of an object are accessible only by functions that are members of that object. For example, a statement like

```
a.rloc = 0;
```

could not be in the **main()** function of the previous program.

 Note   By convention, most C programs have the **main()** function as the first function in the program. However, in the queue program, the member functions of **queue** are defined before the **main()** function. While there is no rule that dictates this (they could be defined anywhere in the program), this is the most common approach used when writing C++ code. This book follows that convention. (Actually, in real applications, the classes associated with a program will usually be contained in a header file.)

A Small Difference Between C and C++

If you look at the preceding program, which implements a queue, you will see that three of the functions, specifically **main()**, **init()**, and **qput()**, take no parameters. In the program, they were declared like this:

```
main()

init()

qput()
```

As you should know, to tell a C compiler that a function takes no parameters requires that **void** be included in that function's parameter list. In C, an empty parameter list simply says *nothing* about the parameters. However, by using **void**, you explicitly tell the C compiler that the function takes *no* parameters. For example, in C, these functions would have most commonly been declared like this:

```
main(void)

init(void)

qput(void)
```

However, in C++, the use of the word **void** in this situation is optional and, indeed, superfluous. That is, in C++, when no parameters are specified in the parameter list, it is implied that the function takes no parameters. Thus, in C++, these two declarations are equivalent:

```
main()

main(void)
```

Since the use of **void** is unnecessary when declaring functions that take no parameters, it will not be used in this context in this book (although it is not an error to do so).

Function Overloading

One way that C++ achieves polymorphism is through the use of function overloading. In C++, two or more functions can share the same name as long as their parameter declarations are different. In this situation, the functions that share the same name are said to be *overloaded,* and the process is referred to as *function overloading.* For example, consider this program:

```
#include <iostream.h>

// sqr_it is overloaded three ways
int sqr_it(int i);
double sqr_it(double d);
long sqr_it(long l);

main(void)
{
  cout << sqr_it(10) << "\n";

  cout << sqr_it(11.0) << "\n";

  cout << sqr_it(9L) << "\n";

  return 0;
}

int sqr_it(int i)
{
  cout << "Inside the sqr_it() function that uses ";
  cout << "an integer argument.\n";

  return i*i;
}

double sqr_it(double d)
{
  cout << "Inside the sqr_it() function that uses ";
  cout << "a double argument.\n";

  return d*d;
}
```

```
long sqr_it(long l)
{
  cout << "Inside the sqr_it() function that uses ";
  cout << "a long argument.\n";

  return l*l;
}
```

This program creates three similar but different functions called **sqr_it()**, each of which returns the square of its argument. As the program illustrates, the compiler knows which function to use in each case because of the type of the argument. The value of overloaded functions is that they allow related sets of functions to be accessed using only one name. In a sense, function overloading lets you create a generic name for some operation with the compiler resolving exactly what function is actually needed to perform the operation.

Functions may be overloaded as long as the type and/or number of parameters differ. It is not sufficient if the functions differ only in their return types.

One reason function overloading is important is that it can help manage complexity. To understand how, consider the following. All C compilers contain the functions **abs()**, **labs()**, and **fabs()** in their standard library. Collectively, these functions return the absolute value of an integer, a long integer, and a floating-point value, respectively. Even though these functions perform almost identical actions, in C, three slightly different names must be used to represent these tasks, which makes the situation more complex, conceptually, than it actually is. Even though the underlying concept of each function is the same, the programmer has three things to remember, not just one. However, in C++, it is possible to use the same name, such as **abs()**, for all three functions. Thus, the name **abs()** represents the *general* action that is being performed. It is left to the compiler to choose the right *specific* version for a particular circumstance. You as programmer need only remember the general action being performed; through the application of polymorphism, the three things to remember have been reduced to one. Although this example is fairly trivial, if you expand the concept, you can see how polymorphism can help you manage very complex programs.

The following program overloads the **abs()** function so that it works with integers, long integers, and floating-point values, as described in the previous paragraph.

```
#include <iostream.h>

int abs(int i);
long abs(long i);
double abs(double i);

main()
{
  cout << abs(-10) << '\n'; // integer
  cout << abs(-100000) << '\n'; // long
  cout << abs(-0.34) << '\n'; // double

  return 0;
}

int abs(int i)
{
  return i<0 ? -i : i;
}

long abs(long i)
{
  return i<0 ? -i : i;
}

double abs(double i)
{
  return i<0 ? -i : i;
}
```

Following is another example of function overloading. As you know, C and C++ do not contain any library functions that prompt the user for input and then wait for a response. However, this program creates three functions called **prompt()** that perform this task for data of types **int**, **double**, and **long**.

```
#include <iostream.h>

void prompt(char *str, int *i);
void prompt(char *str, double *d);
void prompt(char *str, long *l);

main()
{
  int i;
  double d;
  long l;

  prompt("Enter an integer: ", &i);
  prompt("Enter a double: ", &d);
  prompt("Enter a long: ", &l);

  cout << i << " " << d << " " << l;

  return 0;
}

void prompt(char *str, int *i)
{
  cout << str;
  cin >> *i;
}

void prompt(char *str, double *d)
{
  cout << str;
  cin >> *d;
}

void prompt(char *str, long *l)
{
  cout << str;
  cin >> *l;
}
```

One word of warning. You can use the same name to overload unrelated functions, but you should not. For example, you could use the name **sqr_it()** to create functions that return the *square* of an **int** and

the *square root* of a **double**. However, these two operations are funda-
mentally different, and applying function overloading in this manner
defeats its intended purpose. In practice, you should only overload closely
related operations.

Operator Overloading

Another way that polymorphism is achieved in C++ is through operator
overloading. As you know, in C++, it is possible to use the << and >>
operators to perform console I/O operations. The reason for this is that
in the IOSTREAM.H header file, these operators are overloaded. When
an operator is overloaded, it takes on an additional meaning relative to
a certain class. However, it still retains all of its old meanings.

In general, you can overload any of C++'s operators by defining what
they mean relative to a specific class. For example, think back to the
queue class developed earlier in this chapter. It is possible to overload
the + operator relative to objects of type **queue** so that it appends the
contents of one queue to that of another. However, the + still retains its
original meaning relative to other types of data. You will need to know
more about C++ before an actual operator overloading example can be
developed, but this is the general idea.

Inheritance

Inheritance is one of the major traits of an object oriented programming language. C++ supports inheritance by allowing one class to
incorporate another class into its declaration. To see how this works, let's
start with an example. Here is a class, called **road_vehicle**, that defines
very broadly vehicles that travel on the road. It stores the number of
wheels a vehicle has and the number of passengers it can carry.

```
class road_vehicle {
  int wheels;
  int passengers;
```

```
public:
  void set_wheels(int num);
  int get_wheels();
  void set_pass(int num);
  int get_pass();
};
```

This broad definition of a road vehicle can be used to help define specific objects. For example, this declares a class called **truck** using **road_vehicle**:

```
class truck : public road_vehicle {
  int cargo;
public:
  void set_cargo(int size);
  int get_cargo();
  void show();
};
```

Notice how **road_vehicle** is inherited. The general form for inheritance is shown here:

```
class new-class-name : access inherited-class {
  // ... body of derived class
}
```

Here, *access* is optional. However, if present, it must be either **public** or **private**. You will learn more about these options in a later chapter. For now, all inherited classes will be public. When a class is inherited using **public**, all the public elements of the ancester become public elements of the class that inherits it. Therefore, in the example, members of the class **truck** have access to the member functions of **road_vehicle** just as if they had been declared inside **truck**. However, the member functions do *not* have access to the private parts of **road_vehicle**. Following is a program that illustrates inheritance. It creates two sub-classes of **road_vehicle**. One is **truck** and the other is **automobile**.

```
#include <iostream.h>

class road_vehicle {
```

```
  int wheels;
  int passengers;
public:
  void set_wheels(int num);
  int get_wheels();
  void set_pass(int num);
  int get_pass();
};

class truck : public road_vehicle {
  int cargo;
public:
  void set_cargo(int size);
  int get_cargo();
  void show();
};

enum type {car, van, wagon};

class automobile : public road_vehicle {
  enum type car_type;
public:
  void set_type(enum type t);
  enum type get_type();
  void show();
};

void road_vehicle::set_wheels(int num)
{
  wheels = num;
}

int road_vehicle::get_wheels()
{
  return wheels;
}

void road_vehicle::set_pass(int num)
{
  passengers = num;
}
```

```
int road_vehicle::get_pass()
{
  return passengers;
}

void truck::set_cargo(int num)
{
  cargo = num;
}

int truck::get_cargo()
{
  return cargo;
}

void truck::show()
{
  cout << "wheels: " << get_wheels() << "\n";
  cout << "passengers: " << get_pass() << "\n";
  cout << "cargo capacity in cubic feet: " << cargo << "\n";
}

void automobile::set_type(enum type t)
{
  car_type = t;
}

enum type automobile::get_type()
{
  return car_type;
}

void automobile::show()
{
  cout << "wheels: " << get_wheels() << "\n";
  cout << "passengers: " << get_pass() << "\n";
  cout << "type: ";
  switch(get_type()) {
    case van: cout << "van\n";
      break;
    case car: cout << "car\n";
      break;
```

```
      case wagon: cout << "wagon\n";
  }
}

main()
{
  truck t1, t2;
  automobile c;

  t1.set_wheels(18);
  t1.set_pass(2);
  t1.set_cargo(3200);

  t2.set_wheels(6);
  t2.set_pass(3);
  t2.set_cargo(1200);

  t1.show();
  t2.show();

  c.set_wheels(4);
  c.set_pass(6);
  c.set_type(van);

  c.show();

  return 0;
}
```

As this program shows, the major advantage of inheritance is that you can create a base classification that can be incorporated into more specific ones. In this way, each object can precisely represent its own classification.

When referring to inheritance, two terms are commonly used. The class that is inherited is called the *base class*. The class that does the inheriting is called the *derived class.*

One other point: notice that both **truck** and **automobile** include a member function called **show()**, which displays information about each object. This is another aspect of polymorphism. Since each **show()** is linked with it own class, the compiler can easily tell which one to call in any circumstance. There is no reason to use separate names.

Constructors and Destructors

It is very common for some part of an object to require initialization before it can be used. For example, think back to the **queue** class developed earlier in this chapter. Before the queue could be used, the variables **rloc** and **sloc** had to be set to zero. This was performed by using the function **init()**. Because the requirement for initialization is so common, C++ allows objects to initialize themselves, when they are created. This automatic initialization is performed through the use of a constructor function.

A *constructor function* is a special function that is a member of the class and has the same name as that class. For example, here is how the **queue** class looks when converted to use a constructor function for initialization:

```
// this creates the class queue
class queue {
   int q[100];
   int sloc, rloc;
public:
   queue();  // constructor
   void qput(int i);
   int qget();
};
```

Notice that the constructor **queue()** has no return type specified. In C++, constructor functions cannot return values.

The **queue()** function is coded like this:

```
// This is the constructor function.
queue::queue()
{
   sloc = rloc = 0;
   cout << "queue initialized\n";
}
```

As you can see, **queue()** sets **sloc** and **rloc** equal to zero. Keep in mind that the message **queue initialized** is output as a way to illustrate the constructor. In actual practice, most constructor functions will not output or input anything.

An object's constructor is called when the object is created. This means that it is called when the object's declaration is executed. Also, for local objects, the constructor is called each time the object declaration is encountered. For global objects, the constructor is called when the program is started.

The complement of the constructor is the *destructor.* In many circumstances, an object will need to perform some action or actions when it is destroyed. (Keep in mind that local objects are created when their block is entered and destroyed when the block is left.) For example, an object may need to deallocate memory that it had previously allocated. In C++, it is the destructor function that handles deactivation. The destructor has the same name as the constructor, but it is preceded by a tilde (~). For example, here is the **queue** class and its constructor and destructor functions. (Keep in mind that the **queue** class does not require a destructor, so the one shown here is just for illustration.)

```
// this creates the class queue
class queue {
  int q[100];
  int sloc, rloc;
public:
  queue();   // constructor
  ~queue(); // destructor
  void qput(int i);
  int qget();
};

// This is the constructor function.
queue::queue()
{
  sloc = rloc = 0;
  cout << "queue initialized\n";
}

// This is the destructor function.
queue::~queue()
{
  cout << "queue destroyed\n";
}
```

To see how constructors and destructors work, here is a new version of the sample program from earlier in this chapter:

```
#include <iostream.h>

// this creates the class queue
class queue {
  int q[100];
  int sloc, rloc;
public:
  queue();  // constructor
  ~queue(); // destructor
  void qput(int i);
  int qget();
};

// This is the constructor function.
queue::queue()
{
  sloc = rloc = 0;
  cout << "queue initialized\n";
}

// This is the destructor function.
queue::~queue()
{
  cout << "queue destroyed\n";
}

void queue::qput(int i)
{
  if(sloc==100) {
    cout << "queue is full";
    return;
  }
  sloc++;
  q[sloc] = i;
}

int queue::qget()
{
  if(rloc == sloc) {
```

```
      cout << "queue underflow";
      return 0;
    }
  rloc++;
  return q[rloc];
}

main()
{
  queue a, b;  // create two queue objects

  a.qput(10);
  b.qput(19);

  a.qput(20);
  b.qput(1);

  cout << a.qget() << " ";
  cout << a.qget() << " ";
  cout << b.qget() << " ";
  cout << b.qget() << "\n";

  return 0;
}
```

This program displays the following:

```
queue initialized
queue initialized
10 20 19 1
queue destroyed
queue destroyed
```

As you will see in Part II of this book, constructors and destructors play an important role when you are creating Windows applications.

C++ includes all of the keywords defined by C and adds 17 new ones, as shown in Table 1-1. Of these, **catch**, **throw**, and **try** are reserved for future use. The **overload** keyword is obsolete, but it is still accepted to allow older programs to compile without errors. You cannot use any keyword as a name for variables or functions.

TABLE 1-1   The C++ Extended Keywords

asm	private
catch	protected
class	public
delete	template
friend	this
inline	throw
new	try
operator	virtual
overload	

Now that you have been introduced to many of C++'s major features, the remaining chapters in Part I will examine C++ in greater detail.

CHAPTER

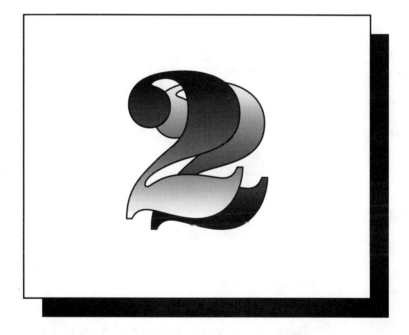

A Closer Look at Classes

As stated in Chapter 1, the class is C++'s most important feature. This chapter examines the class and related issues more closely.

Parameterized Constructors

Often, when an object is created, it is necessary or desirable to initialize various data elements with specific values. As you saw in the previous chapter, by using a constructor function, it is possible to initialize various variables when the object is created. However, in C++, the concept of object initialization is expanded to allow the initialization of specific objects using programmer-defined values. You accomplish this by passing arguments to an object's constructor function. For a simple example, the **queue** class that ended the previous chapter can be enhanced to accept an argument that will act as the queue's ID number. First, **queue** is changed to look like this:

```
// this creates the class queue
class queue {
  int q[100];
  int sloc, rloc;
  int who; // holds the queue's ID number
public:
  queue(int id);  // constructor
  ~queue(); // destructor
  void qput(int i);
  int qget();
};
```

The variable **who** is used to hold an ID number that will identify the queue. Its actual value will be determined by what is passed to the constructor function in **id** when a variable of type **queue** is created. The **queue()** constructor function looks like this:

```
// This is the constructor function.
queue::queue(int id)
{
  sloc = rloc = 0;
```

```
  who = id;
  cout << "queue " << who << " initialized\n";
}
```

To pass an argument to the constructor function, you must associate the value or values being passed with the object when that object is being declared. C++ supports two ways to accomplish this. The first method is illustrated here:

```
queue a = queue(101);
```

This declaration creates a queue called **a** and passes the value 101 to it. However, this form is seldom used because the second method, sometimes called the shorthand method, is shorter and more to the point. In the *shorthand method,* the argument or arguments must follow the object's name and be enclosed between parentheses. For example, this accomplishes the same thing as the previous declaration:

```
queue a(101);
```

Since the shorthand method is used by virtually all C++ programmers, this book also uses the shorthand form exclusively. The general form of passing arguments to constructor functions is shown here:

class-type var(arg-list);

Here, *arg-list* is a comma-separated list of arguments that are passed to the constructor.

The following version of the **queue** program demonstrates passing arguments to constructor functions:

```
#include <iostream.h>

// this creates the class queue
class queue {
  int q[100];
  int sloc, rloc;
  int who, // holds the queue's ID number
```

```cpp
public:
  queue(int id);  // constructor
  ~queue(); // destructor
  void qput(int i);
  int qget();
};

// This is the constructor function.
queue::queue(int id)
{
  sloc = rloc = 0;
  who = id;
  cout << "queue " << who << " initialized\n";
}

// This is the destructor function.
queue::~queue()
{
  cout << "queue " << who << " destroyed\n";
}

void queue::qput(int i)
{
  if(sloc==100) {
    cout << "queue is full";
    return;
  }
  sloc++;
  q[sloc] = i;
}

int queue::qget()
{
  if(rloc == sloc) {
    cout << "queue underflow";
    return 0;
  }
  rloc++;
  return q[rloc];
}

main()
```

```
{
  queue a(1), b(2);   // create two queue objects

  a.qput(10);
  b.qput(19);

  a.qput(20);
  b.qput(1);

  cout << a.qget() << " ";
  cout << a.qget() << " ";
  cout << b.qget() << " ";
  cout << b.qget() << "\n";

  return 0;
}
```

This program produces the following output:

```
queue 1 initialized
queue 2 initialized
10 20 19 1
queue 2 destroyed
queue 1 destroyed
```

As you can see by looking at **main()**, the queue associated with **a** is given the ID number 1 and the queue associated with **b** is given the number 2.

Although the **queue** example passes only a single argument when an object is created, it is, of course, possible to pass several. For example, here, objects of type **widget** are passed two values:

```
#include <iostream.h>

class widget {
  int i;
  int j;
public:
  widget(int a, int b);
  void put_widget();
} ;
```

```
widget::widget(int a, int b)
{
  i = a;
  j = b;
}

void widget::put_widget()
{
  cout << i << " " << j << "\n";
}

main()
{
  widget x(10, 20), y(0, 0);

  x.put_widget();
  y.put_widget();

  return 0;
}
```

This program displays

```
10 20
0 0
```

Friend Functions

A nonmember function can have access to the private parts of a class
if you declare it as a friend of the class. For example, here **frd()** is declared
to be a friend of the class **cl**:

```
class cl {
  .
  .
  .
public:
  friend void frd();
```

```
    .
    .
    .
};
```

As you can see, the keyword **friend** preceeds the entire function decla-ration, which is the case in general.

Friend functions are included in C++ for a number of reasons. For example, friend functions help make overloaded operators more flexible. You can also use them when overloading the C++ I/O system. A discussion of these uses will be deferred until later in this book, but there is one reason for friend functions that can be examined here. This use of a friend function allows one function to have access to the private members of two (or more) classes. This situation most commonly arises when two different classes have some aspect that you desire to compare. For example, you might have two classes—one that stores information about airplanes and one that stores information about automobiles. Assuming that the information contained in each class includes the number of passengers that each carries, you may want to compare the capacity of a specific airplane to a specific car. To do this in the most efficient manner demands that one function have access to the private members of both classes.

To see how two classes can share a friend function, consider a program that defines two classes called **triangle** and **rectangle**. The **triangle** class contains the dimensions of a triangle's base, height, and area. The **rectangle** class contains the box's width, length, and area. Both classes share the **same_size()** function to determine whether a triangle and a rectangle have the same area. These classes are declared as shown here:

```
#include <iostream.h>

class triangle;

class rectangle {
  int area; // area of rectangle
  int width, length; // dimensions
public:
  friend int same_size(triangle t, rectangle b);
  void define(int l, int w);
```

```
   void show_dim();
} ;

class triangle {
  int area; // area of triangle
  int base, height; // dimensions
public:
  friend int same_size(triangle t, rectangle b);
  void define(int b, int h);
  void show_dim();
} ;
```

The **same_size()** function, which is a member of neither but a friend of both, returns true if the **triangle** object and the **rectangle** object, which form its arguments, have the same area; it returns nonzero otherwise. The **same_size()** function is shown here:

```
// Return true if triangle and rectangle have same area.
int same_size(triangle t, rectangle b)
{
  if(t.area==b.area) return 1;
  return 0;
}
```

As you can see, the **same_size()** function needs access to the private parts of both **triangle** and **rectangle** to perform its task efficiently.

Notice the empty declaration of **triangle** at the start of the class declarations. Since **same_size()** in **rectangle** references **triangle** before **triangle** is declared, **triangle** must be forward referenced. If this is not done, the compiler will not know what **triangle** is when encountered in the declaration of **rectangle**. In C++, a *forward reference* to a class is simply the keyword **class** followed by the type name of the class. Usually, the only time forward references are needed is when friend functions are involved.

Here is a program that demonstrates the **triangle** and **rectangle** classes and illustrates how a friend function can access the private parts of a class:

```
#include <iostream.h>
```

```
class triangle;

class rectangle {
  int area; // area of rectangle
  int width, length; // dimensions
public:
  friend int same_size(triangle t, rectangle b);
  void define(int l, int w);
  void show_dim();
} ;

class triangle {
  int area; // area of triangle
  int base, height; // dimensions
public:
  friend int same_size(triangle t, rectangle b);
  void define(int b, int h);
  void show_dim();
} ;

// Return true if triangle and rectangle have same area.
int same_size(triangle t, rectangle b)
{
  if(t.area==b.area) return 1;
  return 0;
}

void rectangle::define(int l, int w)
{
  length = l;
  width =  w;

  area = l * w;
}

void rectangle::show_dim()
{
  cout << "Rectangle is " << length << " by " << width;
  cout << '\n';
}

void triangle::define(int b, int h)
```

```
{
  base = b;
  height = h;

  area = base * height / 2;
}

void triangle::show_dim()
{
  cout << "Triangle is " << base << " by ";
  cout << height << '\n';
}

main()
{
  rectangle b1, b2;
  triangle t1;

  b1.define(10, 10);
  b2.define(5, 7);

  t1.define(10, 20);

  b1.show_dim();
  b2.show_dim();
  t1.show_dim();

  if(same_size(t1, b1)) cout << "b1 and t1 have same area\n";

  return 0;
}
```

It is important to understand that a friend function is not a member function. Therefore, in the preceding program, it would be completely invalid to attempt to execute **same_size()** by using this statement:

```
b1.same_size(t1, b1);   // WRONG!
```

Since a friend is not a member, it cannot be called by using an object and the dot operator. Remember, a friend function is simply a "normal" function that is granted access to the private members of the class or classes for which it is a friend. In general, friend functions are passed the objects upon which they will operate.

Default Function Arguments

C++ allows a function to assign a parameter a default value when no argument corresponding to that parameter is specified in a call to that function. The default value is specified in a manner syntactically similar to a variable initialization. For example, this declares **f()** as taking one integer variable and declares a default value of 1:

```
void f(int i = 1)
{
    .
    .
    .
}
```

Now, **f()** can be called one of two ways, as these examples show:

```
f(10);  // pass an explicit value

f();    // let function use default
```

The first call passes the value 10 to **i**. The second call automatically gives **i** the default value 1. One reason that default arguments are included in C++ is that they provide another method of enabling the programmer to manage greater complexity. In order to handle the widest variety of situations, quite frequently a function contains more parameters than are required for its most common usage. Thus, when the default arguments apply, you need only remember and specify the arguments that are meaningful to the exact situation—not the most general case.

To understand the reason for default arguments, let's develop a practical example. One useful function not found in Turbo C++'s library, called **xyout()**, is shown here:

```
// Output a string at specified X,Y location.
void xyout(char *str, int x = -1, int y = -1)
{
  if(x==-1) x = wherex();
  if(y==-1) y = wherey();
  gotoxy(x, y);
  cout << str;
}
```

This function displays, in text mode, the string pointed to by **str** beginning at the X,Y location defined by **x** and **y**. However, if neither **x** nor **y** is specified, the string is output at the current cursor location. (You can think of this function as a "souped up" version of **puts()**.) The functions **wherex()**, **wherey()**, and **gotoxy()** are part of Turbo C++'s library. The **wherex()** and **wherey()** functions return the current X and Y coordinates of the cursor, respectively. The current X,Y coordinates are where the next output operation will begin. The **gotoxy()** function moves the cursor to the specified X,Y location.

The following short program demonstrates **xyout()**'s use:

```
#include <iostream.h>
#include <conio.h>

void xyout(char *str, int x = -1, int y = -1);

main()
{
  xyout("hello", 10, 10);
  xyout(" there");
  xyout("I like C++", 40);  // this is still on line 10

  xyout("This is on line 11.\n", 1, 11);
  xyout("This follows on line 12.\n");
  xyout("This follows on line 13.");

  return 0;
}

void xyout(char *str, int x, int y)
{
  if(x==-1) x = wherex();
```

```
    if(y==-1) y = wherey();
    gotoxy(x, y);
    cout << str;
}
```

Look closely at how **xyout()** is called inside **main()**. This program produces output similar to that shown in Figure 2-1. As this program illustrates, although it is sometimes useful to specify the exact location where text will be displayed, often you simply want to continue on from the point at which the last output occurred. By using default arguments, you can use the same function to accomplish both goals; there is no need for two separate functions.

Notice that in **main()**, **xyout()** is called with three, two, or one argument. When called with only one argument, both **x** and **y** default. However, when called with two arguments, only **y** defaults. There is no way to call **xyout()** with **x** defaulting and **y** being specified. More generally, when a function is called, all arguments are matched to their respective parameters in order of left to right. Once all existing arguments have been matched, any remaining default arguments are used.

When you create functions that have default argument values, the default values must be specified only once, and this must be the first time the function is declared within the file. For most applications, this means that the values are specified in the function's prototype. It is an error to specify the default values in both the prototype and again in the function's definition—even if the values are the same. This is why only the prototype of **xyout()** in the foregoing program declared the default values.

FIGURE 2-1

Sample output from the xyout() program

```
              hello there           I like C++
      This is on line 11.
      This follows on line 12.
      This follows on line 13.
```

Although default argument values cannot be redefined for the same function, overloaded functions can define separate default arguments for each version of the overloaded function.

All parameters that take default values must appear to the right of those that do not. That is, once you begin to define parameters that take default values, you may not specify a nondefaulting parameter. For example, it would have been incorrect to define **xyout()** like this:

```
// wrong!
void xyout(int x = -1, int y = -1, char *str)
```

Here is another incorrect attempted use of default parameters:

```
// wrong!
int f(int i, int j=10, int k)
```

Once the default parameters begin, no nondefaulting parameter may occur in the list.

You can also use default parameters in an object's constructor function. For example, here is a slightly different version of the **queue()** constructor function shown earlier in this chapter:

```
// This is the constructor function that uses
// a default value.
queue::queue(int id=0)
{
  sloc = rloc = 0;
  who = id;
  cout << "queue " << who << " initialized\n";
}
```

In this version, if an object is declared without any initializing values, **id** defaults to zero. For example,

```
queue a, b(2);
```

creates two objects, **a** and **b**. Here, **a**'s **who** ID value is zero and **b**'s is 2.

Using Default Arguments Correctly

Although default arguments can be a very powerful tool when used correctly, they can actually work against you when misused. The entire point of default arguments is to allow a function to perform its job in an efficient and easy-to-use manner while still allowing considerable flexibility. Toward this end, all default arguments should represent the way the function is used most of the time.

For example, a default argument makes sense if a parameter will contain the same value 90 percent of the time. However, if a common value will occur in only 10 percent of the calls and the rest of the time the arguments corresponding to that parameter vary widely, it is probably not a good idea to use a default argument. The point of using default arguments is that their values are those that the programmer will normally associate with a given function. When there is no single value that is normally associated with a parameter, there is no reason for a default argument. In fact, declaring default arguments when there is an insufficient basis destructures your code because it misleads and confuses anyone reading your program. Where, in between 10 percent and 90 percent, you should elect to use a default argument is, of course, subjective, but 51 percent would seem a reasonable break point.

Classes and Structures Are Related

In C++, the **struct** has some expanded capabilities as compared to its C counterpart. In C++, classes and structures are highly related. In fact, with one exception, they are interchangeable because the C++ **struct** can also include data and the code that manipulates that data in just the same way that a class can. The only difference between a C++ structure and a class is that, by default, the members of a class are private while, by default, the members of a structure are public. Aside from this exception, structures and classes perform exactly the same function. For example, consider this program:

```
#include <iostream.h>

struct cl {
  int get_i(); // these are public
  void put_i(int j); // by default
private:
  int i; // private here
} ;

int cl::get_i()
{
  return i;
}

void cl::put_i(int j)
{
  i = j;
}

main()
{
  cl s;

  s.put_i(10);
  cout << s.get_i();

  return 0;
}
```

This simple program defines a structure type called **cl** in which **get_i()** and **put_i()** are public and **i** is private. Notice that structures use the keyword **private** to introduce the private elements of the structure.

The following program shows an equivalent program that uses a class instead of a structure:

```
#include <iostream.h>

class cl {
  int i; // private by default
```

```
public:
  int get_i();
  void put_i(int j);
} ;

int cl::get_i()
{
  return i;
}

void cl::put_i(int j)
{
  i = j;
}

main()
{
  cl s;

  s.put_i(10);
  cout << s.get_i();

  return 0;
}
```

For the most part, C++ programmers use a class to define the form of an object and use a **struct** in the same way that it is used in C. However, from time to time, you will see C++ code that uses the expanded abilities of structures.

Unions and Classes Are Related

Although the fact that structures and classes are related is not too surprising, you might be surprised to learn that unions are also related to classes. As far as C++ is concerned, a *union* is essentially a structure in which all elements are stored in the same location. A union can contain a constructor and destructor function as well as member and friend functions. For example, this program uses a union to display the characters that make up the low- and high-order bytes of an integer (assuming two-byte integers):

```
#include <iostream.h>

union u_type {
  u_type(int a);   // public by default
  void showchars();
  int i;
  char ch[2];
};

// constructor
u_type::u_type(int a)
{
  i = a;
}

// show the characters that make up an int
void u_type::showchars()
{
  cout << ch[0] << " ";
  cout << ch[1] << "\n";
}

main()
{
  u_type u(1000);

  u.showchars();

  return 0;
}
```

As you can see, since a union resembles a structure, its members are public by default. In fact, the keyword **private** cannot be applied to a union. (Also, as you will learn about later in this chapter, the keyword **protected** cannot be applied to a union either.)

Remember, just because C++ gives unions greater power and flexibilty does not mean you have to use this expanded capability. In cases where you simply need a C-style union, you are free to use one in that manner. However, in cases where you can encapsulate a union along with the routines that manipulate it, you will be adding considerable structure to your program.

Inline Functions

While not pertaining specifically to object oriented programming, C++ contains one very important feature not found in C. This feature is called inline functions. An *inline function* is a function that is expanded inline when it is invoked instead of actually being called. This is similar to a parameterized function-like macro in C, but more flexible.

There are two ways to create an inline function. The first is to use the **inline** modifier. For example, to create an inline function called **f()** that returns an **int** and takes no parameters, you must declare it like this:

```
inline int f()
{
  .
  .
  .
}
```

The general form of **inline** is

inline *function_declaration*

The **inline** modifier precedes all other aspects of a function's declaration.

The reason for **inline** functions is efficiency. Every time a function is called, a series of instructions must be executed to set up the function call, including pushing any arguments onto the stack, and to return from the function. In some cases, many CPU cycles are used to perform these procedures. However, when a function is expanded inline, no such overhead exists and the overall speed of your program will increase. However, in cases where the **inline** function is large, the overall size of your program will also increase. For this reason, the best **inline** functions are those that are very small. Larger functions should be left as normal functions.

For example, the following program uses **inline** to make it more efficient:

```
#include <iostream.h>

class cl {
  int i; // private by default
public:
  int get_i();
  void put_i(int j);
} ;

inline int cl::get_i()
{
  return i;
}

inline void cl::put_i(int j)
{
  i = j;
}

main()
{
  cl s;

  s.put_i(10);
  cout << s.get_i();

  return 0;
}
```

It is important to understand that, technically, **inline** is a *request*, not a *command*, to the compiler to generate inline code. There are various situations that can prevent the compiler from complying with the request. Some of the most common are discussed here. First, if a loop, a **switch**, or a **goto** exists, the compiler will not generate inline code. For functions not returning values, if a **return** statement exists, inline code will not be generated. You cannot have **inline** recursive functions, nor can you create **inline** functions that contain **static** variables.

One last point: it is perfectly fine to inline constructor and destructor functions.

Creating Inline Functions Inside a Class

There is another way, in C++, to create an **inline** function: you can define the code to a function *inside* a class definition. Any function that is defined inside a class is automatically made into an **inline** function. It is not necessary to precede its declaration with the keyword **inline**. For example, the previous program can be rewritten as shown here:

```
#include <iostream.h>

class cl {
  int i; // private by default
public:
  // automatic inline functions
  int get_i() { return i; }
  void put_i(int j) { i = j; }
} ;

main()
{
  cl s;

  s.put_i(10);
  cout << s.get_i();

  return 0;
}
```

Notice the way the function code is arranged. For very short functions, this arrangement reflects common C++ style. However, there is no reason you could not write it as shown here:

```
class cl {
  int i; // private by default
```

```
public:
  // inline functions
  int get_i()
  {
    return i;
  }

  void put_i(int j)
  {
    i = j;
  }
} ;
```

In professionally written C++ code, short functions like those illustrated in the example are commonly defined inside the class definition. This convention is followed in the rest of the C++ examples in this book.

More About Inheritance

As you saw in Chapter 1, it is possible for one class to inherit the attributes of another. This section examines some more details relating to inheritance.

Let's begin by reviewing terminology. A class that is inherited by another class is called the base class. Sometimes this is also referred to as the *parent class.* The class that does the inheriting is called the derived class, sometimes called the *child class.* This book uses the terms "base" and "derived" because they are the most commonly used terms.

In C++, a class can categorize its members into three classifications. The first two you have already seen; they are public and private. The third way a member may be included in a class is as protected. You accomplish this by using the **protected** keyword. As you know, a public member may be accessed by any other function in the program. A private member may be accessed only by member or friend functions. A protected member may also only be accessed by member or friend functions. However, the way a protected member is inherited differs from the way a private member is inherited.

Here is an example to help you understand how protected differs from private. As you know, when one class inherits another class, all private members of the base class are inaccessible to the derived class. For example:

```
class X {
  int i;
  int j;
public:
  void get_ij() { return i*j; }
} ;

class Y : public X {
public:
  Y(int a, int b) { i = a; j = b; } // WRONG, not accessible
  void show() { cout << get_ij(); } // OK, get_ij() is public
} ;
```

Here, the elements of **Y** can access **X**'s public function **get_ij()** but cannot access **i** or **j** because they are private to **X**.

The preceding example gives rise to an interesting question. How do you limit access to a member of a base class yet still grant a derived class access to it? The answer is simple: make those members that you want a derived class to have access to protected members in the base class. When you do this, these members are still private to the base class, but they may be accessed by a derived class. For example:

```
class X {
protected:
  int i; // still private to X
  int j; // but may be used by Y
public:
  void get_ij() { return i*j; }
} ;

class Y : public X {
public:
  Y(int a, int b) { i = a; j = b; } // Now, OK
  void show() { cout << get_ij(); } // OK, get_ij() is public
} ;
```

Now, **Y** has access to **i** and **j** even though they are still inaccessible by the rest of the program. The key point is that when you make an element protected, you are restricting its access to only the member functions of the class, but you are allowing this access to be inherited. When an element is private, access is denied to the derived class.

As you know from the last chapter, the general form for inheriting a class is

class *class-name* : *access class-name* {

 .

 .

 .

} ;

Here, *access* must be either private or public. (It may also be omitted, in which case public is assumed if the base class is a structure or private if the base class is a class.) If *access* is public, all public and protected members of the base class become public and protected members of the derived class, respectively. If *access* is private, all public and protected members of the base class become private members of the derived class. In all cases, private members of the base class remain private to it. To understand the ramifications of these conversions, consider the program shown here:

```
#include <iostream.h>

class X {
protected:
  int i;
  int j;
public:
  void get_ij();
  void put_ij();
} ;


// In Y, i and j of X become protected members.
class Y : public X {
  int k;
public:
```

```
  int get_k() { return k;}
  void make_k() { k = i * j; }
} ;

// Z has access to i and j of X, but not to
// k of Y, since it is private by default.
class Z : public Y {
public:
  void f() { i = 2; j = 3; }
} ;

void X::get_ij()
{
  cout << "Enter two numbers: ";
  cin >> i >> j;
}

void X::put_ij()
{
  cout << i << " " << j << "\n";
}

main()
{
  Y var;
  Z var2;

  var.get_ij();
  var.put_ij();

  var.make_k();
  cout << var.get_k();
  cout << "\n";

  var2.f();
  var2.put_ij();

  return 0;
}
```

Since **Y** inherits **X** as public, the protected members of **X** become protected members of **Y**. This means they may also be inherited by **Z**, and this program compiles and runs correctly. However, if **Y** inherits **X** as private, as shown next, then **Z** is denied access to **i** and **j** because they have become private members of **Y**:

```cpp
// This program contains an error and will not compile.
#include <iostream.h>

class X {
protected:
  int i;
  int j;
public:
  void get_ij();
  void put_ij();
} ;

/* Now, i and j are converted to private members of Y,
   but are still accessible within Y.
class Y : private X {
  int k;
public:
  int get_k() { return k; }
  void make_k() { k = i * j; }
} ;

/* Because i and j are private in Y, they
   may not be inherited by Z, and not available for its use. */
class Z : public Y {
public:
  /* This function no longer works because i and j
     are no longer accessible here. */
  void f() { i = 2; j = 3; } // ERROR!
} ;

void X::get_ij()
{
  cout << "Enter two numbers: ";
  cin >> i >> j;
}

void X::put_ij()
{
```

```
   cout << i << " " << j << "\n";
}
```

When **X** is made private in **Y**'s declaration, it causes **i** and **j** to become private in **Y**. This means they cannot be inherited by **Z**, and thus **Z**'s function **f()** may no longer access them.

One final point about **private**, **protected**, and **public**. These keywords may be appear in any order and any number of times in the declaration of a structure or class. For example, this is perfectly valid:

```
class my_class {
protected:
  int i;
  int j;
public:
  void f1();
  void f2();
protected:
  int a;
public:
  int b;
} ;
```

However, it is usually considered good form to have only one heading inside each class or structure.

Multiple Inheritance

It is possible for one class to inherit the attributes of two or more classes. To accomplish this, use a comma-separated inheritance list in the derived class's base class list. The general form is

class *derived-class-name* : *base-class-list*
{
  .
  .
  .
};

For example, in this program **Z** inherits both **X** and **Y**:

```
#include <iostream.h>

class X {
protected:
  int a;
public:
  void make_a(int i) { a = i; }
};

class Y {
protected:
  int b;
public:
  void make_b(int i) { b = i; }
} ;

// Z inherits both X and Y
class Z : public X, public Y {
public:
  int make_ab() { return a*b; }
} ;

main()
{
  Z i;

  i.make_a(10);
  i.make_b(12);

  cout << i.make_ab();

  return 0;
}
```

In this example, **Z** has access to the public and protected portions of both **X** and **Y**.

Also, in this example, **X**, **Y** and **Z** do not contain constructor functions. However, the situation is more complex when a base class contains a constructor function. For example, let's change the preceding example so that classes **X**, **Y**, and **Z** each have a constructor function, as shown here:

```
#include <iostream.h>

class X {
protected:
  int a;
public:
  X() { a = 10; cout << "Constructing X\n"; }
};

class Y {
protected:
  int b;
public:
  Y() {b = 20; cout << "Constructing Y\n"; }
} ;

// Z inherits both X and Y
class Z : public X, public Y {
public:
  Z() { cout << "Constructing Z\n"; }
  int make_ab() { return a * b; }
} ;

main()
{
  Z i;

  cout << i.make_ab();

  return 0;
}
```

When this program runs, it displays this output:

```
Constructing X
Constructing Y
Constructing Z
200
```

Notice that the base classes are constructed in the order in which they appear in **Z**'s declaration. This result is generalizable because in C++, the constructor functions for any inherited base classes will be called in the order in which they appear. Once the base class or classes have been initialized, the derived class's constructor executes.

As long as no base class takes any arguments, the derived class need not have a constructor function even though one or more base classes do. However, when a base class contains a constructor function that takes one or more arguments, any derived class must also contain a constructor function. The reason for this is to allow a means of passing arguments to the constructor function(s) of the base class or classes. To pass arguments to a base class, you specify them after the derived class's constructor function declaration, as shown in this general form:

derived-constructor(arg-list) :
   base1(arg-list), *base2(arg-list)*, ..., *baseN(arg-list)*
{
     .
     .
     .
}

Here, *base1* through *baseN* are the names of the base classes inherited by the derived class. Notice that the colon is used to separate the derived class's constructor function from the argument lists of the base classes. It is very important to understand that the argument lists associated with the base classes may consist of constants, global variables, and/or the parameters to the derived class's constructor function. Since an object's initialization occurs at run time, you may use as an argument any identifier that is defined within the scope of the class.

The following program illustrates how to pass arguments to the base classes of a derived class by modifying the preceding program:

```
#include <iostream.h>

class X {
protected:
  int a;
public:
```

```
   X(int i) { a = i; }
};

class Y {
protected:
   int b;
public:
   Y(int i) { b = i; }
} ;

// Z inherits both X and Y
class Z : public X, public Y {
public:
   Z(int x, int y);
   int make_ab() { return a * b; }
} ;

/* Initialize X and Y via Z's constructor.
   Notice that Z does not actually use x or y
   itself, but it could, if it so chooses. */
Z::Z(int x, int y) : X(x), Y(y)
{
   cout << "Constructing Z\n";
}

main()
{
   Z i(10, 20);

   cout << i.make_ab();

   return 0;
}
```

Notice that the constructor **Z** does not actually use its parameters directly. Instead, in this example, they are simply passed along to the constructor functions for **X** and **Y**. Keep in mind, however, that there is no reason **Z** could not use these or other arguments.

For the sake of visual clarity, **Z()** was not defined inline within the class **Z** in the foregoing example, but it could have been. It would have been perfectly valid to define the **Z** class like this:

```
// Z inherits both X and Y.
class Z : public X, public Y {
public:
  Z(int x, int y) : X(x), Y(y)
  {
     cout << "Constructing Z\n";
  }
  int make_ab() { return a * b; }
};
```

Passing Objects to Functions

An object may be passed to a function in the same way as any other data type. You pass objects to functions by using the normal C++ call-by-value parameter-passing convention. This means that a copy of the object, not the actual object itself, is passed to the function. Therefore, with one important exception (noted in the next section), any changes made to the object inside the function do not affect the object used to call the function. The following program illustrates this point:

```
#include <iostream.h>

class OBJ {
  int i;
public:
  void set_i(int x) { i = x; }
  void out_i() { cout << i << " "; }
};

void f(OBJ x);

main()
{
  OBJ o;

  o.set_i(10);
  f(o);
  o.out_i();  // still outputs 10, value of i unchanged
```

```
    return 0;
}
void f(OBJ x)
{
  x.out_i();   // outputs 10
  x.set_i(100);   // this affects only local copy
  x.out_i();   // outputs 100
}
```

When passed to a function, the copy of the object is a bitwise clone of the calling object. That is, the data in the copy is equivalent to the data in the argument.

As stated, by default, you pass objects to functions by using the standard call-by-value mechanism. This means that a copy of an object is made when it is passed to a function and that the function operates on the copy, not the original object. However, the fact that a copy is created means, in essence, that another object is created. This raises the question of whether the object's constructor function is executed when the copy is made and whether the destructor function is executed when the copy is destroyed. The answer to these two questions may surprise you. Let's begin with an example:

```
#include <iostream.h>

class myclass {
   int i;
public:
  myclass(int n);
  ~myclass();
  void set_i(int n) { i = n; }
  int get_i() { return i; }
};

myclass::myclass(int n)
{
   i = n;
   cout << "Constructing " << i << "\n";
}

myclass::~myclass()
{
```

```
    cout << "Destroying " << i << "\n";
}
void f(myclass ob);

main()
{
  myclass o(1);

  f(o);
  cout << "This is i in main: ";
  cout << o.get_i() << "\n";

  return 0;
}

void f(myclass ob)
{
  ob.set_i(2);

  cout << "This is local i: " << ob.get_i();
  cout << "\n";
}
```

This program produces this output:

```
Constructing 1
This is local i: 2
Destroying 2
This is i in main: 1
Destroying 1
```

Notice that only one call is made to the constructor function. However, two calls are made to the destructor function. Let's see why. The reason that the constructor function is not called when the copy of the object is made is easy to understand. When you pass an object to a function, you want the current state of that object. If the constructor is called when the copy is created, initialization will occur, possibly changing the object. Thus, the constructor function cannot be executed when the copy of an object is generated in a function call.

Although the constructor function is not called when an object is passed to a function, it is necessary to call the destructor when the copy is destroyed. (The copy is destroyed like any other local variable, when the function terminates.) Remember, the copy of the object does exist as long as the function is executing. This means that the copy could be performing operations that will require its destructor function to be called when the copy is destroyed. For example, it is perfectly valid for the copy to allocate memory that must be freed when it is destroyed. For this reason, the destructor function must be executed when the copy is destroyed.

To summarize: when a copy of an object is generated because it is passed to a function, the object's constructor function is not called. However, when the copy of the object inside the function is destroyed, its destructor function is called.

Troubles Caused by Passing Objects

When an object is passed by value to a function, in theory, modifications to that object within the function affect only the copy of the object that was generated when the function call was made. However, there are a few cases where very troubling side effects can actually affect the object used as an argument in a call-by-value. Remember that a temporary copy of an object is created when an object is used as an argument to a function and that the copy's destructor function is called when that function terminates. This permits a very insidious type of bug to creep into your program. The following program will illustrate:

```
/* WARNING, This program contains an error!
   DO NOT ATTEMPT TO RUN!
*/
#include <iostream.h>
#include <stdlib.h>

class myclass {
  int *p;
public:
  // dynamically allocate memory to store an integer
  myclass(int i) {
    p = (int *) malloc(sizeof(int));
    if(p) *p = i;
  }
```

```
  ~myclass() { if(p) free(p); } // free the memory
  void show() { cout << "Freeing p " << p << '\n'; }
};

void f(myclass o);

main()
{
  myclass o1(100);

  f(o1);

  o1.show(); // logical error, p has already been freed!!!

  return 0;
}

void f(myclass o)
{
  o.show(); // o will be destroyed upon exit.
  /* This means that the memory pointed to by p
     will be freed even though it is still needed
     by o1 in main()!
  */
}
```

Do not attempt to execute this program—it may crash your computer! The dynamic allocation system is destroyed when this program executes. Here is why. When **o1** inside of **main()** is first created, memory is allocated by using **malloc()**; a pointer to this memory is put into **p**; and this memory is used to hold an integer value specified when **o1** is created. So far, this is perfectly valid. However, when **o1** is passed to **f()**, a copy of **o1** is made and copied to parameter **o**. This, in and of itself, still causes no problem. However, when **f()** terminates, the copy stored in **o** is destroyed and its destructor is called. This causes **p** to be freed. However, this frees the same memory that the original **p**, in **main()**, is still using. Thus, when the program terminates, **o1** inside **main()** is destroyed, causing **p** to be freed again. Since the allocation system has already freed this memory, attempting to free it again causes the allocation system to fail.

The key point is that when you pass an object as a parameter, a copy of that object is made. When the function terminates, that copy is destroyed. You must make sure that no side effects are caused by the destruction of the copy. One way around this problem is to pass pointers to these types of objects. In Chapter 3, you will learn another, more convenient, way around this trouble.

Arrays of Objects

You can create arrays of objects in just the same way that you create arrays of any other data types. For example, the following program establishes a class called **display** that holds information about the various display monitors that can be attached to a PC. Specifically, it contains the number of colors that can be displayed and the type of video adapter. Inside **main()**, an array of three **display** objects is created, and the objects that make up the elements of the array are accessed via the normal indexing procedure.

```
// An example of arrays of objects

#include <iostream.h>

enum disp_type {mono, cga, ega, vga};

class display {
  int colors;  // number of colors
  enum disp_type dt; // display type
public:
  void set_colors(int num) {colors = num;}
  int get_colors() {return colors;}
  void set_type(enum disp_type t) {dt = t;}
  enum disp_type get_type() {return dt;}
} ;

char names[4][5] = {
  "mono",
  "cga",
  "ega",
  "vga"
} ;
```

```
main()
{
  display monitors[3];
  register int i;

  monitors[0].set_type(mono);
  monitors[0].set_colors(1);

  monitors[1].set_type(cga);
  monitors[1].set_colors(4);

  monitors[2].set_type(vga);
  monitors[2].set_colors(16);

  for(i=0; i<3; i++) {
    cout << names[monitors[i].get_type()] << " ";
    cout << "has " << monitors[i].get_colors();
    cout << " colors" << "\n";
  }

  return 0;
}
```

This program produces the following output:

```
mono has 1 colors
cga has 4 colors
vga has 16 colors
```

Although this is not related to arrays of objects, notice how the two-dimensional character array **names** is used to convert between an enumerated value and its equivalent character string. In all enumerations that do not contain explicit initializations, the first constant has the value zero, the second 1, and so on. Therefore, the value returned by **get_type()** can be used to index the **names** array, causing the appropriate name to be printed.

Multidimensional arrays of objects are indexed in precisely the same way as arrays of other types of data.

Pointers to Objects

As you know, in C, you may access a structure directly or through a pointer to that structure. In like fashion, in C++, you may reference an object either directly (as has been the case in all preceding examples) or by using a pointer to that object. As you will see later on, pointers to objects are among C++'s most important features.

To access a member of an object when using the actual object itself, you use the dot (.) operator. To access a specific member of an object when using a pointer to the object, you must use the arrow operator (->). (The use of the dot and arrow operators for objects parallels their use for structures and unions.)

You declare an object pointer by using the same declaration syntax that you use for any other type of data. The following program creates a simple class called **P_example** and defines an object of that class called **ob** and a pointer to an object of type **P_example** called **p**. It then illustrates how to access **ob** directly and indirectly by using a pointer.

```
// A simple example using an object pointer.

#include <iostream.h>

class P_example {
  int num;
public:
  void set_num(int val) {num = val;}
  void show_num();
};

void P_example::show_num()
{
  cout << num << "\n";
}

main()
{
  P_example ob, *p; // declare an object and pointer to it
```

```
ob.set_num(1); // access ob directly

ob.show_num();

p = &ob; // assign p the address of ob
p->show_num();   // access ob using pointer

return 0;
}
```

Notice that the address of **ob** is obtained by using the & (address of) operator in the same way the address is obtained for any type of variable.

As you know, when a pointer is incremented or decremented, it is increased or decreased in such a way that it will always point to the next element of its base type. The same thing occurs when a pointer to an object is incremented or decremented: the next object is pointed to. To illustrate this, the preceding program has been modified so that **ob** is a two-element array of type **P_example**. Notice how **p** is incremented and decremented to access the two elements in the array.

```
// Incrementing an object pointer
#include <iostream.h>

class P_example {
  int num;
public:
  void set_num(int val) {num = val;}
  void show_num();
};

void P_example::show_num()
{
  cout << num << "\n";
}

main()
{
  P_example ob[2], *p;

  ob[0].set_num(10);   // access objects directly
  ob[1].set_num(20);
```

```
    p = &ob[0];   // obtain pointer to first element
    p->show_num(); // show value of ob[0] using pointer

    p++;   // advance to next object
    p->show_num(); // show value of ob[1] using pointer

    p--;   // retreat to previous object
    p->show_num(); // again show value of ob[0]

    return 0;
}
```

The output from this program is 10, 20, 10.

CHAPTER

Function and Operator Overloading

*F*unction and operator overloading are two of C++'s most important and versatile features. In fact, they are used in virtually all but the smallest C++ programs. You were introduced to function overloading in Chapter 1. This chapter examines further issues related to this topic and then moves on to operator overloading. Along the way, several other important features are introduced, including references.

Overloading Constructor Functions

Although they perform a unique service, constructor functions are not much different from other types of functions, and they too can be overloaded. To overload a class's constructor function, simply declare the various forms it will take and define its action relative to these forms. For example, the following program declares a class called **timer** that acts as a countdown timer (such as a darkroom timer). When an object of type **timer** is created, it is given an initial time value. When the **run()** function is called, the timer counts down to zero and then rings the bell. In this example, the constructor has been overloaded to allow the time to be specified as an integer, a string, or as two integers corresponding to minutes and seconds.

This program makes use of Turbo C++'s **clock()** function, which returns the number of system clock ticks since the program began running. Dividing this value by the macro **CLK_TCK** converts the return value of **clock()** into seconds. Both the prototype for **clock()** and the definition of **CLK_TCK** are found in the header file TIME.H.

```
#include <iostream.h>
#include <stdlib.h>
#include <time.h>

class timer{
  int seconds;
public:
  // seconds specified as a string
  timer(char *t) { seconds = atoi(t); }

  // seconds specified as integer
```

```
    timer(int t) { seconds = t; }

    // time specified in minutes and seconds
    timer(int min, int sec) { seconds = min*60 + sec; }

    void run();
} ;

void timer::run()
{
  clock_t t1, t2;

  t1 = t2 = clock()/CLK_TCK;
  while(seconds) {
    if(t1/CLK_TCK+1 <= (t2=clock())/CLK_TCK) {
        seconds--;
        t1 = t2;
        cout << '.';
    }
  }
  cout << "\a\n"; // ring the bell
}

main()
{
  timer a(10), b("20"), c(1, 10);

  a.run(); // count 10 seconds
  b.run(); // count 20 seconds
  c.run(); // count 1 minute, 10 seconds

  return 0;
}
```

As you can see, when **a**, **b**, and **c** are created inside **main()**, they are given initial values using the three different methods supported by the overloaded constructor functions. Each approach causes the appropriate constructor to be utilized, thus properly initializing all three variables.

In the program just shown, you may see little value in overloading a constructor function because it is not difficult to simply decide on a single way to specify the time. However, if you were creating a library of classes for someone else to use, you might want to supply constructors for the most common forms of initialization to give the user the most flexibility. Also, as you will shortly see, there is one C++ attribute that makes overloaded constructors quite valuable.

Before the discussion of overloading continues, a few short digressions are in order. The topics of the next few sections relate, ultimately, to how overloading is used.

Local Variable Declaration in C++

In C, you must declare all local variables used within a block at the start of that block. You cannot declare a variable in a block after an action statement has occurred. For example, in C, this fragment is incorrect:

```
/* incorrect in C */
f()
{
  int i;

  i = 10;

  int j;
  .
  .
  .
}
```

Because the statement **i=10** intervenes between the declaration of **i** and that of **j**, a C compiler will flag an error and refuse to compile this function. However, in C++, this fragment is perfectly acceptable and will compile without error. For example:

```
#include <iostream.h>
#include <string.h>

main()
{
  int i;
```

```
i = 10;

int j = 100; // perfectly legal in C++

cout << i*j << "\n";

cout << "Enter a string: ";
char str[80]; // declare str when it is needed
cin >> str;

// display the string in reverse order
int k;  // declare k where it is needed
k = strlen(str);
k--;
while(k>=0) {
  cout << str[k];
  k--;
}

  return 0;
}
```

As this program illustrates, in C++, you may declare local variables anywhere within a block of code. Since much of the philosophy behind C++ is the encapsulation of code and data, it makes sense that you can declare variables close to where they are used instead of just at the beginning of the block. In this example, the declarations of **i** and **j** are separated simply for illustration. However, you can see how the localization of **str** amd **k** to their relevant code helps encapsulate each routine. Declaring variables close to their use can help you avoid accidental side effects.

 Remember   In C++, you may declare local variables anywhere within a block, not just at the beginning of it. Declaring variables close to where they are used is often called *variable localization.*

Dynamic Initialization

In both C and C++, local variables can be initialized at run time using any valid expression. This means that local variables can be initialized using constants, function calls, and global variables. When global variables or function calls are used to initialize a variable, the process is sometimes referred to as *dynamic initialization* because these values are known only at run time. In C, although local variables may be dynamically initialized, global variables must be initialized using a constant expression. This is because a C compiler fixes a global variable's initialization code at compile time. However, in C++, this restriction no longer applies. In C++, a global variable can be initialized at run time using any expression valid at the time the variable is declared. For example, these are perfectly valid local or global variable initializations in C++:

```
        .
        .
        .
int n = atoi(gets(str));

long pos = ftell(fp);

double d = 1.02 * count / deltax;
```

Because of the ability to apply dynamic initialization to both global and local variables, you can create more flexible constructor functions, as the next section describes.

Applying Dynamic Initialization to Constructors

Like simple variables, objects can be initialized dynamically when they are created. This feature means that you can create exactly the type of object you need by using information that is known only at run time—whether that object is local or global. To illustrate how dynamic initialization works, this section reworks the timer program shown earlier in this chapter.

As stated, in the first example of the timer program, there appeared little to be gained by overloading the **timer()** constructor. However, in cases when an object will be initialized at run time, there may be significant advantages in allowing various initialization formats to be used because doing so allows you the flexibility of using the constructor that most closely matches the format of the data. For example, in the version of the timer program given here, two objects, **b** and **c**, are constructed at run time using dynamic initialization. One object, **a**, is constructed using a constant.

```cpp
#include <iostream.h>
#include <stdlib.h>
#include <time.h>

class timer{
  int seconds;
public:
  // seconds specified as a string
  timer(char *t) { seconds = atoi(t); }

  // seconds specified as integer
  timer(int t) { seconds = t; }

  // time specified in minutes and seconds
  timer(int min, int sec) { seconds = min*60 + sec; }

  void run();
} ;

void timer::run()
{
  clock_t t1, t2;

  t1 = t2 = clock()/CLK_TCK;
  while(seconds) {
    if(t1/CLK_TCK+1 <= (t2=clock())/CLK_TCK) {
      seconds--;
      t1 = t2;
      cout << '.';
    }
  }
  cout << "\a\n"; // ring the bell
}

main()
{
```

```
timer a(10); // construct using constant

a.run();

cout << "Enter number of seconds: ";
char str[80];
cin >> str;
timer b(str); // initialize at run time
b.run();

cout << "Enter minutes and seconds: ";
int min, sec;
cin >> min >> sec;
timer c(min, sec); // initialize at run time
c.run();

return 0;
}
```

As you can see, object **a** is constructed using an integer constant. However, objects **b** and **c** are constructed with information entered by the user. For **b**, since the user enters a string, it makes sense for **timer()** to be overloaded to accept it. In similar fashion, object **c** is also constructed at run time with user-input information. In this case, since the time is entered as minutes and seconds, it is logical to use this form to construct object **c**. Because various initialization formats are allowed, you need not perform any unnecessary conversions from one form to another when initializing an object. Instead, you may choose the best method of creating an object based upon the form of the data present at that point in your program. Furthermore, because variables can be declared close to where they are used, it makes sense to initialize them dynamically when appropriate. Thus, the combination of dynamic initialization, localization of variable declarations, and constructor overloading forms a powerful programming tool.

Keep in mind that the point of overloading constructor functions is to help you handle greater complexity by allowing objects to be constructed in the most natural manner relative to their specific use. Since there are three common ways to pass timing values to an object, it makes sense that **timer()** be overloaded to accept each way. However, overloading **timer()** to accept hours or days, or even nanoseconds, is probably not a good idea. Littering your code with constructors to handle seldom-used contingencies has a destabilizing influence on your program. The point here is that you must decide what constitutes valid constructor overloading and what is frivolous.

The this Keyword

Before the discussion moves on to operator overloading, it is necessary for you to learn about another C++ keyword, called **this**. It is an essential ingredient for many overloaded operators.

Each time a member function is invoked, it is automatically passed a pointer to the object that invoked it. You can access this pointer by using **this**. Further, this pointer is automatically passed to a member function when it is called. That is, the **this** pointer is an *implicit parameter* to all member functions.

As you know, a member function may directly access the private data of its class. For example, given this class:

```
class cl {
  int i;
  .
  .
  .
};
```

a member function can assign **i** the value 10 by using this statement:

```
i = 10;
```

In actuality, this statement is shorthand for

```
this->i = 10;
```

To see how the **this** pointer works, examine this short program:

```
#include <iostream.h>

class cl {
  int i;
```

```
public:
  void load_i(int val) { this->i = val; } // same as i = val
  int get_i() { return this->i; } // same as return i
} ;

main()
{
  cl o;

  o.load_i(100);
  cout << o.get_i();

  return 0;
}
```

This program displays the number **100**.

While the preceding example is trivial—in fact, no one would actually use the **this** pointer in this way—in the next section you will see why the **this** pointer is so important.

To review, the **this** pointer is a pointer to the object that generated a call to a member function.

Operator Overloading

Another feature of C++, which is related to function overloading, is called *operator overloading*. With very few exceptions, most of C++'s operators may be given special meanings relative to specific classes. For example, a class that defines a linked list might use the + operator to add an object to the list. Another class might use the + operator in an entirely different way. When an operator is overloaded, none of its original meaning is lost. It is simply that a new operation relative to a specific class is defined. Therefore, overloading the + to handle a linked list does not cause its meaning relative to integers (that is, addition) to be changed.

To overload an operator, you must define what that operation means relative to the class to which it is applied. To do this, you create an operator function, which defines its action. The general form of an operator function is shown here.

type classname::operator#(*arg-list*)
{
  // operation defined relative to the class
}

Here, *type* is the type of value returned by the specified operation. Often, the return value is of the same type as the class (although it could be of any type you choose). Overloaded operators often have a return value that is of the same type as the class for which the operator is overloaded because it facilitates their use in complex expressions, as you will soon see. The # will be replaced by the operator you are overloading.

Operator functions must be either members or friends of the class for which they are being used. Although the methods are very similar, there are some differences between the way a member operator function is overloaded and the way a friend operator function is overloaded. In this section, only member functions are overloaded. Later in this chapter, you will see how to overload friend operator functions.

Let's start with a simple example that creates a class called **three_d** that maintains the coordinates of an object in three-dimensional space. This program overloads the + and the = operators relative to the **three_d** class. Examine it closely.

```
#include <iostream.h>

class three_d {
  int x, y, z; // 3-d coordinates
public:
  three_d operator+(three_d t);
  three_d operator=(three_d t);

  void show() ;
  void assign(int mx, int my, int mz);
} ;

// Overload the +.
three_d three_d::operator+(three_d t)
{
  three_d temp;

  temp.x = x + t.x; // these are integer additions
```

```
    temp.y = y + t.y; // and the + retains its original
    temp.z = z + t.z; // meaning relative to them
    return temp;
}


// Overload the =.
three_d three_d::operator=(three_d t)
{
  x = t.x; // these are integer assignments
  y = t.y; // and the = retains its original
  z = t.z; // meaning relative to them
  return *this;
}


// Show the X,Y,Z coordinates.
void three_d::show()
{
  cout << x << ", ";
  cout << y << ", ";
  cout << z << "\n";
}


// Assign coordinates.
void three_d::assign(int mx, int my, int mz)
{
  x = mx;
  y = my;
  z = mz;
}


main()
{
  three_d a, b, c;

  a.assign(1, 2, 3);
  b.assign(10, 10, 10);

  a.show();
  b.show();

  c = a+b;   // now add a and b together
  c.show();
```

```
  c = a+b+c; // add a, b, and c together
  c.show();

  c = b = a;  // demonstrate multiple assignment
  c.show();
  b.show();

  return 0;
}
```

This program produces the following output:

```
1, 2, 3
10, 10, 10
11, 12, 13
22, 24, 26
1, 2, 3
1, 2, 3
```

As you examined this program, you may have been surprised to see that both operator functions had only one parameter each, even though they overloaded binary operations. The reason for this apparent contradiction is that when a binary operator is overloaded using a member function, only one argument needs to be explicitly passed to it. The other argument is implicitly passed using the **this** pointer. Thus, in the line

```
temp.x = x + t.x;
```

the **x** refers to **this–>x**, which is the **x** associated with the object that prompted the call to the operator function. In all cases, it is the object on the left side of an operation that causes the call to the operator function. The object on the right side is passed to the function.

In general, when you use a member function, no parameters are needed when you are overloading a unary operator, and only one parameter is required when you are overloading a binary operator. (You cannot overload the ? ternary operator.) In either case, the object that causes the activation of the operator function is implicitly passed via the **this** pointer.

To understand how operator overloading works, let's examine this program carefully, beginning with the overloaded operator +. When two objects of type **three_d** are operated on by the + operator, the magnitudes of their respective coordinates are added together, as shown in the **operator+()** function associated with this class. Notice, however, that this function does not modify the value of either operand. Instead, an object of type **three_d** is returned by the function that contains the result of the operation. This is an important point. To understand why the + operation must not change the contents of either object, think about the standard arithmetic + operation as applied like this: 10+12. The outcome of this operation is 22, but neither 10 nor 12 is changed by it. Although there is no rule that states an overloaded operator must perform the same way as it does for any of C++'s built-in types, it usually makes sense to stay within the spirit of its original use.

Another key point about how the + operator is overloaded is that it returns an object of type **three_d**. Although the function could have returned any valid C++ type, the fact that it returns a **three_d** object allows the + operator to be used in more complex expressions, such as **a+b+c**.

Contrasting with the + operator, the assignment operator does, indeed, cause one of its arguments to be modified. (This is, after all, the very essence of assignment.) Since the **operator=()** function is called by the object that occurs on the left side of the assigment, it is this object that is modified by the assignment operation. However, even the assignment operation must return a value because, in C++ (as well as in C), the assignment operation produces the value that occurs on the right side. Thus, to allow statements like

```
a = b = c = d;
```

operator=() must return the object pointed to by **this**, which will be the object that occurs on the left side of the assignment statement, thus allowing a string of assignments to be made.

Overloading the ++ and – – Operators

You may also overload unary operators, such as ++ or – –. As stated earlier, when overloading a unary operator, no object is explicitly passed to the operator function. That is, a unary operator function takes no objects as parameters. Instead, the operation is performed on the object that generates the call to the function through the implicitly passed **this** pointer. For example, here is an expanded version of the previous example program that defines the prefix increment operation for objects of type **three_d**:

```
#include <iostream.h>

class three_d {
  int x, y, z; // 3-d coordinates
public:
  three_d operator+(three_d op2);  // op1 is implied
  three_d operator=(three_d op2);  // op1 is implied
  three_d operator++(); // op1 is also implied here

  void show() ;
  void assign(int mx, int my, int mz);
} ;

three_d three_d::operator+(three_d op2)
{
  three_d temp;

  temp.x = x+op2.x;  // these are integer additions
  temp.y = y+op2.y;  // and the + retains its original
  temp.z = z+op2.z;  // meaning relative to them
  return temp;
}


three_d three_d::operator=(three_d op2)
{
  x = op2.x; // these are integer assigments
  y = op2.y; // and the = retains its original
  z = op2.z; // meaning relative to them
  return *this;
}

// Overload the ++ prefix operator.
three_d three_d::operator++()
{
  x++; // ++ retains its original meaning
```

```
  y++; // relative to integers
  z++;
  return *this; // return incremented value
}

// Show the X,Y,Z coordinates.
void three_d::show()
{
  cout << x << ", ";
  cout << y << ", ";
  cout << z << "\n";
}

// Assign coordinates.
void three_d::assign(int mx, int my, int mz)
{
  x = mx;
  y = my;
  z = mz;
}

main()
{
  three_d a, b, c;

  a.assign(1, 2, 3);
  b.assign(10, 10, 10);

  a.show();
  b.show();

  c = a+b;   // now add a and b together
  c.show();

  c = a+b+c; // add a, b, and c together
  c.show();

  c = b = a; // demonstrate multiple assignment
  c.show();
  b.show();

  ++c; // increment c
```

```
c.show();

return 0;
}
```

The − − prefix is overloaded the same way, except, of course, the values of **x**, **y**, and **z** are decremented. You might want to try this on your own.

As stated, the preceding program overloads the ++ as a prefix operator. As you should know, in both C and C++, the following operations are slightly different:

```
x = i++; // postfix
x = ++i; // prefix
```

In the postfix assignment, the value of **i** is first assigned to **x**, and then it is incremented. In the prefix version, the value of **i** is first incremented and then assigned to **x**. In the preceding program, in which ++ was overloaded for objects of type **three_d**, only the prefix version of ++ was implemented. This is the form automatically created when using this general form of the operator function:

// Generic form for the prefix ++ or − −
type operator##()
{
  // ...
}

Here, *type* is the class type for which the ++ or − − is defined, and ## is either ++ or − −.

To overload the increment or decrement operators so they operate as a postfix operator, you must create another operator function that takes a slightly different form. For example, the general form for the postfix version of the ++ or − − is shown here:

// Generic form for postfix ++ or − −
type operator##(int i)
{
  // ...
}

This version is called when an object of type *type* is incremented using the postfix ++ operation. The parameter **i** is a placeholder and is not used. It simply distinguishes between the prefix and postfix functions. Here is another version of the preceding program that includes both a prefix and a postfix form of the ++ operator:

```
// Demonstrate how to create prefix and postfix unary operators.
#include <iostream.h>

class three_d {
  int x, y, z; // 3-d coordinates
 public:
   three_d operator+(three_d op2); // op1 is implied
   three_d operator=(three_d op2); // op1 is implied
   three_d operator++(); // prefix
   three_d operator++(int i); // postfix
   void show() ;
   void assign(int mx, int my, int mz);
} ;

// Overload + for three_d.
three_d three_d::operator+(three_d op2)
{
   three_d temp;

   temp.x = x + op2.x; // these are integer additions
   temp.y = y + op2.y; // and the + retains its original
   temp.z = z + op2.z; // meaning relative to them
   return temp;
}

// Overload = for three_d.
three_d three_d::operator=(three_d op2)
{
  x = op2.x; // these are integer assigments
  y = op2.y; // and the = retains its original
  z = op2.z; // meaning relative to them
  return *this;
}

// Overload a prefix unary operator.
three_d three_d::operator++()
```

```
{
  x++; // ++ retains original meaning relative
  y++; // to integers
  z++;
  return *this; // return incremented value
}

// Overload a postfix unary operator.
three_d three_d::operator++(int i)
{
  three_d temp = *this; // make copy of operand
  x++;
  y++;
  z++;
  return temp; // return original value
}

// Show the X,Y,Z coordinates.
void three_d::show()
{
  cout << x << ", ";
  cout << y << ", ";
  cout << z << "\n";
}

// Assign coordinates.
void three_d::assign(int mx, int my, int mz)
{
  x = mx;
  y = my;
  z = mz;
}

main()
{
  three_d a, b, c;

  a.assign(1, 2, 3);
  b.assign(10, 10, 10);

  a.show();
  b.show();
```

```
c = a+b; // now add a and b together
c.show();

c = a+b+c; // add a, b, and c together
c.show();

c = b = a; // demonstrate multiple assignment
c.show();
b.show();

cout << "Postfix increment: ";
a = c++; // demonstrate postfix operation
a.show();
c.show();

cout << "Prefix increment: ";
a = ++c; // demonstrate prefix operation
a.show();
c.show();

return 0;
}
```

Notice that in this version, the postfix form of ++ returns a temporary object that holds the original contents of the object that generates the call. This is necessary because it is this value that is used by a larger expression, not the one that is incremented.

 Remember   In general, a member unary operator function takes no parameters. However, when it is applied to the increment or decrement operators, it causes the prefix version of the operator to be overloaded. To create the postfix version, add the dummy integer parameter.

Using Overloaded Operators Correctly

The action of an overloaded operator as applied to the class for which it is defined need not bear any relationship to that operator's default usage as applied to C++'s built-in types. For example, the << and >> as applied to **cout** and **cin** have nothing in common with the same operators applied to integer types. However, for the purposes of the structure and readability of your code, an overloaded operator should reflect, when possible, the spirit of the operator's original use. For example, the + relative to **three_d** is conceptually similar to the + relative to integer types. There is little benefit, for example, in defining the + operator relative to some classes so it acts more the way you would expect the % operator to perform. The key concept here is that while you may give an overloaded operator any meaning you like, it is best, for clarity, when that new meaning is related to the original meaning.

Some restrictions to overloading operators also apply. First, you may not alter the precedence of any operator. Second, you cannot alter the number of operands required by the operand, although your operator function could choose to ignore an operand. Finally, except for the =, overloaded operators are inherited by any derived classes. (Of course, you may overload operators relative to the derived class if necessary.) However, each class must define explicitly its own overloaded = operator if one is needed.

The only operators you may not overload are shown here:

```
.  ::  .*  ?
```

The .* is a rarely used operator. Its purpose is to dereference a pointer to a class (not an object) member, and its use is beyond the scope of this book.

Friend Operator Functions

It is possible for an operator function to be a friend of a class rather than a member. As you learned earlier in this chapter, friend functions do not have the implied argument **this**. Therefore, when a friend is used to overload an operator, both operands are passed explicitly when binary operators are overloaded and a single operand is passed when unary operators are overloaded. The only operators that cannot use friend functions are =, (), [], and ->. The rest may use either member or friend functions to implement the specified operation relative to its class. For example, here is a modified version of the preceding program that uses a friend instead of a member function to overload the + operation:

```
// Demonstrate friend operator function.
#include <iostream.h>

class three_d {
  int x, y, z; // 3-d coordinates
public:
  // now, operator+ is a friend
  friend three_d operator+(three_d op1, three_d op2);

  three_d operator=(three_d op2);  // op1 is implied
  three_d operator++(); // prefix
  three_d operator++(int i); // postfix

  void show() ;
  void assign(int mx, int my, int mz);
} ;

/* Overload + for three_d as a friend. Both operands
   are now passed explicitly. */
three_d operator+(three_d op1, three_d op2)
{
  three_d temp;

  temp.x = op1.x + op2.x; // these are integer additions
  temp.y = op1.y + op2.y; // and the + retains its original
  temp.z = op1.z + op2.z; // meaning relative to them
  return temp;
}

// Overload = for three_d.
three_d three_d::operator=(three_d op2)
{
  x = op2.x; // these are integer assignments
  y = op2.y; // and the = retains its original
  z = op2.z; // meaning relative to them
  return *this;
}

// Overload a prefix unary operator.
three_d three_d::operator++()
{
  x++; // ++ retains original meaning relative
```

```
  y++; // to integers.
  z++;
  return *this; // return incremented value
}
// Overload a postfix unary operator.
three_d three_d::operator++(int i)
{
  three_d temp = *this; // make copy of operand
  x++;
  y++;
  z++;
  return temp; // return original value
}

// Show the X,Y,Z coordinates.
void three_d::show()
{
  cout << x << ", ";
  cout << y << ", ";
  cout << z << "\n";
}

// Assign coordinates.
void three_d::assign(int mx, int my, int mz)
{
  x = mx;
  y = my;
  z = mz;
}

main()
{
  three_d a, b, c;

  a.assign(1, 2, 3);
  b.assign(10, 10, 10);

  a.show();
  b.show();

  c = a+b; // now add a and b together
  c.show();
```

```
c = a+b+c; // add a, b, and c together
c.show();

c = b = a; // demonstrate multiple assignment
c.show();
b.show();

cout << "Postfix increment: ";
a = c++; // demonstrate postfix operation
a.show();
c.show();

cout << "Prefix increment: ";
a = ++c; // demonstrate prefix operation
a.show();
c.show();

return 0;
}
```

As you can see by looking at **operator+()**, now both operands are passed to it. The left operand is passed in **op1** and the right operand in **op2**.

In many cases, there is no benefit to using a friend function instead of a member function when overloading an operator. However, there is one situation in which you must use a friend function. As you know, a pointer to the object that invokes a member operator function is passed in **this**. In the case of binary operators, the object on the left invokes the function. This is fine, provided that the object on the left defines the specified operation. For example, assuming some object called **O** that has assignment and addition defined for it, this is a perfectly valid statement:

```
O = O + 10; // will work
```

Since the object **O** is on the left of the + operator, it invokes its overloaded operator function, which (presumably) is capable of adding an integer value to some element of **O**. However, this statement won't work:

```
O = 10 + O; // won't work
```

The statement won't work because the object on the left is an integer, which is a built-in type for which no operation involving an integer and an object of **O**'s type is defined.

The problem of built-in types on the left side of an operation can be eliminated if the + is overloaded by using two friend functions. In this case, the operator function is explicitly passed both arguments, and it is invoked like any other overloaded function, based upon the types of its arguments. Overloading the + (or any other binary operator) by using a friend allows a built-in type to occur on the left side of the operator. The following program illustrates how to accomplish this:

```
#include <iostream.h>

class CL {
public:
  int count;
  CL operator=(int i);
  friend CL operator+(CL ob, int i);
  friend CL operator+(int i, CL ob);
};

CL CL::operator=(int i)
{
  count = i;
  return *this;
}

// This handles ob + int.
CL operator+(CL ob, int i)
{
  CL temp;

  temp.count = ob.count + i;
  return temp;
}

// This handles int + ob.
CL operator+(int i, CL ob)
{
  CL temp;
```

```
    temp.count = ob.count + i;
    return temp;
}

main()
{
    CL obj;

    obj = 10;
    cout << obj.count << " "; // outputs 10

    obj = 10 + obj; // add object to integer
    cout << obj.count << " "; // outputs 20

    obj = obj + 12; // add integer to object
    cout << obj.count;        // outputs 32

    return 0;
}
```

As you can see, the **operator+()** function is overloaded twice to accommodate the two ways in which an integer and an object of type **CL** may occur in the addition operation.

Although you may use a friend function to overload a unary operator, such as ++, you first need to know about another feature of C++, called the reference, which is the subject of the next section.

References

By default, C and C++ pass arguments to a function by using call-by-value. As you know, passing an argument by using call-by-value causes a copy of that argument to be used by the function and prevents the argument used in the call from being modified by the function. In C (and optionally in C++), when a function needs to be able to alter the values of the variables used as arguments, the parameters need to be explicitly declared as pointer types, and the function must operate on the calling variables by using the * pointer operator. For example, the following program implements a function called **swap()**, which exchanges its two integer arguments:

```
#include <iostream.h>

void swap(int *a, int *b);

main()
{
  int i, j;

  i = 10;
  j = 20;

  cout << i << " " << j << "\n";

  swap(&i, &j); // exchange their values

  cout << i << " " << j << "\n";

  return 0;
}

// C-like, explicit pointer version of swap().
void swap(int *a, int *b)
{
  int t;

  t = *a;
  *a = *b;
  *b = t;
}
```

When **swap()** is called, the variables used in the call must be preceded by the & operator in order to produce a pointer to each argument. This is the way that a call-by-reference is generated in C. However, even though C++ still allows this syntax, it supports a cleaner, more transparent method of generating a call-by-reference, using what is called a *reference* parameter.

In C++, it is possible to tell the compiler to automatically generate a call-by-reference rather than a call-by-value for one or more parameters of a particular function. You accomplish this by preceding the parameter name in the function's declaration with the &. For example, here is a function called **f()**, which takes one reference parameter of type **float**:

```
void f(int &f)
{
  f = rand(); // this modifies calling argument
}
```

This declaration form is also used in the function's prototype. Notice that the statement **f = rand()** does not use the * pointer operator. When you declare a reference parameter, the C++ compiler automatically knows it is a pointer and dereferences it for you.

Once the compiler has seen this declaration, it will automatically pass **f()** the *address* of any argument it is called with. For example, given this fragment

```
int val;

f(val);  // get random value
printf("%d", val);
```

the address of **val**, not its value, will be passed to **f()**. Thus, **f()** may modify the value of **val**.

If you are familar with Pascal, it may help to know that a reference parameter in C++ is similar to a **VAR** parameter in Pascal.

To demonstrate reference parameters in actual use, the **swap()** function is rewritten here with references. Look carefully at how **swap()** is declared and called.

```
#include <iostream.h>

void swap(int &a, int &b); // declare as reference parameters

main()
{
  int i, j;

  i = 10;
  j = 20;

  cout << i << " " << j << "\n";

  swap(i, j); // exchange their values
```

```
    cout << i << " " << j << "\n";

    return 0;
}

/* Here, swap() is defined as using call-by-reference,
   not call-by-value. */
void swap(int &a, int &b)
{
  int t;

  t = a;
  a = b;   // this swaps i
  b = t;   // this swaps j
}
```

Returning References

A second way that a reference can be used is when one is returned by a function. To declare a function as returning a reference, simply follow the return type name with the &. For example, this prototype states that **f()** will return a reference to an integer:

```
int &f();
```

Inside a function that returns a reference, to return a reference, simply return an object. The compiler will automatically return that object's address. For example, here **f()** returns a reference to **i**:

```
int &f()
{
  int i;

  cin >> i:   // get a value for i

  return i; // automatically returns reference to i
}
```

Later in this book you will see how valuable functions returning references can be.

Stylistic Note

Some C++ programmers associate the & with the type rather than the variable. For example, here is another way to write the prototype to **swap()**:

```
void swap(int& a, int& b);
```

Further, some C++ programmers also specify pointers by associating the * with the type rather the variable, as shown here:

```
float* p;
```

These types of declarations reflect the desire by some programmers for C++ to contain a separate pointer type. However, the trouble with associating the & or * with the type rather than the variable is that, according to formal C++ syntax, neither the & nor the * is transitive over a list of variables, and this can lead to confusing declarations. For example, the following declaration creates one, not two, integer pointers. Here, **b** is declared as an integer (not an integer pointer) because, as specified by the C++ syntax, when used in a declaration, the * and & are linked to the individual variable they precede, not to the type they follow:

```
int* a, b;
```

It is important to understand that as far as the C++ compiler is concerned, it doesn't matter whether you write **int *p** or **int* p**. Thus, if you prefer to associate the * or & with the type rather than with the variable, feel free to do so. However, to avoid confusion, this book will continue to associate the * and the & with the variable that it modifies rather than the type.

Independent References

It is possible to declare a reference variable that is not a parameter to a function or a return type from a function. You do this by using what is called an independent reference. It must be stated at the outset, however, that independent references are seldom a good idea because they tend to confuse and destructure your program. With these reservations in mind, let's take a short look at them here.

An *independent reference* is, essentially, just another name for another variable. An independent reference must be initialized when it is declared. This means it will be assigned the address of a previously declared variable. Once this is done, the reference variable may be used anywhere that the variable it references may. In fact, there is virtually no distinction between the two. For example, consider this program:

```
#include <iostream.h>

main()
{
  int j, k;
  int &i = j;

  j = 10;

  cout << j << " " << i; // outputs 10 10

  k = 121;
  i = k; // copies k's value into j
      // not k's address

  cout << "\n" << j;  // outputs 121

  return 0;
}
```

This program displays this output:

```
10 10
121
```

The key point is that the object pointed to by the reference variable is fixed. Thus, when the statement **i = k** is evaluated, it is **k**'s value that is copied into **j** (pointed to by **i**), not its address. In other words, references are not pointers!

There are several restrictions that apply to stand-alone reference variables. First, you cannot reference a reference variable. That is, you cannot take its address. Second, references are not allowed on bit-fields. Third, you cannot create arrays of references. Finally, you cannot create a pointer to a reference.

You may also use an independent reference to point to a constant. For example, this is valid:

```
int &i = 100;
```

In this case, **i** references the location in your program's constant table where the value 100 is stored.

As stated earlier, in general it is not a good idea to use independent references because they are not necessary and tend to confuse your code.

Using a Reference to Overload a Unary Operator

In the final version of the timer program from the preceding section, the ++ operator was not overloaded using a friend function because it required the use of a reference. In this section you learn why.

To begin, consider the original version of the overloaded prefix ++ operator relative to the **three_d**. It is shown here for your convenience:

```
// Overload prefix ++ operator.
three_d three_d::operator++()
{
  x++;
  y++;
  z++;
```

```
   return *this;
}
```

As you know, all member functions have as an implicit first argument a pointer to themselves that is referenced inside the member function by using the keyword **this**. This is why, when you overload a unary operator by using a member function, no argument is explicitly declared. The only argument needed in this situation is the implicit pointer to the object that activated the call to the overloaded operator function. Since **this** is a pointer to the object, any changes made to the object's private data will affect the object that generates the call to the operator function. Unlike member functions, a friend function does not receive a **this** pointer and therefore cannot reference the object that activated it. For this reason, trying to create a friend **operator++()** function as shown here will not work.

```
// THIS WILL NOT WORK
three_d operator++(three_d op1)
{
   op1.x++;
   op1.y++;
   op1.z++;
   return op1;
}
```

This function will not work because only a *copy* of the object that activated the call to **operator++()** is passed to the function in parameter **op1**. Thus, the changes inside **operator++()** will not affect the called object.

You might at first think that the solution to the preceding program is to define the friend operator function as shown here, using a pointer to the object which activates the call:

```
// THIS WILL NOT WORK
three_d operator++(three_d *op1)
{
   op1->x++;
   op1->y++;
   op1->z++;
   return *op1;
}
```

While this function is correct as far as it goes, C++ does not know how to correctly activate it. For example, assuming this version of the **operator++()** function, this code fragment will not compile:

```
three_d ob(1, 2, 3);

&ob++; // will not compile
```

The trouble is that the statement **&ob++** is inherently ambiguous.

The way to use a friend when overloading a unary ++ or − − is to use a reference parameter. In this way, the compiler knows in advance that it must generate an address when it calls the function. This avoids the ambiguity introduced by the previous attempt. Here is the entire **three_d** program that uses friend **operator++()** functions. Notice the difference between the prefix and postfix forms.

```
// This version uses friend operator++() functions.
#include <iostream.h>

class three_d {
  int x, y, z; // 3-d coordinates
public:
  friend three_d operator+(three_d op1, three_d op2);
  three_d operator=(three_d op2); // op1 is implied

  // use a reference to overload the ++
  friend three_d operator++(three_d &op1); // prefix
  friend three_d operator++(three_d &op1, int i); // postfix

  void show() ;
  void assign(int mx, int my, int mz);
} ;

// Overload + using friend function.
three_d operator+(three_d op1, three_d op2)
{
  three_d temp;

  temp.x = op1.x + op2.x; // these are integer additions
  temp.y = op1.y + op2.y; // and the + retains its original
  temp.z = op1.z + op2.z; // meaning relative to them
```

```
    return temp;
}

// Overload = for three_d.
three_d three_d::operator=(three_d op2)
{
  x = op2.x; // these are integer assigments
  y = op2.y; // and the = retains its original
  z = op2.z; // meaning relative to them
  return *this;
}

/* Overload a prefix unary operator using a friend function.
   This requires the use of a reference parameter.
*/
three_d operator++(three_d &op1)
{
  op1.x++; // ++ retains its original meaning
  op1.y++; // relative to integers
  op1.z++;
  return op1; // return incremented value
}

/* Overload a postfix unary operator using a friend function.
   This requires the use of a reference parameter.
*/
three_d operator++(three_d &op1, int i)
{
  three_d temp = op1; // make copy of operand
  op1.x++;
  op1.y++;
  op1.z++;
  return temp; // return original value
}

// show X,Y,Z coordinates
void three_d::show()
{
  cout << x << ", ";
  cout << y << ", ";
  cout << z << "\n";
}
```

```
// Assign coordinates
void three_d::assign(int mx, int my, int mz)
{
  x = mx;
  y = my;
  z = mz;
}

main()
{
  three_d a, b, c;

  a.assign(1, 2, 3);
  b.assign(10, 10, 10);

  a.show();
  b.show();

  c = a+b; // now add a and b together
  c.show();

  c = a+b+c; // add a, b, and c together
  c.show();

  c = b = a; // demonstrate multiple assignment
  c.show();
  b.show();

  ++c; // prefix increment c
  c.show();

  c++; // postfix increment c
  c.show();

  return 0;
}
```

Because a friend operator function has its operands passed explicitly, the prefix version of the ++ operator function takes one parameter: the object that generates the call. The postfix version adds the dummy integer parameter, which is used to distinguish the two.

Keep in mind one important point: in general, you should use member functions to implement overloaded operators. Remember, friend functions are allowed in C++ mostly to handle some special-case situations.

Another Example of Operator Overloading

To close this chapter, another example of operator overloading is developed that implements a string type and defines several operations relative to that type. As you might know, many newcomers to C (and C++) complain about the lack of an explicit string type. C strings are more flexible and efficiently implemented as character arrays rather than as a spearate type. However, to beginners, this approach can still lack the conceptual clarity of the way strings are implemented in languages such as BASIC. By using C++, it is possible to combine the best of both worlds by defining a string class and operations that relate to that class.

To begin, the following class declares the type **str_type**:

```
#include <iostream.h>
#include <string.h>

class str_type {
  char string[80];
public:
  str_type(char *str = "\0") { strcpy(string, str); }

  str_type operator+(str_type str); // concatenate
  str_type operator=(str_type str); // assign

  // output the string
  void show_str() { cout << string; }
} ;
```

As you can see, **str_type** declares one string in its private portion. For the sake of this example, no string can be longer than 80 bytes. The class has one constructor function that can be used to initialize the array **string** with a specific value or assign it a null string in the absence of any initializer. It also declares two overloaded operators that will perform concatenation and assignment. Finally, it declares the function **show_str()**, which outputs **string** to the screen. The overloaded operator functions are shown here:

```
// Concatenate two strings.
str_type str_type::operator+(str_type str) {
  str_type temp;

  strcpy(temp.string, string);
  strcat(temp.string, str.string);
  return temp;
}

// Assign one string to another.
str_type str_type::operator=(str_type str) {
  strcpy(string, str.string);
  return *this;
}
```

Given these definitions, the following **main()** illustrates their use:

```
main()
{
  str_type a("Hello "), b("There"), c;

  c = a + b;

  c.show_str();

  return 0;
}
```

This program outputs **Hello There** on the screen. It first concatenates **a** with **b** and then assigns this value to **c**.

Keep in mind that both the = and the + are defined only for objects of type **str_type**. For example, this statement is invalid because it tries to assign object **a** a normal C++ string:

```
a = "this is currently wrong";
```

However, the **str_type** class can be enhanced to allow such a statement, as you will see next.

To expand the types of operations supported by the **str_type** class so you can assign strings to objects or concatenate a string with an object, you need to overload the + and = operations a second time. First, the class declaration is changed, as shown here:

```
class str_type {
  char string[80];
public:
  str_type(char *str = "\0") { strcpy(string, str); }

  str_type operator+(str_type str); // concatenate objects
  str_type operator+(char *str); // concatenate object with
                                 // a string

  str_type operator=(str_type str); // assign object to
                                     // object
  char *operator=(char *str); // assign string to object

  void show_str() { cout << string; }
} ;
```

Next, the overloaded **operator+()** and **operator=()** are implemented, as shown here:

```
// Assign a string to an object
str_type str_type::operator=(char *str)
{
  str_type temp;

  strcpy(string, str);
  strcpy(temp.string, string);
  return temp;
}

// Add a string to an object
str_type str_type::operator+(char *str)
{
  str_type temp;
```

```
  strcpy(temp.string, string);
  strcat(temp.string, str);
  return temp;
}
```

Look carefully at these functions. Notice that the right-side argument is not an object of type **str_type** but rather simply a pointer to a null-terminated character array—that is, a normal string in C++. However, notice that both functions return an object of type **str_type**. Although the functions could, in theory, have returned some other type, it makes the most sense to return an object since the targets of these operations are also objects. The advantage of defining string operations that accept normal C++ strings as the right-side operand is that doing so allows some statements to be written in a natural way. For example, these are now valid statements:

```
str_type a, b, c;

a = "hi there"; // assign an object a string

c = a + " George"; // concatenate an object with a string
```

The following program incorporates the additional meanings for the + and = operations and illustrates their use:

```
// Expanding the string type.
#include <iostream.h>
#include <string.h>

class str_type {
  char string[80];
public:
  str_type(char *str = "\0") { strcpy(string, str); }

  str_type operator+(str_type str);
  str_type operator+(char *str);

  str_type operator=(str_type str);
  str_type operator=(char *str);

  void show_str() { cout << string; }
} ;
```

```
// Overload + for strings.
str_type str_type::operator+(str_type str) {
  str_type temp;

  strcpy(temp.string, string);
  strcat(temp.string, str.string);
  return temp;
}

// Overload = for strings.
str_type str_type::operator=(str_type str) {
  strcpy(string, str.string);
  return *this;
}

// Overload = for char *.
str_type str_type::operator=(char *str)
{
  str_type temp;

  strcpy(string, str);
  strcpy(temp.string, string);
  return temp;
}

// Overload + for char *.
str_type str_type::operator+(char *str)
{
  str_type temp;

  strcpy(temp.string, string);
  strcat(temp.string, str);
  return temp;
}

main()
{
  str_type a("Hello "), b("There"), c;

  c = a + b;
```

```
   c.show_str();
   cout << "\n";

   a = "to program in because";
   a.show_str();
   cout << "\n";

   b = c = "C++ is fun";

   c = c+" "+a+" "+b;
   c.show_str();

   return 0;
}
```

This program displays the following on the screen:

```
Hello There
to program in because
C++ is fun to program in because C++ is fun
```

Before continuing, make sure you understand how this output is created. Also, on your own, try creating other string operations. You might try defining the − − so that it performs a substring deletion. For example, if object **A**'s string is "This is a test" and object **B**'s string is "is", then **A–B** yields "th a test". In this case, all occurrences of the substring are removed from the original string.

CHAPTER

Inheritance, Virtual Functions, and Polymorphism

Crucial to object oriented programming is polymorphism. As applied to C++, polymorphism is the term used to describe the process by which different implementations of a function can be accessed via the same name. For this reason, polymorphism is sometimes characterized by the phrase "one interface, multiple methods." This means that a general class of operations may be accessed in the same fashion even though the specific actions associated with each operation may differ.

In C++, polymorphism is supported both at run time and at compile time. Operator and function overloading are examples of compile-time polymorphism. However, as powerful as operator and function overloading are, they cannot perform all tasks required by a true object oriented language. Therefore, C++ also allows run-time polymorphism through the use of derived classes and virtual functions, and these are the major topics of this chapter.

This chapter begins with a short discussion of pointers to derived types because they are needed to support run-time polymorphism.

Pointers to Derived Types

Pointers to base types and derived types are related. Assume that you have a base type called **B_class** and a type called **D_class**, which is derived from **B_class**. In C++, any pointer declared as a pointer to **B_class** may also be a pointer to **D_class**. For example, given

```
B_class *p; // pointer to object of type B_class
B_class B_ob; // object of type B_class
D_class D_ob; // object of type D_class
```

then the following is perfectly valid:

```
p = &B_ob;  // p points to object of type B_class

p = &D_ob;  /* p points to object of type D_class,
                which is an object derived from B_class. */
```

Through the use of **p**, all elements of **D_ob** inherited from **B_ob** may be accessed. However, elements specific to **D_ob** may not be referenced by using **p**.

It is important to understand that in general, in C++, a pointer of one type cannot be used (without a type cast) to point to an object of another type. Therefore, the fact that a base pointer can point to an object of a derived type is an exception to C++'s strict type-checking rules.

For a concrete example of a base pointer accessing a derived object, consider this short program, which defines a base class called **B_class** and a derived class called **D_class**. The derived class implements a simple automated telephone book.

```cpp
// Using pointers on derived class objects.

#include <iostream.h>
#include <string.h>

class B_class {
  char name[80];
public:
  void put_name(char *s) {strcpy(name, s); }
  void show_name() {cout << name << " ";}
} ;

class D_class : public B_class {
  char phone_num[80];
public:
  void put_phone(char *num) {
    strcpy(phone_num, num);
  }
  void show_phone() {cout << phone_num << "\n";}
};

main()
{
  B_class *p;
  B_class B_ob;

  D_class *dp;
  D_class D_ob;

  p = &B_ob;  // address of base

  // Access B_class via pointer.
  p->put_name("Thomas Edison");
```

```
// Access D_class via base pointer.
p = &D_ob;
p->put_name("Albert Einstein");

// Show that each name went into proper object.
B_ob.show_name();
D_ob.show_name();

// may also call show_name() using p
p = &B_ob; // point to base object
p->show_name();
p = &D_ob; // point to derived object
p->show_name();

cout << "\n";

/* Since put_phone and show_phone are not part of the
   base class, they are not accessible via the base
   pointer p and must be accessed either directly
   or, as shown here, through a pointer to the
   derived type.
*/
dp = &D_ob;
dp->put_phone("555 555-1234");
p->show_name(); // either p or dp can be used in this line
dp->show_phone();
return 0;
}
```

In this example, the pointer **p** is defined as a pointer to **B_class**. However, it can point to an object of the derived class **D_class** and can be used to access those elements of the derived class that are defined by the base class. However, remember that a base pointer cannot access those elements specific to the derived class without the use of a type cast. This is why **show_ phone()** is accessed by using the **dp** pointer, which is a pointer to the derived class.

If you want to access elements defined by a derived type by using a base pointer, you must cast it into a pointer of the derived type. For example, this line of code will properly call the **show_ phone()** function of **D_ob**:

```
((D_class *)p)->show_phone();
```

The outer set of parentheses is necessary to associate the cast with **p** and not the return type of **show_ phone()**. While there is technically nothing wrong with casting a pointer in this manner, it is probably best avoided because it simply adds confusion to your code.

Another point to understand is that while you can use a base pointer to point to any type of derived object, the reverse is not true. That is, you cannot use a pointer to a derived class to access an object of the base type.

One final point: a pointer is incremented and decremented relative to its base type. Therefore, when a pointer to a base class is pointing at a derived class, incrementing or decrementing it will *not* make it point to the next object of the derived class. Instead, it would be pointing to what it thought was the next object of the base class. Therefore, you should consider it invalid to increment or decrement a pointer when it is pointing to a derived object.

The fact that a pointer to a base type may be used to point to any object derived from that base is extremely important and fundamental to C++. In fact, as you will soon learn, it is crucial to the way C++ implements run-time polymorphism.

Virtual Functions

As stated earlier in this chapter, run-time polymorphism is achieved through the use of derived types and virtual functions. In short, a *virtual function* is a function that is declared as virtual in a base class and redefined in one or more derived classes. What makes virtual functions special is that when one is accessed using a base pointer to an object of a derived class, C++ determines which function to call at run time based upon the type of object pointed to. Thus, when different objects are pointed to, different versions of the virtual function are automatically executed. This is how run-time polymorphism is achieved.

You declare a virtual function as virtual inside the base class by preceding its declaration with the keyword **virtual**. However, when a virtual function is redefined by a derived class, the keyword **virtual** need not be repeated (although it is not an error to do so).

As a first example of virtual functions, examine this short program:

```
// A short example that uses virtual functions.
#include <iostream.h>

class Base {
public:
  virtual void who() { // specify a virtual
    cout << "Base\n";
  }
};

class first_d : public Base {
public:
  void who() { // define who() relative to first_d
    cout << "First derivation\n";
  }
};

class second_d : public Base {
public:
  void who() { // define who() relative to second_d
    cout << "Second derivation\n";
  }
};

main()
{
  Base base_obj;
  Base *p;
  first_d first_obj;
  second_d second_obj;

  p = &base_obj;
  p->who();   // access Base's who

  p = &first_obj;
  p->who(); // access first_d's who
```

```
  p = &second_obj;
  p->who();  // access second_d's who

  return 0;
}
```

This program produces the following output:

```
Base
First derivation
Second derivation
```

Let's examine it in detail to understand how it works.

As you can see, in **Base**, the function **who()** is declared as virtual. This means that the function may be redefined by a derived class. Inside both **first_d** and **second_d**, **who()** is redefined relative to each class. Inside **main()**, four variables are declared: **base_obj**, which is an object of type **Base**; **p**, which is a pointer to **Base** objects; and **first_obj** and **second_obj**, which are objects of the two derived classes. Next, **p** is assigned the address of **base_obj** and the **who()** function is called. Since **who()** is declared as virtual, C++ determines, at run time, which version of **who()** is referred to by the type of object pointed to by **p**. In this case, it is an object of type **Base**, so it is the version of **who()** declared in **Base** that is executed. Next, **p** is assigned the address of **first_obj**. Remember, a base class pointer may be used to reference any derived class. Now, when **who()** is called, C++ again examines what type of object is pointed to by **p** to determine what version of **who()** to call. Since **p** points to an object of type **first_d**, that version of **who()** is used. Likewise, when **p** is assigned the address **second_obj**, the version of **who()** declared inside **second_d** is executed.

The key point about using virtual functions to achieve run-time polymorphism is that you must access those functions through the use of a pointer declared as a pointer to the base class. Although you can call a virtual function explicitly by using the object name like you would call any other member function, it is only when a virtual function is accessed through a base pointer that run-time polymorphism is achieved.

The redefinition of a virtual function in a derived class is, in some ways, like function overloading. However, the reason this term is not used in the preceding discussion is that several restrictions apply. First, the prototypes for virtual functions must match. As you know, when you overload normal functions, the return type and the number and type of parameters may differ. (Indeed, for a function to be overloaded, the type and/or number of parameters *must* differ.) However, when you overload a virtual function, these elements must be unchanged. If the prototypes of the functions differ, the function is simply considered overloaded, and its virtual nature is lost. Another restriction is that a virtual function must be a member, not a friend, of the class for which it is defined. However, a virtual function can be a friend of another class. Also, destructor functions may be virtual, but constructors may not.

Because of the restrictions and differences between overloading normal functions and "overloading" virtual functions, the term *overriding* is used to describe the virtual function redefinition.

Once a function is declared as virtual, it stays virtual no matter how many layers of derived classes it may pass through. For example, if **second_d** is derived from **first_d** instead of **Base**, as shown here, **who()** is still virtual, and the proper version is still correctly selected:

```
// Derive from first_d, not Base
class second_d : public first_d {
public:
  void who() { // define who() relative to second_d
    cout << "Second derivation\n";
  }
};
```

When a derived class does not override a virtual function, the version of the function in the base class is used. For example, try this version of the preceding program:

```
#include <iostream.h>

class Base {
public:
  virtual void who() {
    cout << "Base\n";
  }
};
```

```
class first_d : public Base {
public:
  void who() {
    cout << "First derivation\n";
  }
};

class second_d : public Base {
// who() not defined
};

main()
{
  Base base_obj;
  Base *p;
  first_d first_obj;
  second_d second_obj;

  p = &base_obj;
  p->who(); // access Base's who()

  p = &first_obj;
  p->who(); // access first_d's who()

  p = &second_obj;
  p->who(); /* access Base's who() because
               second_d does not redefine it */

  return 0;
}
```

This program now outputs the following:

```
Base
First derivation
Base
```

Keep in mind that inherited characteristics are hierarchical. Therefore, if, in the preceding example, **second_d** is derived from **first_d** instead of **Base**, then when **who()** is referenced relative to an object of type **second_d**, it is the version of **who()** declared inside **first_d** that is called, since it is the class closest to **second_d**, rather than the **who()** inside **Base**.

Why Virtual Functions?

As stated at the start of this chapter, virtual functions in combination with derived types allow C++ to support run-time polymorphism. And polymorphism is essential to object oriented programming for one reason: it allows a generalized class to specify those functions that will be common to any derivative of that class while allowing a derived class to specify the specific implementation of some or all of those functions. Sometimes this idea is expressed like this: the base class dictates the general *interface* that any object derived from that class will have but lets the derived class define the actual *method*, itself. This is why the phrase "one interface, multiple methods" is often used to describe polymorphism.

Part of the key to successfully applying polymorphism is understanding that base and derived classes form a hierarchy that moves from greater to lesser generalization (base to derived). Hence, when used correctly, the base class provides all elements that a derived class can use directly plus those functions that the derived class must implement on its own. However, since the form of the interface is defined by the base class, any derived class will still share that common interface. Hence, when properly designed using virtual functions, the base class defines the generic interface that will be used by all derived classes.

At this point you might be asking yourself why a consistent interface with multiple implementations is important. The answer, again, goes back to the central driving force behind object oriented programming: it helps you handle increasingly complex programs. For example, if you develop your program correctly, then you know that all objects you derive from some base class are accessed in the same general way, even if the specific actions vary from one derived class to the next. This means that you need to remember only one interface rather than several. Further, the separation of interface and implementation allows the creation of class libraries, which can be provided by a third party. If these libraries are implemented correctly, they will provide a common interface that you can use to derive classes of your own that meet your specific needs.

To get an idea of the power of the "one interface, multiple methods" concept, examine the following short program. It creates a base class called **figure**. This class is used to store the dimensions of various two-dimensional objects and to compute their areas. The function **set_dim()** is a standard member function because this operation will be common to all derived classes. However, **show_area()** is declared as virtual because the way the area of each object is computed will vary. The program uses the base class **figure** to derive two specific classes called **square** and **triangle**.

```
#include <iostream.h>

class figure {
protected:
  double x, y;
public:
  void set_dim(double i, double j) {
    x = i;
    y = j;
  }
  virtual void show_area() {
    cout << "No area computation defined ";
    cout << "for this class.\n";
  }
} ;

class triangle : public figure {
public:
  void show_area() {
    cout << "Triangle with height ";
    cout << x << " and base " << y;
    cout << " has an area of ";
    cout << x * 0.5 * y << ".\n";
  }
};

class square : public figure {
public:
  void show_area() {
    cout << "Square with dimensions ";
    cout << x << "x" << y;
    cout << " has an area of ";
```

```
    cout << x *  y << ".\n";
  }
};

main()
{
  figure *p;   /* create a pointer to base type */

  triangle t;   /* create objects of derived types */
  square s;

  p = &t;
  p->set_dim(10.0, 5.0);
  p->show_area();

  p = &s;
  p->set_dim(10.0, 5.0);
  p->show_area();

  return 0;
}
```

As you can see by examining this program, the interface to both **square**
and **triangle** is the same even though each provides its own methods for
computing the area of each of its objects.

Given the declaration for **figure**, is it possible to derive a class called
circle that will compute the area of a circle given its radius? The answer
is yes. All you need to do is to create a new derived type that computes
the area of a circle. The power of virtual functions is based on the fact
that you can easily derive a new type that will still share the same
common interface as other related objects. For example, here is one way
to do it:

```
class circle : public figure {
public:
  void show_area() {
    cout << "Circle with radius ";
    cout << x;
    cout << " has an area of ";
    cout <<  3.14 * x * x;
  }
};
```

Before trying to use **circle**, look closely at the definition of **show_area()**. Notice that it uses only the value of **x**, which is assumed to hold the radius. (Remember, the area of a circle is computed by using the formula πr^2.) However, the function **set_dim()** as defined in **figure** assumes that it will be passed two values, not just one. Since **circle** does not require this second value, what course of action can be taken?

There are two ways to resolve this problem. First and worst, you could simply call **set_dim()** using a dummy value as the second parameter when using a **circle** object. This has the disadvantage of being sloppy as well as requiring you to remember a special exception, which violates the "one interface, many methods" approach.

A better way to resolve this problem is to give the **y** parameter inside **set_dim()** a default value. In this way, when calling **set_dim()** for a circle, you need specify only the radius. When calling **set_dim()** for a triangle or a square, you would specify both values. The expanded program is shown here:

```
#include <iostream.h>

class figure {
protected:
  double x, y;
public:
  void set_dim(double i, double j=0) {
    x = i;
    y = j;
  }
  virtual void show_area() {
    cout << "No area computation defined ";
    cout << "for this class.\n";
  }
} ;

class triangle : public figure {
  public:
    void show_area() {
      cout << "Triangle with height ";
      cout << x << " and base " << y;
      cout << " has an area of ";
      cout << x * 0.5 * y << ".\n";
    }
```

```
};

class square : public figure {
public:
  void show_area() {
    cout << "Square with dimensions ";
    cout << x << "x" << y;
    cout << " has an area of ";
    cout << x *  y << ".\n";
  }
};

class circle : public figure {
public:
  void show_area() {
    cout << "Circle with radius ";
    cout << x;
    cout << " has an area of ";
    cout << 3.14 * x * x;
  }
} ;

main()
{
  figure *p;  /* create a pointer to base type */

  triangle t;  /* create objects of derived types */
  square s;
  circle c;

  p = &t;
  p->set_dim(10.0, 5.0);
  p->show_area();

  p = &s;
  p->set_dim(10.0, 5.0);
  p->show_area();

  p = &c;
  p->set_dim(9.0);
  p->show_area();
```

```
    return 0;
}
```

This points out a very important point about defining base classes: be as flexible as possible. Don't make unnecessarily harsh restrictions.

Pure Virtual Functions and Abstract Types

As stated, when a virtual function that is not overridden in a derived class is called for an object of that derived class, the version of the function as defined in the base class is used. However, in many circumstances there will be no meaningful definition of a virtual function inside the base class. For example, in the base class **figure** used in the preceding example, the definition of **show_area()** is simply a placeholder. It will not compute and display the area of any type of object.

As you will see as you create your own class libraries, it is not uncommon for a virtual function to have no meaningful definition in the context of its base class. When this occurs, there are two ways you can handle it. One way, as shown in the example, is to simply have it report a warning message. While this approach can be useful in certain situations, it will not be appropriate for all circumstances. For example, there may be virtual functions that simply must be defined by the derived class in order for the derived class to have any meaning. Consider the class **triangle**; it simply has no meaning if **show_area()** is not defined. In this sort of case, you want some method to ensure that a derived class does, indeed, define all necessary functions. C++'s solution to this problem is the pure virtual function.

A *pure virtual function* is a function declared in a base class that has no definition relative to the base. Since it has no definition relative to the base, any derived type must define its own version; it cannot simply use the version defined in the base. To declare a pure virtual function, use this general form:

virtual *type func-name(parameter-list)* = 0;

where *type* is the return type of the function and *func-name* is the name of the function. For example, in this version of **figure**, **show_area()** is a pure virtual function:

```
class figure {
protected:
  double x, y;
public:
  void set_dim(double i, double j=0) {
    x = i;
    y = j;
  }
  virtual void show_area() = 0; // pure
} ;
```

By declaring a virtual function as pure, you force any derived class to define its own implementation. If a class fails to do so, Turbo C++ will report an error. For example, try to compile this modified version of the figures program in which the definition for **show_area()** has been removed from the **circle** class:

```
/*
   This program will not compile because the class
   circle does not override show_area().
*/
#include <iostream.h>

class figure {
protected:
  double x, y;
public:
  void set_dim(double i, double j) {
    x = i;
    y = j;
  }
  virtual void show_area() = 0; // pure
} ;

class triangle : public figure {
public:
  void show_area() {
    cout << "Triangle with height ";
```

```
    cout << x << " and base " << y;
    cout << " has an area of ";
    cout << x * 0.5 * y << ".\n";
  }
};

class square : public figure {
public:
  void show_area() {
    cout << "Square with dimensions ";
    cout << x << "x" << y;
    cout << " has an area of ";
    cout << x *  y << ".\n";
  }
};

class circle : public figure {
// ERROR! No definition of show_area().
};

main()
{
  figure *p;   /* create a pointer to base type */

  triangle t;  /* create objects of derived types */
  square s;

  p = &t;
  p->set_dim(10.0, 5.0);
  p->show_area();

  p = &s;
  p->set_dim(10.0, 5.0);
  p->show_area();

  return 0;
}
```

If a class has at least one pure virtual function, that class is said to be *abstract*. Abstract classes have one important feature: there can be no objects of that class. Instead, an abstract class must be used only as a base that other classes will inherit. The reason that an abstract class cannot be used to declare an object is, of course, that one or more of its functions have no definition. However, even if the base class is abstract, you still may use it to declare pointers, which are needed to support run-time polymorphism.

Early Versus Late Binding

There are two terms that are commonly used when object oriented programming languages are discussed: *early binding* and *late binding*. Relative to C++, these terms refer to events that occur at compile time and events that occur at run time, respectively.

In object oriented terms, early binding means that an object is bound to its function call at compile time. That is, all information necessary to determine which function will be called is known when the program is compiled. Examples of early binding include standard function calls, overloaded function calls, and overloaded operator function calls. The principal advantage of early binding is efficiency—it is faster and (often) requires less memory. Its disadvantage is lack of flexibility.

Late binding means that an object is bound to its function call at run time. This means that precisely which function relates to an object will be determined "on the fly" at run time. As you now know, you achieve late binding in C++ by using virtual functions and derived types. The advantage of late binding is that it provides greater flexibility by allowing your program to respond to events that are known only at run time. You can use late binding to support a common interface while allowing various objects that utilize that interface to define their own implementations. Further, it can help you create class libraries, which may be reused and extended.

Whether your program uses early or late binding depends upon what your program is designed to do. (Actually, most large programs will use a combination of both.) Late binding is one of C++'s most powerful additions to the C language. However, the price you pay for this power is that your program will run slightly more slowly. Therefore, it is best to use late binding only when it meaningfully adds to the structure and manageability of your program. (In essence, use, but don't abuse, the power.) Keep in mind that the loss of performance is very small, so when the situation calls for late binding, you should most definitely use it.

Constructors and Destructors in Derived Classes

Since elements of C++'s polymorphism rely heavily upon derived classes, it is appropriate to take a closer look at them at this time. One important consideration related to a derived class is when its constructor and destructor functions are executed. Let's begin with constructors.

It is possible for a base class and a derived class to each have a constructor function. (In fact, in the case of multiple inheritance, it is possible for all involved classes to have constructors, but this discussion starts with the simplest case.) When a base class contains a constructor, that constructor is executed before the constructor in the derived class. For example, consider this short program:

```
#include <iostream.h>

class Base {
public:
  Base() {cout << "\nBase created\n";}
};

class D_class1 : public Base {
public:
  D_class1() {cout << "D_class1 created\n";}
};

main()
{
  D_class1 d1;

  // do nothing but execute constructors
  return 0;
}
```

This program creates an object of type **D_class1**. It displays this output:

```
Base created
D_class1 created
```

Here, **d1** is an object of type **D_class1** that is derived using **Base**. Thus, when **d1** is created, first **Base()** is executed, and then **D_class1()** is called. This result can be generalized: constructors are called in the order of derivation, base to derived.

If you think about it, it makes sense for constructors to be called in the same order in which the derivation takes place. Because the base class has no knowledge of the derived class, any initialization that it needs to perform is obviously separate from and possibly prerequisite to any derived class, so it must be executed first.

Opposite from constructors, a destructor function in a derived class is executed before the destructor in the base. The reason for this is also easy to understand. Since the destruction of the base class implies the destruction of the derived class, the derived destructor must be executed before it is destroyed. Generalizing, destructors are called in reverse order of derivation. This program illustrates the order in which constructors and destructors are executed:

```cpp
#include <iostream.h>

class Base {
public:
  Base() {cout << "\nBase created\n";}
  ~Base() {cout << "Base destroyed\n\n";}
};

class D_class1 : public Base {
public:
  D_class1() {cout << "D_class1 created\n";}
  ~D_class1() {cout << "D_class1 destroyed\n";}
};

main()
{
  D_class1 d1;
```

```
  cout << "\n";

  return 0;
}
```

The program produces this output:

```
Base created
D_class1 created

D_class1 destroyed
Base destroyed
```

As you know, it is possible for a derived class, itself, to be used as a base class in the creation of another derived class. When this happens, constructors are executed in the order of the derivation and destructors in the reverse order. For example, consider this program, which uses **D_class1** to derive **D_class2**:

```
#include <iostream.h>

class Base {
public:
  Base() {cout << "\nBase created\n";}
  ~Base() {cout << "Base destroyed\n\n";}
};

class D_class1 : public Base {
public:
  D_class1() {cout << "D_class1 created\n";}
  ~D_class1() {cout << "D_class1 destroyed\n";}
};

class D_class2 : public D_class1 {
public:
  D_class2() {cout << "D_class2 created\n";}
  ~D_class2() {cout << "D_class2 destroyed\n";}
};

main()
{
```

```
   D_class1 d1;
   D_class2 d2;

   cout << "\n";

   return 0;
}
```

This program produces this output:

```
Base created
D_class1 created

Base created
D_class1 created
D_class2 created

D_class2 destroyed
D_class1 destroyed
Base destroyed

D_class1 destroyed
Base destroyed
```

Remember   In class hierarchies, constructors are executed in order of their derivation. Destructors are executed in reverse order.

Multiple Base Classes

It is possible to specify more than one base class when creating a derived type. To do so, use a comma-separated list of the classes that will be inherited. For example, consider this program:

```
#include <iostream.h>

class Base1 {
public:
  Base1() {cout << "\nBase1 created\n";}
  ~Base1() {cout << "Base1 destroyed\n\n";}
```

```
};

class Base2 {
public:
  Base2() {cout << "Base2 created\n";}
  ~Base2() {cout << "Base2 destroyed\n";}
};

// multiple base classes
class D_class1 : public Base1, public Base2 {
public:
  D_class1() {cout << "D_class1 created\n";}
  ~D_class1() {cout << "D_class1 destroyed\n";}
};

main()
{
  D_class1 d1;

  cout << "\n";

  return 0;
}
```

In this program, **D_class1** is derived from both **Base1** and **Base2**. It produces this output:

```
Base1 created
Base2 created
D_class1 created

D_class1 destroyed
Base2 destroyed
Base1 destroyed
```

As you can see, when a list of base classes is used, the constructors are called in order of left to right. Destructors are called in order of right to left.

CHAPTER

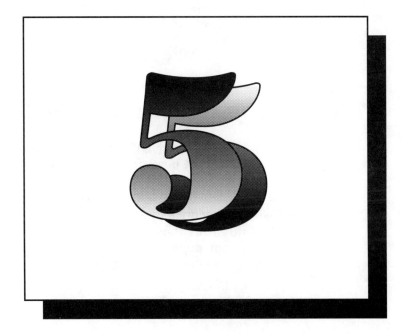

Using C++'s I/O Class Library

ince Chapter 1, you have been performing console input and output by using C++'s overloaded operators >> and <<. Although Turbo C++ supports all of C's rich set of I/O functions, the past few chapters have ignored them in favor of C++'s I/O operators. There is one main reason for this: using C++'s method of I/O helps you to think in an object oriented manner and to see the value of the "one interface, multiple methods" philosophy. In this chapter you learn more about C++'s I/O system, including how to overload the << and >> operators so you can input or output objects of classes that you design. C++'s I/O system is very large, and it won't be possible to talk about every function and feature, but this chapter introduces you to the most important and commonly used ones. Let's begin with a short look at why C++ defines its own I/O system.

Why C++ Has Its Own I/O System

If you have programmed in other languages, you know that C has one of the most flexible yet powerful I/O systems. (In fact, it may be safe to say that among the world's structured languages, C's I/O system is unparalleled.) Given the power of C's I/O functions, you might be asking yourself why C++ defines its own I/O functions, which, as you will see, in large part duplicate those already contained in C. The answer is that the C I/O system provides no support for user-defined objects. For example, in C, if you create this structure:

```
struct my_struct {
  int count;
  char s[80];
  double balance;
} cust;
```

there is no way to customize or extend C's I/O system so that it knows about and can perform I/O operations directly on a variable of **my_struct**. That is, you cannot create a new format specifier that is defined for data of type **my_struct** and use it to call **printf()**. However, by using C++'s approach to I/O, it is possible to overload the << and >> operators so that they know about classes that you create. This includes both the console I/O operations you have been using for the past four chapters and file I/O. (Console and file I/O are linked in C++ as they are in C and are really just two sides of the same coin.)

Although there is no I/O operation that you can perform by using C++'s I/O system that you cannot perform by using C's, the fact that C++'s system can be made aware of user-defined types greatly increases its flexibility and helps to prevent bugs. To see how, consider this call to **printf()**:

```
printf("%d%s", "Hello", 10);
```

In this call, the string and the integer are inverted in the argument list; the **%d** will be matched with **Hello** and the **%s** with **10**. However, this is not technically an error in C. It is conceivable that in some highly unusual situation, you might actually *want* to use a call to **printf()** like that shown. (After all, C was designed to allow you to do just about anything you want, whether it makes sense or not.) However, it is most likely the case that this call to **printf()** is, indeed, an error. In short, when calling **printf()**, C has no means of providing strong type checking. However, in C++, I/O operations for all built-in types are defined relative to the << and >> operators, so there is no way for an inversion such as that shown in the **printf()** call to take place. Instead, the correct operation is automatically determined by the type of the operand. This feature can also be extended to user-defined objects.

C++ Streams

You will be happy to know that the C and the C++ I/O systems do have one important thing in common: they both operate on streams. The fact that C and C++ streams are similar means that what you know about streams is completely applicable to C++.

The C++ Predefined Streams

Like C, C++ contains several predefined streams that are automatically opened when your C++ program begins execution. These are **cin**, **cout**, **cerr**, and **clog**. As you know, **cin** is the stream associated with standard input and **cout** is the stream associated with standard output. The **cerr** stream is linked to standard output and so is **clog**. The difference between **cerr** and **clog** is that **cerr** is not buffered, so any output sent to it is immediately output. Alternately, **clog** is buffered, and output is written only when a buffer is full.

By default, the C++ standard streams are linked to the console, but they may be redirected to other devices or files by your program. Also, they may be redirected by the operating system.

The C++ Stream Classes

The Turbo C++ I/O system is defined by a hierarchy of classes that relate to streams. These definitions are found in the header file IOSTREAM.H. The lowest level class is called **streambuf**, and it provides the basic stream operations but no formatting support. The next class in the hierarchy is called **ios**. The **ios** class provides the basic support for formatted I/O. It is also used to derive three classes that you can use to create streams. They are **istream**, **ostream**, and **iostream**. By using **istream**, you can create an input stream; by using **ostream**, you can create an output stream; and by using **iostream**, you can create a stream capable of both input and output.

Creating Your Own Inserters and Extractors

Up to this point, when a program needed to output or input the data associated with a class, special member functions were created, the only purpose of which was to output or input the class's data. While there is nothing, in and of itself, wrong with this approach, C++ allows a much better way of performing I/O operations on classes by overloading the << and the >> operators.

In the language of C++, the << operator is usually referred to as the *insertion operator* because it inserts characters into a stream. Likewise, the >> operator is called the *extraction operator* because it extracts characters from a stream. The operator functions that overload the insertion and extraction operators are generally called *inserters* and *extractors*, respectively.

As you know, the insertion and extraction operators are already overloaded (in IOSTREAM.H) so that they are capable of performing stream I/O on any of C++'s built-in types. However, as the beginning of the chapter indicated, it is possible to define these operators relative to classes you define. In this section you will see how.

Creating Inserters

One of the nicest features of C++ is how easily you can create inserters for classes that you create. As a simple first example, let's create an inserter for the **three_d** class, shown here:

```
class three_d {
public:
  int x, y, z; // 3-d coordinates
  three_d(int a, int b, int c) {x=a; y=b, z=c;}
} ;
```

To create an inserter function for an object of type **three_d**, you must define what an insertion operation is relative to it. To do this, you must overload the << operator, as shown here:

```
// Display X,Y,Z coordinates (three_d's inserter).
ostream &operator<<(ostream &stream, three_d obj)
{
  stream << obj.x << ", ";
  stream << obj.y << ", ";
  stream << obj.z << "\n";
  return stream;  // return the stream
}
```

Let's look closely at this function because many of its features are common to all inserter functions. First, notice that it is declared as returning a reference to an object of type **ostream**. This is necessary to allow several inserters of this type to be strung together in a single statement. Next, the function has two parameters. The first is a reference to the stream that occurs on the left side of the << operator. The second parameter is the object that occurs on the right side. Inside the function, the three values contained in an object of type **three_d** are output, and **stream** is returned. Here is a short program that demonstrates the inserter:

```
#include <iostream.h>

class three_d {
public:
  int x, y, z; // 3-d coordinates
  three_d(int a, int b, int c) {x=a; y=b, z=c;}
} ;

// Display X,Y,Z coordinates - three_d inserter
ostream &operator<<(ostream &stream, three_d obj)
{
  stream << obj.x << ", ";
  stream << obj.y << ", ";
  stream << obj.z << "\n";
  return stream;  // return the stream
}

main()
{
  three_d a(1, 2, 3), b(3, 4, 5), c(5, 6, 7);

  cout << a << b << c;

  return 0;
}
```

If you eliminate the code that is specific to the **three_d** class, you are left with the skeleton for an inserter function, as shown here:

```
ostream &operator<<(ostream &stream, class_type obj)
{
  // type specific code goes here
  return stream;  // return the stream
}
```

Keep in mind that the second parameter may be passed by reference, using a reference parameter, instead of by value. This may be important in situations in which you do not want a temporary copy created that will be destroyed when the inserter terminates.

Within wide boundaries, what an inserter function actually does is up to you. Just make sure that you return **stream**. You might be wondering why the function was not coded as shown here:

```
// Limited version - don't use.
ostream &operator<<(ostream &stream, three_d obj)
{
  cout << obj.x << ", ";
  cout << obj.y << ", ";
  cout << obj.z << "\n";
  return stream;  // return the stream
}
```

In this version, the **cout** stream is hardcoded into the function. However, remember that the << operator can be applied to *any* stream. Therefore, you must use the stream passed to the function if it is to work correctly in all cases.

In the preceding program, the overloaded inserter function is not a member of **three_d**. In fact, neither inserter nor extractor functions can be members of a class. The reason for this is that when an operator function is a member of a class, the left operand (implicitly passed using the **this** pointer) is assumed to be an object of the class that generated the call to the operator function. There is no way to change this. However, when overloading inserters, the left argument is a stream and the right argument is an object of the class. Therefore, overloaded inserters must be nonmember functions.

The fact that inserters must not be members of the class they are defined to operate on raises a serious question: how can an overloaded inserter access the private elements of a class? In the previous program, the variables **x**, **y**, and **z** were made public so the inserter could access them. But hiding data is an important part of OOP, and forcing all data to be public is a serious inconsistency. However, there is a solution: an inserter may be a friend of a class. As a friend of the class it is defined for, it has access to private data. To see an example of this, the **three_d** class and sample program are reworked here, with the overloaded inserter declared as a friend:

```
#include <iostream.h>

class three_d {
  int x, y, z; // 3-d coordinates - - now private
public:
  three_d(int a, int b, int c) {x=a; y=b, z=c;}
  friend ostream &operator<<(ostream &stream, three_d obj);
} ;

// Display X,Y,Z coordinates - three_d inserter
ostream &operator<<(ostream &stream, three_d obj)
{
  stream << obj.x << ", ";
  stream << obj.y << ", ";
  stream << obj.z << "\n";
  return stream;  // return the stream
}

main()
{
  three_d a(1, 2, 3), b(3, 4, 5), c(5, 6, 7);

  cout << a << b << c;

  return 0;
}
```

Notice that the variables **x**, **y**, and **z** are now private to **three_d** but can still be directly accessed by the inserter. Making inserters (and extractors) friends of the class they are defined for preserves the data-hiding principle of OOP.

 Remember Although the example just shown passes its second parameter by value, you may also pass it by reference if this is required by your application.

Overloading Extractors

To overload an extractor, use the same general approach as when overloading an inserter. For example, this extractor inputs 3-D coordinates. Notice that it also prompts the user.

```
// Get three dimensional values - extractor.
istream &operator>>(istream &stream, three_d &obj)
{
  cout << "Enter X,Y,Z values: ";
  stream >> obj.x >> obj.y >> obj.z;
  return stream;
}
```

Extractors must return a reference to an object of type **istream**. Also, the first parameter must be a reference to an object of type **istream**. Notice that the second parameter is a reference. This is necessary so that the variable receiving input can be modified.

The general form of an extractor is shown here:

istream &operator>>(istream &*stream*, *object_type* &*obj*)
{
  // *put your extractor code here*
  return *stream*;
}

Here is a program that demonstrates the extractor for objects of type **three_d**:

```
#include <iostream.h>

class three_d {
  int x, y, z; // 3-d coordinates
public:
  three_d(int a, int b, int c) {x=a; y=b, z=c;}
  friend ostream &operator<<(ostream &stream, three_d obj);
  friend istream &operator>>(istream &stream, three_d &obj);
} ;

// Display X,Y,Z coordinates - inserter.
ostream &operator<<(ostream &stream, three_d obj)
{
  stream << obj.x << ", ";
  stream << obj.y << ", ";
  stream << obj.z << "\n";
  return stream; // return the stream
```

```
}

// Get three dimensional values - extractor
istream &operator>>(istream &stream, three_d &obj)
{
  cout << "Enter X,Y,Z values: ";
  stream >> obj.x >> obj.y >> obj.z;
  return stream;
}

main()
{
  three_d a(1, 2, 3);

  cout << a;

  cin >> a;
  cout << a;

  return 0;
}
```

Like inserters, extractor functions may not be members of the class they are designed to operate upon. They may, as shown in the example, be friends or simply independent functions.

Except for the fact that you must return a reference to an object of type **istream**, you may do anything you like inside an extractor function. However, for the sake of structure and clarity, it is best to limit the actions of an extractor to the input operation.

Formatting I/O

As you know, by using **printf()**, you can control the format of information displayed on the screen. For example, you can specify field widths and left or right justification. By using C++'s approach to I/O, you can also accomplish the same type of formatting. There are two ways to format output. The first uses member functions of the **ios** class. The second uses

a special type of function called a manipulator. This discussion begins
by looking at formatting using the member functions of **ios**.

Formatting Using the ios Member Functions

In IOSTREAM.H is defined the following enumeration:

```
// formatting flags
enum      {
  skipws = 0x0001,
  left = 0x0002,
  right = 0x0004,
  internal = 0x0008,
  dec = 0x0010,
  oct = 0x0020,
  hex = 0x0040,
  showbase = 0x0080,
  showpoint = 0x0100,
  uppercase = 0x0200,
  showpos = 0x0400,
  scientific = 0x0800,
  fixed = 0x1000,
  unitbuf = 0x2000,
  stdio = 0x4000
};
```

The values defined by this enumeration are used to set or clear flags that
control some of the ways information is formatted by a stream.

When the **skipws** flag is set, leading whitespace characters (spaces,
tabs, and newlines) are discarded when performing input on a stream.
When **skipws** is cleared, whitespace characters are not discarded.

When the **left** flag is set, output is left justified. When **right** is set,
output is right justified. When the **internal** flag is set, a numeric value
is padded to fill a field by the insertion of spaces between any sign or
base characters. (You will learn how to specify a field width shortly.)

By default, numeric values are output in decimal. However, you can
override this default. Setting the **oct** flag causes output to be displayed

in octal. Setting **hex** causes output to be displayed in hexadecimal. Setting **dec** returns output to decimal.

Setting **showbase** causes the base of numeric values to be shown.

By default, when scientific notation is displayed, the "e" is in lowercase. Also, when a hexadecimal value is displayed, the "x" is in lowercase. When **uppercase** is set, these characters are displayed in uppercase.

Setting **showpos** causes a leading plus sign to be displayed before positive integer values.

Setting **showpoint** causes a decimal point and trailing zeros to be displayed for all floating-point output, whether needed or not.

When the **scientific** flag is set, floating-point numeric values are displayed using scientific notation. When **fixed** is set, floating-point values are displayed using normal notation. By default, when **fixed** is set, six decimal places are displayed. When neither flag is set, the compiler chooses an appropriate method.

For reasons that are beyond the scope of this book, when **unitbuf** is set, the C++ I/O system performance is improved. This flag is on by default in Turbo C++.

When **stdio** is set, each stream is flushed after each output. *Flushing* a stream causes output to actually be written to the physical device linked to the stream.

The format flags are held in a long integer. To set a flag, use the **setf()** member function, the most common form of which is shown here:

long setf(long *flags*);

This function returns the previous settings of the format flags and turns on those flags specified by *flags*. For example, to turn on the **showbase** flag, you can use this statement:

stream.setf(ios::showbase);

Here, *stream* is the stream you wish to affect. It is important to understand that **setf()** and other I/O functions may be used only in conjunction with a stream. There is no concept in C++ of calling **setf()** by itself. Further, any format changes affect only that specific stream. There is no way to effect a global format change.

Here is another example. This program turns on both the **showpos** and **scientific** flags relative to **cout**:

```
#include <iostream.h>

main()
{
  cout.setf(ios::showpos);
  cout.setf(ios::scientific);
  cout << 123 << " " << 123.23 << " ";

  return 0;
}
```

The output produced by this program is shown here:

```
+123 +1.2323e+02
```

You may OR together as many flags as you like in a single call. For example, you can change the program so that only one call is made to **setf()** by ORing together **scientific** and **showpos**, as shown here:

```
cout.setf(ios::scientific | ios::showpos);
```

To turn off a flag, use the **unsetf()** function. Its prototype is shown here:

long unsetf(long *flags*);

The function returns the previous flag settings and turns off those flags specified by *flags*.

Sometimes it is useful to know the current flag settings. You can retrieve the current flag values by using the **flags()** functions. The prototype is shown here:

long flags();

This function returns the current value of the flags relative to the associated stream.

This form of **flags()** sets the flag values to those specified by *flags* and returns the previous flag values:

long flags(long *flags*);

To see how **flags()** and **unsetf()** work, examine this program. It includes a function called **showflags()** that displays the state of the flags.

```
#include <iostream.h>

void showflags(long f);

main()
{
  long f;

  f = cout.flags();

  showflags(f);
  cout.setf(ios::showpos);
  cout.setf(ios::scientific);

  f = cout.flags();
  showflags(f);

  cout.unsetf(ios::scientific);

  f = cout.flags();
  showflags(f);

  return 0;
}

void showflags(long f)
{
  long i;

  for(i=0x4000; i; i = i >> 1)
    if(i & f) cout << "1 ";
```

```
      else cout << "0 ";

   cout << "\n";
}
```

When run, the program produces this output:

```
0 1 0 0 0 0 0 0 0 0 0 0 0 0 1
0 1 0 1 1 0 0 0 0 0 0 0 0 0 1
0 1 0 0 1 0 0 0 0 0 0 0 0 0 1
```

In addition to the formatting flags, you can also set the field width, the fill character, and the number of digits displayed after a decimal point by using these functions:

int width(int *len*);
char fill(char *ch*);
int precision(int *num*);

The **width()** function returns the current field width and sets the field width to *len*. By default, the field width varies, depending upon the number of characters it takes to represent the data. The **fill()** function returns the current fill character, which is a space by default, and makes the current fill character the same as *ch*. The fill character is the character used to pad output to fill a specified field width. The **precision()** function returns the number of digits displayed after a decimal point and sets that value to *num*. Here is a program that demonstrates these three functions:

```
#include <iostream.h>

main()
{
  cout.setf(ios::showpos);
  cout.setf(ios::scientific);
  cout << 123 << " " << 123.23 << "\n";

  cout.precision(2); // two digits after decimal point
  cout.width(10);   // in a field of ten characters
  cout << 123 << " " << 123.23 << "\n";

  cout.fill('#');   // fill using #
```

```
   cout.width(10);   // in a field of ten characters
   cout << 123 << " " << 123.23;

   return 0;
}
```

The program displays this output:

```
+123 +1.2323e+02
      +123 +1.23e+02
######+123 +1.23e+02
```

Using Manipulators

The C++ I/O system includes a second way in which you may alter the format parameters of a stream. This way uses special functions called *manipulators* that can be included in an I/O statement. The standard manipulators are shown in Table 5-1. To access manipulators that take arguments, you must include IOMANIP.H in your program.

Here is an example program that uses manipulators to change the format of output:

```
#include <iostream.h>
#include <iomanip.h>

main()
{
   cout << setprecision(2) << 1000.243 << endl;
   cout << setw(20) << "Hello there.";

   return 0;
}
```

It produces this output:

```
1000.24
        Hello there.
```

ABLE
5-1
The C++ Manipulators

Manipulator	Purpose	Input/Output
dec	Format numeric data in decimal	Input and output
endl	Output a newline character and flush the stream	Output
ends	Output a null	Output
flush	Flush a stream	Output
hex	Format numeric data in hexadecimal	Input and output
oct	Format numeric data in octal	Input and output
resetiosflags (long f)	Turn off the flags specified in f	Input and output
setbase (int base)	Set the number base to base	Output
setfill (int ch)	Set the fill character to ch	Output
setiosflags (long f)	Turn on the flags specified in f	Output
setprecision (int p)	Set the number of digits displayed after a decimal point	Output
setw(int w)	Set the field width to w	Output
ws	Skip leading whitespace	Input

Notice how the manipulators occur in the chain of I/O operations. Also, notice that when a manipulator does not take an argument, such as **endl** in the example, it is not followed by parentheses. The reason for this is that it is the address of the manipulator that is passed to the overloaded << operator.

This program uses **setiosflags()** to set the **scientific** and **showpos** flags:

```
#include <iostream.h>
#include <iomanip.h>
```

```
main()
{
  cout << setiosflags(ios::showpos);
  cout << setiosflags(ios::scientific);
  cout << 123 << " " << 123.23;

  return 0;
}
```

This program uses **ws** to skip any leading whitespace when inputting a string into **s**:

```
#include <iostream.h>

main()
{
  char s[80];

  cin >> ws >> s;
  cout << s;
}
```

Creating Your Own Manipulator Functions

You can create your own manipulator functions. The easiest ones to create are those that don't take arguments, and it is these types of manipulators you learn to create here. (The creation of parameterized manipulators is beyond the scope of this book.)

All nonargument manipulator output functions have this skeleton:

```
ostream &manip-name(ostream &stream)
{
  // your code here
```

return *stream*;
}

Here, *manip-name* is the name of the manipulator. It is important to understand that even though the manipulator has as its single argument a reference to the stream upon which it is operating, no argument is used when the manipulator is inserted in an output operation.

This program creates a manipulator called **setup()** that turns on left justification, sets the field width to 10, and specifies that the dollar sign will be the fill character:

```
#include <iostream.h>
#include <iomanip.h>

ostream &setup(ostream &stream)
{
  stream.setf(ios::left);
  stream << setw(10) << setfill('$');
  return stream;
}

main()
{
  cout << 10 << " " << setup << 10;

  return 0;
}
```

Custom manipulators are useful for two reasons. First, you might need to perform an I/O operation on a device for which none of the predefined manipulators apply—a plotter, for example. In this case, creating your own manipulators will make it more convenient when outputting to the device. Second, you may find you are repeating the same sequence of operations many times. You can consolidate these operations into a single manipulator, as the foregoing program illustrates.

All nonargument input manipulator functions have this skeleton:

```
istream &manip-name(istream &stream)
{
  // your code here

  return stream;
}
```

For example, this program creates the **prompt()** manipulator, which converts to hexadecimal input and prompts the user to enter a value using hexadecimal:

```
#include <iostream.h>
#include <iomanip.h>

istream &prompt(istream &stream)
{
  cin >> hex;
  cout << "Enter number using hex format: ";

  return stream;
}

main()
{
  int i;

  cin >> prompt >> i;
  cout << i;

  return 0;
}
```

File I/O

You can use the C++ I/O system to perform file I/O. Although the end result is the same, C++'s approach to file I/O differs in places from the standard C I/O system. For this reason, you will want to pay special attention to this section.

In order to perform file I/O, you must include the header file
FSTREAM.H in your program. It defines several important classes and
values.

Opening and Closing a File

In C++, you open a file by linking it to a stream. There are three types
of streams: input, output, and input/output. To open an input stream,
you must declare the stream to be of class **ifstream**. To open an output
stream, it must be declared as class **ofstream**. Streams that will be
performing both input and output operations must be declared as class
fstream. For example, this fragment creates one input stream, one
output stream, and one stream capable of both input and output:

```
ifstream in;  // input

ofstream out; // output

fstream both; // input and output
```

Once you have created a stream, one way to associate it with a file is
by using the function **open()**. This function is a member of each of the
three stream classes. Its prototype is shown here:

void open(char *filename, int mode, int access);

Here, filename is the name of the file, which may include a path
specifier. The value of mode determines how the file is opened. It must
be one (or more) of these values (defined in FSTREAM.H):

ios::app
ios::ate
ios::in
ios::nocreate
ios::noreplace
ios::out
ios::trunc

You can combine two or more of these values by ORing them together. Let's see what each of these values means.

Including **ios::app** causes all output to that file to be appended to the end. This value can be used only with files capable of output. Including **ios::ate** causes a seek to the end of the file to occur when the file is opened.

The **ios::in** value specifies that the file is capable of input. The **ios::out** value specifies that the file is capable of output. However, creating a stream using **ifstream** implies input and creating a stream using **ofstream** implies output, so in these cases, it is unnecessary to supply these values.

Including **ios::nocreate** causes the **open()** function to fail if the file does not already exist. The **ios::noreplace** value causes the **open()** function to fail if the file does already exist.

The **ios::trunc** value causes the contents of a preexisting file by the same name to be destroyed, and the file is truncated to zero length.

The value of *access* determines how the file can be accessed. This value corresponds to DOS's file attribute codes. They are

Attribute	Meaning
0	Normal file—open access
1	Read-only file
2	Hidden file
4	System file
8	Archive bit set

You can OR two or more of these together.

The following fragment opens a normal output file:

```
ofstream out;

out.open("test", ios::out, 0);
```

However, you will seldom (if ever) see **open()** called as shown because both the *mode* and *access* parameters have default values. For both

ifstream and **ofstream**, the *mode* parameter has a default value. For **ifstream**, it is **ios::in** and for **ofstream** it is **ios::out**. The *access* parameter also has a default value of zero (normal file). Therefore, the preceding statement will usually look like this:

```
out.open("test");   // defaults to output and normal file
```

To open a stream for input and output, you must specify both the **ios::in** and the **ios::out** *mode* values, as shown in this example:

```
fstream mystream;

mystream.open("test", ios::in | ios::out);
```

If **open()** fails, **mystream** will be zero.

Although it is entirely proper to open a file by using the **open()** function, most of the time you will not do so because the **ifstream**, **ofstream**, and **fstream** classes have constructor functions that automatically open the file. The constructor functions have the same parameters and defaults as the **open()** function. Therefore, the most common way you will see a file opened is shown in this example:

```
ifstream  mystream("myfile"); // open file for input
```

If, for some reason, the file cannot be opened, the value of the associated stream variable will be zero. Therefore, to confirm that the file has actually been opened, you will use code like that shown here:

```
ifstream  mystream("myfile"); // open file for input
if(!mystream) {
  cout << "cannot open file";
  //  process error
}
```

To close a file, use the member function **close()**. For example, to close the file linked to a stream called **mystream**, use this statement:

```
mystream.close();
```

The **close()** function takes no parameters and returns no value.

Reading and Writing Text Files

To read from or write to a text file is a simple matter because you can simply use the << and >> operators. For example, this program writes an integer, a floating-point value, and a string to a file called TEST:

```
#include <iostream.h>
#include <fstream.h>

main()
{
  ofstream out("test");
  if(!out) {
    cout << "Cannot open file";
    return 1;
   }

  out << 10 << " " << 123.23 << "\n";
  out << "This is a short text file.";

  out.close();

  return 0;
}
```

The following program reads an integer, a floating-point value, a character, and a string from the file created by the foregoing program:

```
#include <iostream.h>
#include <fstream.h>

main()
{
  char ch;
  int i;
  float f;
  char str[80];

  ifstream in("test");
  if(!in) {
    cout << "Cannot open file";
```

```
    return 1;
  }

  in >> i;
  in >> f;
  in >> ch;
  in >> str;

  cout << i << " " << f << " " << ch << "\n";
  cout << str;

  in.close();
  return 0;
}
```

When reading text files using the >> operator, keep in mind that certain character translations will occur. For example, whitespace characters are omitted. If you want to prevent any character translations, you must use C++'s binary I/O functions, discussed in the next section.

Binary I/O

There are two ways to write and read binary data to or from a file. First, you may write a byte by using the member function **put()** and read a byte by using the member function **get()**. The **get()** function has many forms, but the most commonly used version is shown here along with **put()**:

istream &get(char &*ch*);
ostream &put(char *ch*);

The **get()** function reads a single character from the associated stream and puts that value in *ch*. It returns a reference to the stream. It returns null when the end of the file is encountered. The **put()** function writes *ch* to the stream and returns a reference to the stream.

This program will display the contents of any file on the screen. It uses the **get()** function.

```
#include <iostream.h>
#include <fstream.h>
```

```
main(int argc, char *argv[])
{
  char ch;

  if(argc!=2) {
    cout << "Usage: PR <filename>\n";
    return 1;
  }

  ifstream in(argv[1]);
  if(!in) {
    cout << "Cannot open file";
    return 1;
  }

  while(in) { // in will be 0 when eof is reached
    in.get(ch);
    cout << ch;
  }

  return 0;
}
```

When **in** reaches the end of the file, it will be null, causing the **while** loop to stop.

There is actually a more compact way to code the loop that reads and displays a file, as shown here:

```
while(in.get(ch))
  cout << ch;
```

This works because **get()** returns a reference to the stream **in** and **in** will be null when the end of the file is encountered.

This program uses **put()** to write a string to a file:

```
#include <iostream.h>
#include <fstream.h>

main()
{
```

```
    char *p = "hello there";

    ofstream out("test");
    if(!out) {
      cout << "Cannot open file";
      return 1;
     }

    while(*p) out.put(*p++);

    out.close();

    return 0;
}
```

To read and write blocks of binary data, use C++'s **read()** and **write()** member functions. Their prototypes are shown here:

istream &read(unsigned char *buf, int num);
ostream &write(const unsigned char *buf, int num);

The **read()** function reads numbytes from the associated stream and puts them in the buffer pointed to by buf. The **write()** function writes num bytes to the associated stream from the buffer pointed to by buf.

The following program writes and then reads an array of integers:

```
#include <iostream.h>
#include <fstream.h>

main()
{
  int n[5] = {1, 2, 3, 4, 5};
  register int i;

  ofstream out("test");
  if(!out) {
    cout << "Cannot open file",
    return 1;
   }

  out.write((unsigned char *) &n, sizeof n);
```

```
    out.close();

    for(i=0; i<5; i++) // clear array
      n[i] = 0;

    ifstream in("test");
    in.read((unsigned char *) &n, sizeof n);

    for(i=0; i<5; i++) // show values read from file
      cout << n[i] << " ";

    in.close();

    return 0;
}
```

Note that the type casts inside the calls to **read()** and **write()** are necessary when operating on a buffer that is not defined as a character array.

If the end of the file is reached before *num* characters have been read, then **read()** simply stops and the buffer contains as many characters as were available. You can find out how many characters have been read by using another member function, called **gcount()**, which has this prototype:

int gcount();

It returns the number of characters read by the last binary read operation.

Detecting EOF

You can detect when the end of the file is reached by using the member function **eof()**, which has this prototype:

int eof();

It returns nonzero when the end of the file has been reached; otherwise it returns zero.

Random Access

In C++'s I/O system, you perform random access by using the **seekg()** and **seekp()** functions. Their most common forms are shown here:

istream &seekg(streamoff *offset*, seek_dir *origin*);
ostream &seekp(streamoff *offset*, seek_dir *origin*);

Here, **streamoff** is a type defined in IOSTREAM.H that is capable of containing the largest valid value that *offset* can have. Also, **seek_dir** is an enumeration that may have these values:

ios::beg
ios::cur
ios::end

The C++ I/O system manages two pointers associated with a file. One is the *get pointer*, which specifies where in the file the next input operation will occur. The other is the *put pointer*, which specifies where in the file the next output operation will occur. Each time an input or output operation takes place, the appropriate pointer is automatically advanced. However, by using the **seekg()** and **seekp()** functions, it is possible to access the file in a nonsequential fashion.

The **seekg()** function moves the associated file's current get pointer *offset* number of bytes from the specified *origin*, which must be one of these three values:

ios::beg	Beginning of file
ios::cur	Current location
ios::end	End of file

The **seekp()** function moves the associated file's current put pointer *offset* number of bytes from the specified *origin*, which must be one of the values just shown.

The following program demonstrates the **seekp()** function. It allows you to specify a file name on the command line followed by the specific byte in the file you want to change. It then writes an "X" at the specified location.

```
#include <iostream.h>
#include <fstream.h>
#include <stdlib.h>

main(int argc, char *argv[])
{
  if(argc!=3) {
    cout << "Usage: CHANGE <filename> <byte>\n";
    return 1;
  }

  fstream out(argv[1], ios::in|ios::out);
  if(!out) {
    cout << "Cannot open file";
    return 1;
  }

  out.seekp(atoi(argv[2]), ios::beg);

  out.put('X');
  out.close();

  return 0;
}
```

The next program uses **seekg()**. It displays the contents of a file beginning with the location you specify.

```
#include <iostream.h>
#include <fstream.h>
#include <stdlib.h>

main(int argc, char *argv[])
```

```
{
  char ch;

  if(argc!=3) {
    cout << "Usage: NAME <filename> <starting location>\n";
    return 1;
  }

  ifstream in(argv[1]);
  if(!in) {
    cout << "Cannot open file";
    return 1;
  }

  in.seekg(atoi(argv[2]), ios::beg);

  while(in.get(ch))
    cout << ch;

  return 0;
}
```

You can determine the current position of each file pointer using these functions:

streampos tellg();
streampos tellp();

Here, **streampos** is a type defined in IOSTREAM.H that is capable of holding the largest value that either function can return.

As you have seen, C++'s I/O system is both powerful and flexible. Although this chapter discussed the most important and commonly used functions, C++ includes several other I/O functions. You should consult your Turbo C++ user manuals to see what other "goodies" are contained within the C++ I/O system.

CHAPTER

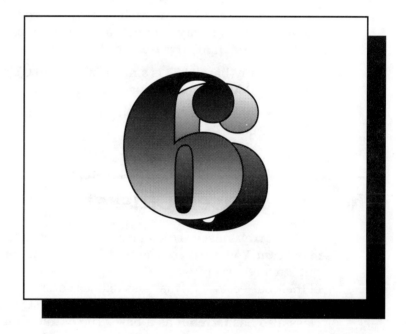

Array-based I/O

*I*n addition to console and file I/O, C++'s stream-based I/O system allows array-based I/O. *Array-based I/O* uses RAM as either the input device, the output device, or both. Array-based I/O is performed through normal C++ streams. In fact, all the information presented in the preceding chapter is applicable to array-based I/O. The only thing that makes array-based I/O unique is that the device linked to the stream is memory.

In some C++ literature, array-based I/O is referred to as *in-RAM I/O*. Also, because the streams are, like all C++ streams, capable of handling formatted information, sometimes array-based I/O is called *in-RAM formatting*. (Sometimes the archaic term *incore formatting* is also used. But since core memory is largely a thing of the past, this book uses the terms "in-RAM" and "array-based.")

C++'s array-based I/O is similar in effect to C's **sprintf()** and **sscanf()** functions. Both approaches use memory as an input or output device.

To use array-based I/O in your programs, you must include STRSTREAM.H.

The Array-based Classes

The array-based I/O classes are **istrstream**, **ostrstream**, and **strstream**. You use these classes to create input, output, and input/output streams, respectively. All of these classes have **strstreambuf** as one of their base classes. This class defines several low-level details that are used by the derived classes. In addition to **strstreambuf**, the **istrstream** class also has **istream** as a base. The **ostrstream** class is also derived from **ostream** and the **strstream** class also contains the **iostream** classes. Therefore, all array-based classes also have access to the same member functions that the "normal" I/O classes do.

Creating an Array-based Output Stream

To link an output stream to an array, use this **ostrstream** constructor:

ostrstream *ostr*(char **buf*, int *size*, int *mode*=ios::out)

Here, *buf* is a pointer to the array that will be used to collect characters written to the stream *ostr*. The size of the array is passed in the *size* parameter. By default, the stream is opened for normal output, but you can OR various other options (discussed in Chapter 5) with it to create the mode you need. (For example, you might include the **ios::app** to cause output to be written at the end of any information already contained in the array.) For most purposes, *mode* will be allowed to default.

Once you have opened an array-based output stream, all output to that stream is put into the array. However, no output will be written outside the bounds of the array. An attempt to do so results in an error.

Here is a simple program that demonstrates an array-based output stream:

```
#include <strstream.h>
#include <iostream.h>

main()
{
  char str[80];
  int a = 10;

  ostrstream outs(str, sizeof(str));

  outs << "Hello there ";
  outs << a+44 << hex << " ";
  outs.setf(ios::showbase);
  outs << 100 << ends;

  cout << str;  // display string on console

  return 0;
}
```

This program displays **Hello there 54 0x64**. Keep in mind that **outs** is a stream like any other stream and that it has the same capabilities as any of the other types of streams you saw earlier. The only difference is that the device it is linked to is memory. Because **outs** is a stream, manipulators like **hex** and **ends** are perfectly valid. Also, **ostream** member functions, such as **setf()**, are also available for use.

If you want the output array to be null terminated, you must explicitly write a null. In this program, the **ends** manipulator was used to null terminate the string, but you could also have used \0.

If you're not quite sure what is really happening in the preceding program, compare it to the following C program. This program is functionally equivalent to the C++ version. However, it uses **sprintf()** to construct an output array.

```
#include <stdio.h>

main()
{
  char str[80];
  int a = 10;

  sprintf(str, "Hello there %d %#x", a+44, 100);

  printf(str);

  return 0;
}
```

You can determine how many characters are in the output array by calling the **pcount()** member function. It has this prototype:

```
int pcount();
```

The number returned by **pcount()** also includes the null terminator, if it exists.

The next program illustrates **pcount()**. It reports that 17 characters are in **outs**—16 characters plus the null terminator.

```
#include <strstream.h>
#include <iostream.h>

main()
```

```
{
  char str[80];

  ostrstream outs(str, sizeof(str));

  outs << "Hello ";
  outs << 34 << " " << 1234.23;
  outs << ends;   // null terminate

  cout << outs.pcount(); // display how many chars in outs

  cout << " " << str;

  return 0;
}
```

Using an Array as Input

To link an input stream to an array, use this **istrstream** constructor:

istrstream *istr*(const char *buf*);

Here, *buf* is a pointer to the array that will be used as a source of characters each time input is performed on the stream *istr*. The contents of the array pointed to by *buf* must be null terminated. However, the null terminator is never read from the array.

Here is an example that uses a string as input:

```
#include <iostream.h>
#include <strstream.h>

main()
{
  char s[] = "One 2 3.00";

  istrstream ins(s);

  int i;
```

```
    char str[80];
    float f;

    // reading: one 2
    ins >> str;
    ins >> i;
    cout << str << " " << i << endl;

    // reading 3.00
    ins >> f;
    cout << f << '\n';

    return 0;
}
```

If you wish only part of a string to be used for input, use this form of the **istrstream** constructor:

istrstream *istr*(const char **buf*, int *size*);

Here, only the first *size* elements of the array pointed to by *buf* will be used. This string need not be null terminated since it is the value of *size* that determines the size of the string.

Streams linked to memory behave just like those linked to other devices. For example, the following program illustrates the way that contents of any text array may be read. When the end of the array (same as end-of-file) is reached, **ins** will be zero.

```
/* This program shows how to read the contents of any
   array that contains text. */
#include <iostream.h>
#include <strstream.h>

main()
{
  char s[] = "C++ arrays are fun! 123.23 0x23\n";

  istrstream ins(s);

  char ch;
```

```
// This will read and display the contents of any text array.
ins.unsetf(ios::skipws); // don't skip spaces
while (ins) {  // 0 when end of array is reached
  ins >> ch;
  cout << ch;
}

return 0;
}
```

Using Binary I/O

Arrays linked to array-based streams may also contain binary information. When reading binary information, you may need to use the **eof()** function to determine when the end of the array has been reached. For example, this program shows how to read the contents of any array—binary or text—by using the binary input function **get()**:

```
#include <iostream.h>
#include <strstream.h>

main()
{
  char s[] = "text and binary mixed\23\22\21\a\t\n";

  istrstream ins(s);

  char ch;

  // This will read the contents of any type of array.
  while (!ins.eof()) {
    ins.get(ch);
    cout << ch;
  }

  return 0;
}
```

In this example, the values formed by **\23\22\21** are the nontext control characters CTRL-W, CTRL-V, and CTRL-U. The **\a** is the bell character, and the **\t** is a tab. However, any type of binary data could have been read.

To output binary characters, use the **put()** function. If you need to read buffers of binary data, you can use the **read()** member function. To write buffers of binary data, use the **write()** function.

Input/Output Array-based Streams

To create an array-based stream that can perform both input and output, use this **strstream** constructor function:

strstream *iostr*(char **buf*, int *size*, int *mode*);

Here, *buf* points to the string that will be used for I/O operations. The value of *size* specifies the size of the array. The value of *mode* determines how the stream operates. For normal input/output operations, *mode* will be **ios::in | ios::out**. For input, the array must be null terminated.

Here is a program that uses an array to perform both input and output:

```
// Perform both input and output.
#include <iostream.h>
#include <strstream.h>

main()
{
  char iostr[80];

  strstream ios(iostr, sizeof(iostr), ios::in | ios::out);

  int a, b;
  char str[80];

  ios << "1734 534abcdefghijklmnopqrstuvwxyz";
  ios >> a >> b >> str;
  cout << a << " " << b << " " << str << endl;
```

This program first writes two integers and the alphabet to the file and then reads it back in again.

Random Access Within Arrays

It is important to remember that all normal I/O operations apply to array-based I/O. This also includes random access using **seekg()** and **seekp()**. For example, the next program seeks to the eighth character inside **iostr** and displays what it is. (It outputs **h**.)

```
#include <iostream.h>
#include <strstream.h>

main()
{
  char iostr[80];

  strstream ios(iostr, sizeof(iostr), ios::in | ios::out);

  char ch;

  ios << "abcdefghijklmnopqrstuvwxyz";
  ios.seekg(7, ios::beg);
  ios >> ch;
  cout << "Character at 7: " << ch;

  return 0;
}
```

You can seek anywhere *inside* the I/O array, but you are not allowed to seek past an array boundary.

You can also apply functions like **tellg()** and **tellp()** to array-based streams.

Using Dynamic Arrays

In the first part of this chapter, when you linked a stream to an output array, the array and its size were passed to the **ostrstream** constructor.

This approach is fine as long as you know the maximum number of characters you will be outputting to that array. However, what if you don't know how large the output array needs to be? The solution to this problem is to use a second form of the **ostrstream** constructor, shown here:

ostrstream();

When this constructor is used, **ostrstream** creates and maintains a dynamically allocated array. This array is allowed to grow in length to accommodate the output it must store.

Notice that the **ostrstream** constructor does *not* return a pointer to the allocated array. Accessing the dynamically allocated array requires the use of a second function called **str()**. This function "freezes" the array and returns a pointer to it. Once a dynamic array is frozen, it may not be used for output again. Therefore, you will not want to freeze the array until you are through outputting characters to it.

Here is a program that uses a dynamic output array:

```
#include <strstream.h>

#include <iostream.h>

main()
{
  char *p;

  ostrstream outs;   // dynamically allocate array

  outs << "I like C++ ";
  outs << -10 << hex << " ";
  outs.setf(ios::showbase);
  outs << 100 << ends;

  p = outs.str(); // Freeze dynamic buffer and return
                  // pointer to it.

  cout << p;

  delete p;   // Free dynamic buffer created by ostrstream().
```

```
    return 0;
}
```

As this program illustrates, once a dynamic array has been frozen, it is your responsibility to release its memory back to the system when you are through with it. However, if you never freeze the array, the memory is automatically freed when the stream is destroyed.

You can also use dynamic I/O arrays with the **strstream** class, which may perform both input and output on an array.

Manipulators and Array-based I/O

Since array-based streams are the same as any other stream, manipulators that you create for I/O in general can be used with array-based I/O with no changes whatsoever. For example, in Chapter 5, the output manipulator **setup()** was created, which turned on left justification and set the field width to 10 and the fill character to the dollar sign. This manipulator can be used unchanged when using an array as output, as shown here:

```
/* This program uses a custom manipulator with
   array-based I/O. */

#include <strstream.h>
#include <iostream.h>
#include <iomanip.h>

// Custom output manipulator.
ostream &setup(ostream &stream)
{
  stream.setf(ios::left);
  stream << setw(10) << setfill('$');
  return stream;
}


main()
{
  char str[80];
```

```
    ostrstream outs(str, sizeof(str));

    outs << setup << 99 << ends;

    cout << str << '\n';

    return 0;
}
```

Custom Extractors and Inserters

As has been said many times in this chapter, since array-based streams are just that—streams—you can create your own extractor and inserter functions in just the same way you do for other types of streams. For example, the following program creates a class called **plot** that maintains the X,Y coordinates of a point in two-dimensional space. The overloaded inserter for this class displays a small coordinate plane and plots the location of the point. For simplicity, the range of the X,Y coordinates is restricted to 0 through 5.

```
#include <iostream.h>
#include <strstream.h>

const int size=5;

class plot {
  int x, y;
public:
  plot(int i, int j) {
    // For simplicity, restrict x and y to 0 through size.
    if(i>size) i = size;  if (i<0) i=0;
    if(j>size) j = size;  if (j<0) j=0;
    x=i; y=j;
  }
  // An inserter for plot.
```

```
    friend ostream &operator<<(ostream &stream, plot o);
};

ostream &operator<<(ostream &stream, plot o)
{
  register int i, j;

  for(j=size; j>=0; j--) {
    stream << j;
    if(j == o.y) {
      for(i=0; i<o.x; i++) stream << "  ";
      stream << '*';
    }
    stream << "\n";
  }

  for(i=0; i<=size; i++) stream << " " << i;
  stream << "\n";

  return stream;
}

main()
{
  plot a(2, 3), b(1, 1);

  // output first using cout
  cout << "Output using cout:\n";
  cout << a << "\n" << b << "\n\n";

  char str[200];   // now use RAM-based I/O
  ostrstream outs(str, sizeof(str));

  // now output using outs and in-RAM formatting
  outs << a << b << ends;

  cout << "Output using in-RAM formatting:\n";
  cout << str;
}
```

This program produces the following output:

```
Output using cout:
5
4
3      *
2
1
0
 0  1  2  3  4  5


5
4
3
2
1   *
0
 0  1  2  3  4  5


Output using in-RAM formatting:
5
4
3      *
2
1
0
 0  1  2  3  4  5
5
4
3
2
1  *
0
 0  1  2  3  4  5
```

Uses for Array-based Formatting

In C, the in-RAM I/O functions **sprintf()** and **sscanf()** were particularly useful for preparing output or reading input from nonstandard devices.

However, because of C++'s ability to overload inserters and extractors relative to a class and to create custom manipulators, you can handle many exotic devices easily by using these features, making the need for in-RAM formatting less important. Nevertheless, there are still many uses for array-based I/O.

One common use of array-based formatting is to construct a string that will be used as input by either a standard library or a third-party function. For example, you may need to construct a string that will be parsed by the **strtok()** standard library function. (The **strtok()** function *tokenizes*—that is, decomposes to its elements—a string.) Another place where you can use array-based I/O is in text editors that perform complex formatting operations. Often it is easier to use C++'s array-based formatted I/O to construct a complex string than it is to do so by "manual" means.

Perhaps the single most important use of RAM-based I/O as it relates to Windows programming is that it allows you to fully construct and maintain a complete screen image in memory. As you will soon see, all Windows applications must be able to restore their screens after they have been overwritten by another window. You might find array-based I/O the easiest way to accomplish this task.

CHAPTER

Miscellaneous C++ Topics

*T*his chapter discusses several aspects of C++ not covered in the previous chapters. It also looks at some differences between C and C++ and at two of Turbo C++'s built-in classes.

Dynamic Allocation Using new and delete

As you know, C uses the functions **malloc()** and **free()** (among others) to dynamically allocate memory and to free dynamically allocated memory. However, C++ contains two operators that perform the function of allocating and freeing memory in a better and easier way. The operators are **new** and **delete**. Their general form is shown here:

pointer_var = new *var_type*;
delete *pointer_var*;

Here, *pointer_var* is a pointer of type *var_type*. The **new** operator allocates sufficient memory to hold a value of type *var_type* and returns an address to it. Any valid data type may be allocated by using **new**. The **delete** operator frees the memory pointed to by *pointer_var*.

Like **malloc()**, **new** returns a null pointer if the allocation request fails. Therefore, you must always check the pointer produced by **new** before using it. Also, like **malloc()**, **new** allocates memory from the heap.

Because of the way dynamic allocation is managed, you must use **delete** only with a pointer to memory that was previously allocated by using **new**. Using **delete** with any other type of address will cause serious problems.

There are several advantages to using **new** over **malloc()**. First, **new** automatically computes the size of the type being allocated. You don't have to make use of the **sizeof** operator, which saves you some effort. More importantly, it prevents the wrong amount of memory from being accidentally allocated. Second, it automatically returns the correct pointer type—you don't need to use a type cast. Third, as you will soon see, it is possible to initialize the object being allocated by using **new**.

Finally, it is possible to overload **new** (and **delete**) relative to a class you create.

Here is a simple example of **new** and **delete**:

```
#include <iostream.h>

main()
{
  int *p;

  p = new int; // allocate memory for integer
  if(!p) {
    cout << "allocation failure\n";
    return 1;
  }

  *p = 20; // assign that memory the value 20
  cout << *p; // prove that it works by displaying value

  delete p; // free the memory

  return 0;
}
```

This program assigns to **p** an address in memory that is large enough to hold an integer. It then assigns that memory the value 20 and displays the contents of that memory on the screen. Finally, it frees the dynamically allocated memory.

As stated, you can initialize the memory by using the **new** operator. To do this, specify the initial value inside parentheses after the type name. For example, this program uses initialization to give the memory pointed to by **p** the value 99:

```
#include <iostream.h>

main()
{
  int *p;

  p = new int (99);  // initialize to 99
```

```
  if(!p) {
    cout << "allocation failure\n";
    return 1;
  }

  cout << *p;

  delete p;

  return 0;
}
```

You can allocate one-dimensional arrays by using **new**. The general form for a one-dimensional array is shown here:

pointer-var = new *var-type* [*size*];

Here, *size* specifies the number of elements in the array.

This program allocates space for 10 floats, assigns the array the values 100 to 109, and displays the contents of the array on the screen:

```
#include <iostream.h>

main()
{
  float *p;
  int i;

  p = new float [10]; // get a 10-element array
  if(!p) {
    cout << "allocation failure\n";
    return 1;
  }

  // assign the values 100 through 109
  for(i=0; i<10; i++) p[i] = 100.00 + i;

  // display the contents of the array
  for(i=0; i<10; i++)  cout << p[i] << " ";

  delete p; // delete the entire array
```

```
   return 0;
}
```

There is one important point to remember about allocating an array:
you cannot initialize it.

As stated, you can allocate memory for any valid type. This includes
objects of classes you create. For example, in this program, **new** allocates
memory for an object of type **three_d**:

```
#include <iostream.h>

class three_d {
public:
  int x, y, z; // 3-d coordinates
  three_d(int a, int b, int c);
  ~three_d() {cout << "destructing\n";}
} ;

three_d::three_d(int a, int b, int c)
{
  cout << "constructing\n";
  x = a;
  y = b;
  z = c;
}

// Display X,Y,Z coordinates - three_d inserter
ostream &operator<<(ostream &stream, three_d &obj)
{
  stream << obj.x << ", ";
  stream << obj.y << ", ";
  stream << obj.z << "\n";
  return stream;  // return the stream
}

main()
{
  three_d *p;

  p = new three_d (5, 6, 7);
  if(!p) {
```

```
      cout << "allocation failure\n";
      return 1;
    }

    cout << *p;

    delete p;

    return 0;
}
```

Notice that this program makes use of the inserter function for the **three_d** class created earlier. When you run the program, you will see that **three_d**'s constructor function is called when **new** is encountered and that its destructor function is called when **delete** is reached. Also note that the initializers are automatically passed to the constructor by **new**.

You can also allocate arrays of objects dynamically. However, when you free a dynamically allocated array of class objects that contain destructor functions, you must use this form of **delete**:

delete [*size*] *pointer-var*;

Here, *size* specifies the number of elements in the array. The reason you must specify the size of the array is that when you free the memory of an array containing objects, the destructor function (if existent) for each object must be executed. However, if you are freeing an array of objects that has no destructors (such as an array of a built-in type), the *size* specifier is not required.

This program illustrates how an array of user-defined objects can be dynamically allocated and freed:

```
#include <iostream.h>
class three_d {
public:
  int x, y, z; // 3-d coordinates
  three_d(int a, int b, int c) ;
  three_d(){cout << "constructing\n";} // needed for arrays
  ~three_d() {cout << "destructing\n";}
```

```
} ;

three_d::three_d(int a, int b, int c)
{
  cout << "constructing\n";
  x = a;
  y = b;
  z = c;
}

// Display X,Y,Z coordinates - three_d inserter
ostream &operator<<(ostream &stream, three_d &obj)
{
  stream << obj.x << ", ";
  stream << obj.y << ", ";
  stream << obj.z << "\n";
  return stream;  // return the stream
}

main()
{
  three_d *p;
  int i;

  p = new three_d [10];
  if(!p) {
    cout << "allocation failure\n";
    return 1;
  }

  for(i=0; i<10; i++) {
    p[i].x = 1;
    p[i].y = 2;
    p[i].z = 3;
  }

  for(i=0; i<10; i++) cout << *p;

  delete [10] p;

  return 0;
}
```

Notice that a second constructor function has been added to the **three_d** class. Because allocated arrays cannot be initialized, a constructor function that does not have any parameters is needed. If you don't supply this constructor, an error message will be displayed.

In this example, **delete** uses the *size* specifier to force the destructor for each element in the array to be called.

Remember   When you deallocate an array of objects that have destructors, you must specify the size of the array in order for each object to be correctly destroyed. However, if the objects do not have destructors, it is not necessary to specify the size of the array. In both cases, the correct amount of memory is returned to the system.

Overloading new and delete

It is possible to overload **new** and **delete**. You might want to do this because you want to use some special allocation method. For example, you may want allocation routines that automatically begin using a disk file as virtual memory when the heap has been exhausted. Whatever the reason, it is a very simple matter to overload these operators.

The skeletons for the functions that overload **new** and **delete** are shown here:

```
void *operator new(size_t size)
{
  // perform allocation
  return pointer_to_memory;
}
void operator delete(void *p)
{
  // free memory pointed to by p
}
```

The type **size_t** is defined by Turbo C++ as a type capable of containing the largest single piece of memory that can be allocated. **size_t** is an integer type. The parameter *size* will contain the number of bytes needed to hold the object being allocated. The overloaded **new** function must return a pointer to the memory that it allocates or zero if an allocation error occurs. Beyond these constraints, the overloaded **new** function can do anything else you require.

The **delete** function receives a pointer to the region of memory to free.

In general, **new** and **delete** are overloaded relative to a class you create. To overload the **new** and **delete** operators relative to a class, simply make the overloaded operator functions members of that class.

The following example overloads **new** and **delete** relative to the **three_d** type. For the purposes of illustration, no new allocation scheme will be used. Instead, the overloaded functions will simply invoke **malloc()** and **free()**. However, you are free to implement any alternative allocation scheme you like.

```
#include <iostream.h>
#include <stdlib.h>

class three_d {
public:
  int x, y, z; // 3-d coordinates
  three_d(int a, int b, int c) ;
  ~three_d() {cout << "destructing\n";}
  void *operator new(size_t size);
  void operator delete(void *p);
} ;

three_d::three_d(int a, int b, int c)
{
  cout << "constructing\n";
  x = a;
  y = b;
  z = c;
}

// Overload new relative to three_d
void * three_d::operator new(size_t size)
{
```

```
    cout << "in three_d new\n";
    return malloc(size);
}

// Overload delete relative to three_d
void three_d::operator delete(void *p)
{
    cout << "in three_d delete\n";
    free(p);
}

// Display X,Y,Z coordinates - three_d inserter.
ostream &operator<<(ostream &stream, three_d &obj)
{
    stream << obj.x << ", ";
    stream << obj.y << ", ";
    stream << obj.z << "\n";
    return stream;  // return the stream
}

main()
{
    three_d *p, *p1;

    p = new three_d (1, 2, 3);
    p1 = new three_d (4, 5, 6);
    if(!p || !p1) {
        cout << "allocation failure\n";
        return 1;
    }

    cout << *p << *p1;

    delete p;
    delete p1;

    return 0;
}
```

It is important to understand that when **new** and **delete** are used to allocate data of any type other than the class for which they are overloaded, the original **new** or **delete** is employed. The overloaded operators are used only when allocating data of the type for which they are defined. This means that if you add this line to **main()**, the global **new** will be executed:

```
int *i = new int;
```

Static Class Members

You can apply the keyword **static** to members of a class. Its meaning in this context is similar to its original C-like meaning. When you declare a member of a class as static, you are telling the compiler that no matter how many objects of the class are created, there is only one copy of the static member. A static member is shared by all objects of the class. All static data is initialized to zero when the first object of its class is created if no other initialization is specified.

When you declare a static data member within a class, you are *not* defining it. Instead, you must provide a global definition for it elsewhere, outside the class. You do this by redeclaring the static variable, using the scope resolution operator to identify which class it belongs to.

As a first example, examine the following program and try to understand how it works:

```
#include <iostream.h>

class counter {
  static int count;
public:
  void setcount(int i) {count = i;};
  void showcount() {cout << count << " ";}
};
int counter::count; // declare storage for count

main()
{
  counter a, b;
```

```
a.showcount(); // prints 0
b.showcount(); // prints 0

a.setcount(10); // set static count to 10

a.showcount(); // prints 10
b.showcount(); // also prints 10

return 0;
}
```

As stated, Turbo C++ initializes **count** to zero. This is why the first calls to **showcount()** both display zero. Next, object **a** sets **count** to 10. Next, both **a** and **b** use **showcount()** to display its value. Because there is only one copy of **count**, shared by both **a** and **b**, both cause the value 10 to be displayed.

 Remember When you declare a member of a class as static, you are causing only one copy of that member to be created and then shared by all objects of that class.

You can also have static member functions. Static member functions may only access other static data and static functions declared in a class. They cannot manipulate nonstatic data nor call nonstatic functions. The reason for this is that a static member function does not have a **this** pointer. This means that it has no way of knowing which object's nonstatic data to access. For example, if there are two objects of a class that contains a static function called **f()**, and if **f()** attempts to access a nonstatic variable called **var**, defined in the class, which copy of **var** should the call be routed to? The compiler has no way of knowing. This is why static functions can access only other static functions or data.

To see an example of static functions, here is a short program that gives you the flavor of their usage. It is not uncommon for an object to require access to some scarce resource, such as a shared file in a network. As the program illustrates, the use of static data and functions provides a method by which an object can check on the status of the resource and access it if it is available.

```
#include <iostream.h>
```

```
enum access_t {shared, in_use, locked, unlocked};

// a scarce resource control class
class access {
  static enum access_t acs;
  // ...
public:
  static void set_access(enum access_t a) {acs = a;}
  static enum access_t get_access()
  {
    return acs;
  }
  // ...
};
enum access_t access::acs; // declare storage for acs

main()
{
  access  obj1, obj2;

  obj1.set_access(locked);

  // ... intervening code

  // see if obj2 can access resource
  if(obj2.get_access()==unlocked) {
    obj2.set_access(in_use);
    cout << "access resource\n";
  }
  else cout << "locked out\n";

  // ...
}
```

If you compile this skeleton, you will see that **locked out** is displayed. You might want to play with the program a little until you are sure you understand the effect of **static** on both data and functions.

As stated, static functions can access only other static functions or static data within the same class. To prove this, try compiling this version of the program:

```
// This program will not compile!
#include <iostream.h>

enum access_t {shared, in_use, locked, unlocked};

// a scarce resource control class
class access {
  static enum access_t acs;
  int i;  // nonstatic
  // ...
public:
  static void set_access(enum access_t a) {acs = a;}
  static enum access_t get_access()
  {
    i = 100; // this will not compile!!!
    return acs;
  }
  // ...
};
enum access_t access::acs; // declare storage for acs

main()
{
  access  obj1, obj2;

  obj1.set_access(locked);

  // ... intervening code

  // see if obj2 can access resource
  if(obj2.get_access()==unlocked) {
    obj2.set_access(in_use);
    cout << "access resource\n";
  }
  else cout << "locked out\n";

  // ...
}
```

Turbo C++ will issue an error message and not compile your program because **getaccess()** is attempting to access a nonstatic variable.

Although you may not see an immediate need for static members, as you continue to write programs in C++, you will find static members very useful in certain situations because they allow you to avoid the use of global variables.

Virtual Base Classes

As you know, in C++, you use the **virtual** keyword to declare virtual functions that will be overridden by a derived class. However, **virtual** also has a another use. This second use enables you to specify *virtual base classes*. To understand what a virtual base class is and why the keyword **virtual** has a second meaning, let's begin with the short, incorrect program shown here:

```
// This program contains an error and will not compile.
#include <iostream.h>

class base {
public:
  int i;
};

// d1 inherits base.
class d1 :  public base {
public:
  int j;
};

// d2 inherits base.
class d2 : public base {
public:
  int k;
};

// d3 inherits both d1 and d2. This means there
// are two copies of base in d3!
class d3 : public d1, public d2 {
```

```
public:
  int m;
};

main()
{
  d3 d;

  d.i = 10;   // this is ambiguous, which i???
  d.j = 20;
  d.k = 30;
  d.m = 40;


  // also ambiguous, which i???
  cout << d.i << " ";
  cout << d.j << " " << d.k << " ";
  cout << d.m;

  return 0;
}
```

As the comments in the program indicate, both **d1** and **d2** inherit **base**. However, **d3** inherits both **d1** and **d2**. This means there are two copies of **base** present in an object of type **d3**. Therefore, in an expression like

```
d.i = 20;
```

which **i** is being referred to—the one in **d1** or the one in **d2**? Since there are two copies of **base** present in object **d**, there are two **d.i**'s. As you can see, the statement **d.i = 10** is inherently ambiguous.

There are two ways to remedy the preceding program. The first is to apply the scope resolution operator to **i** and manually select one **i**. For example, this version of the program does compile and run as expected:

```
#include <iostream.h>

class base {
public:
  int i;
};
```

```
// d1 inherits base.
class d1 :  public base {
public:
  int j;
};

// d2 inherits base.
class d2 : public base {
public:
  int k;
};

// d3 inherits both d1 and d2. This means there
// are two copies of base in d3!
class d3 : public d1, public d2 {
public:
  int m;
};

main()
{
  d3 d;

  d.d2::i = 10; // scope resolved, using d2's i
  d.j = 20;
  d.k = 30;
  d.m = 40;

  // scope resolved, using d2's i
  cout << d.d2::i << " ";
  cout << d.j << " " << d.k << " ";
  cout << d.m;

  return 0;
}
```

As you can see, by the application of the :: scope resolution operator, the program has manually selected **d2**'s version of **base**. However, this solution raises a deeper issue: What if only one copy of **base** is actually required? Is there some way to prevent two copies from being included in **d3**? The answer, as you probably have guessed, is yes. And this solution is achieved by using virtual base classes.

When two or more objects are derived from a common base class, you can prevent multiple copies of the base class from being present in an object derived from those objects by declaring the base class as virtual when it is inherited. For example, here is another version of the example program in which **d3** contains only one copy of **base**:

```
#include <iostream.h>

class base {
public:
  int i;
};

// d1 inherits base as virtual.
class d1 : virtual public base {
public:
  int j;
};

// d2 inherits base as virtual.
class d2 : virtual public base {
public:
  int k;
};

/* d3 inherits both d1 and d2. However, now
   there is only one copy of base in d3. */
class d3 : public d1, public d2 {
public:
  int m;
};

main()
{
  d3 d;

  d.i = 10; // no longer ambiguous
  d.j = 20;
  d.k = 30;
  d.m = 40;
```

```
cout << d.i << " "; // no longer ambiguous
cout << d.j << " " << d.k << " ";
cout << d.m;

return 0;
}
```

As you can see, the keyword **virtual** precedes the rest of the inherited class's specification. Now that both **d1** and **d2** have inherited **base** as virtual, any multiple inheritance involving them will cause only one copy of **base** to be present. Therefore, in **d3**, there is only one copy of **base**, and therefore **d.i = 10** is perfectly valid and unambiguous.

One further point to keep in mind: even though both **d1** and **d2** specify **base** as virtual, **base** is still present in any objects of either type. For example, the following sequence is perfectly valid:

```
// define a class of type d1
d1 myclass;

myclass.i = 100;
```

The only difference between a normal base class and a virtual one is when an object inherits the base more than once. If virtual base classes are used, then only one base class is present in the object. Otherwise, multiple copies will be found.

Using the asm Keyword

You can embed assembly language directly into your Turbo C++ program by using the **asm** keyword. The **asm** keyword has three slightly different general forms, which are shown here:

asm *instruction* ;
asm *instruction newline*
asm {
    instruction sequence
}

Here, *instruction* is any valid 80x86 assembly language instruction. Unlike any other Turbo C++ statement, an **asm** statement does not have to end with a semicolon. It may end with either a semicolon or a newline.

The assembly language instructions that you embed in your program are passed automatically and unaltered to BASM (Borland's built-in assembler). Depending upon how you compile, they might also be passed to TASM (Turbo Assembler). Either way, the result is the same: the instructions are assembled as is into your C++ program.

As a first simple example, this program uses **asm** to execute an **INT 5** instruction, which invokes the PC's print screen function:

```
// Print the screen.
#include <iostream.h>

main()
{
  asm INT 5;
  return 0;
}
```

If you want to use a sequence of assembly language statements, enclose them in braces, as shown in this do-nothing (but harmless) example.

```
#include <iostream.h>

main()
{
  // this effectively does nothing
  asm {
    push ds
    pop ds
  }

  return 0;
}
```

If you want to put a comment on the same line as an assembly language statement, use C-like, not assembler-like, comments. (For both

BASM and TASM, a comment begins with a semicolon, but this just won't work in Turbo C++.)

 Caution   A thorough working knowledge of assembly language programming is required to use the **asm** statement. If you are not proficient at assembly language, it is best to avoid using it because very nasty errors may result.

Linkage Specification

In Turbo C++, you may specify how a function is linked. Specifically, you can tell Turbo C++ to link a function as a C function or as a C++ function. By default, functions are linked as C++ functions. However, by using a *linkage specification,* you can cause a function to be linked as defined by a different language. The general form of a linkage specifier is shown here:

extern "*language*" *function-prototype*

where *language* denotes the desired language. In Turbo C++, *language* must be either C or C++, but other implementations may allow other language types.

This program causes **myCfunc()** to be linked as a C function:

```
#include <iostream.h>

extern "C" void myCfunc();

main()
{
  myCfunc();

  return 0;
}

// This will link as a C function.
```

```
void myCfunc()
{
  cout << "This links as a C function.\n";
}
```

 Note   The **extern** keyword is a necessary part of the linkage specification. Further, the linkage specification must be global; it cannot be used
inside a function.

You can specify more than one function at a time by using this form
of the linkage specification:

extern "*language*" {
    prototypes
}

The use of a linkage specification is rare, and you will probably not
need to use one.

Creating Conversion Functions

Sometimes you will create a class that you want to be able to freely
mix in an expression with other types of data. While overloaded operator
functions can provide a means of mixing types, sometimes a simple
conversion to another type is all that you want. In these cases, you can
use a *type conversion function* to convert your class into a type compatible
with that of the rest of the expression. The general format of a type
conversion function is shown here:

operator (*type*)() {return *value*;}

Here, *type* is the target type you are converting your class to, and *value*
is the value of the class after conversion. A conversion function must be
a member of the class for which it is defined.

To illustrate how to create a conversion function, let's use the **three_d**
class once again. Suppose for some reason you want to be able to convert

an object of type **three_d** into an integer so it can be used in an integer expression. Further, the conversion will take place by using the product of the three dimensions. To accomplish this, you will use a conversion function that looks like this:

```
operator int() { return x * y * z; }
```

Here is a program that illustrates how the conversion function works:

```
#include <iostream.h>

class three_d {
  int x, y, z; // 3-d coordinates
public:
  three_d(int a, int b, int c) {x=a; y=b, z=c;}

  three_d operator+(three_d op2) ;
  friend ostream &operator<<(ostream &stream, three_d &obj);

  operator int() {return x*y*z;} // conversion function
} ;

// Display X,Y,Z coordinates - three_d inserter
ostream &operator<<(ostream &stream, three_d &obj)
{
  stream << obj.x << ", ";
  stream << obj.y << ", ";
  stream << obj.z << "\n";
  return stream;  // return the stream
}


three_d three_d::operator+(three_d op2)
{
  three_d temp(0, 0, 0);

  temp.x = x+op2.x;  // these are integer additions
  temp.y = y+op2.y;  // and the   retains its original
  temp.z = z+op2.z;  // meaning relative to them
  return temp;
}
```

```
main()
{
  three_d a(1, 2, 3), b(2, 3, 4);

  cout << a << b;

  cout <<  b+100;   // displays 124 because of conversion to int
  cout << "\n";
  cout << a+b;   // displays 3, 5, 7 - no conversion

  return 0;
}
```

This program displays this output:

```
1, 2, 3
2, 3, 4
124
3, 5, 7
```

As the program illustrates, when a **three_d** object is used in an integer expression, such as **cout << b+100**, the conversion function is applied to the object. In this specific case, the conversion function returns the value 24, which is then added to 100. However, when no conversion is needed, as in **cout << a+b**, the conversion function is not called.

Remember, you can create different conversion functions to meet different needs. You could define one that converts to double or long, for example. Each will be applied automatically.

The overload Anachronism

In early versions of C++, when a function was overloaded, you had to first tell the compiler this by preceding its prototype with the keyword **overload**. However, this has not been necessary for several years. The **overload** keyword is still supported by Turbo C++ in order to provide compatibility with older programs, but it is completely unnecessary for new programs.

Differences Between C and C++

For the most part, C++ is a superset of ANSI standard C, and virtually all C programs are also C++ programs. However, a few differences do exist, the most important of which are discussed here.

Perhaps the most important yet subtle difference between C and C++ was discussed in Chapter 1. It is reviewed here for your convenience. In C, a function declared like this:

```
int f();
```

says *nothing* about any parameters to that function. That is, when there is nothing specified between the parentheses following the function's name, in C, this means that nothing is being stated, one way or the other, about any parameters to that function. It might have parameters; it might not have parameters. However, in C++, a function declaration like this means that the function does *not* have parameters. That is, in C++, these two declarations are equivalent:

```
int f();
```

```
int f(void);
```

In C++, the **void** keyword is optional. Many C++ programmers include **void** as a means of making it completely clear to anyone reading the program that a function does not have any parameters, but this is technically unnecessary.

In C++, all functions must be prototyped. This is an option in C (although good programming practice suggests full prototyping be used in a C program).

A small, but potentially important, difference between C and C++ is that in C, a character constant is automatically elevated to an integer. In C++, it is not.

In C, it is not an error to declare a global variable several times, even though this is bad programming practice. In C++, this is an error.

As you learned earlier, in C, an identifier may be up to 31 characters long. In C++, no such limit exists. However, from a practical point of view, extremely long identifiers are unwieldy and are seldom needed.

Turbo C++'s Complex and BCD Classes

In addition to the classes and overloaded operators defined by IOSTREAM.H and its derivatives, Turbo C++ includes two additional class libraries that perform complex and BCD arithmetic. Let's take a quick look at these now.

As you may know, a *complex number* has two parts: a real half and an imaginary half. The real half is an ordinary number; the imaginary part is a multiple of the square root of –1. To use complex numbers, you must include COMPLEX.H in your program.

To construct a complex number, use the **complex()** constructor function. It has this prototype:

complex(double *real-part*, double *imaginary-part*);

The << and >> operators are overloaded relative to complex numbers. For example, this program constructs an imaginary number and displays it on the screen:

```
#include <iostream.h>
#include <complex.h>

main()
{
  complex num(10, 1);

  cout << num;

  return 0;
}
```

The program outputs the following:

```
(10, 1)
```

This output also illustrates the general format used when displaying complex numbers.

You may mix complex numbers with any other type of number, including integers, **float**s, and **double**s. The arithmetic operators +, −, *, and / are overloaded relative to complex numbers, as are the relational operators == and !=. This program illustrates how complex and regular numbers can be mixed in an expression:

```
#include <iostream.h>
#include <complex.h>

main()
{
  complex num(10, 1);

  num = 123.23 + num / 3;

  cout << num;

  return 0;
}
```

Turbo C++ has overloaded many mathematical functions, such as **sin()** (which returns the sine of its argument), relative to complex numbers. It also defines several functions that apply specifically to complex numbers. The complex functions are shown in Table 7-1.

Turbo C++ also defines the **bcd** class. As you may know, real numbers can be represented inside the computer a number of different ways. The most common is as binary floating-point values. However, another way to represent a real number is to use *binary coded decimal,* or BCD for short. In BCD, base 10, rather than base 2, is used to represent a number. The major advantage of the BCD representation is that no round-off errors occur. For example, if you use binary floating point, the number 100.23 cannot be accurately represented and is rounded to 100.230003. However, if you use BCD, no rounding occurs. For this reason, BCD numbers are often used in accounting programs and the like. The major disadvantage of BCD numbers is that BCD calculations are slower than binary floating-point calculations. To use BCD numbers, you must include BCD.H in your programs.

TABLE 7-1 The Complex Functions

Function	Purpose
complex abs(complex n)	Returns the absolute value of n
double acos(complex n)	Returns the arc cosine of n
double arg(complex n)	Returns the angle of n in the complex coordinate plane
complex asin(complex n)	Returns the arc sine of n
complex atan(complex n)	Returns the arc tangent of n
complex atan2(complex n)	Returns the arc tangent2 of n
double conj(complex n)	Returns the conjugate of n
complex cos(complex n)	Returns the cosine of n
complex cosh(complex n)	Returns the hyperbolic cosine of n
complex exp(complex n)	Returns e to the nth
double imag(complex n)	Returns the imaginary part of n
complex log(complex n)	Returns the natural log of n
complex log10(complex n)	Returns the log base 10 of n
double norm(complex n)	Returns the square of n
complex polar(double *magnitude*, double *angle*)	Returns the complex number given its polar coordinates
complex pow (complex x, complex y)	Returns x to the y power
complex pow (complex x, double y)	Returns x to the y power
complex pow (double x, complex y)	Returns x to the y power
double real(complex n)	Returns the real part of n
complex sin(complex n)	Returns the sine of n

TABLE 7-1	The Complex Functions *(continued)*	
	Function	**Purpose**
	complex sinh(complex *n*)	Returns the hyperbolic sine of *n*
	complex sqrt(complex *n*)	Returns the square root of *n*
	complex tan(complex *n*)	Returns the tangent of *n*
	complex tanh(complex *n*)	Returns the hyperbolic tangent of *n*

The **bcd** class has these constructor functions:

bcd(int *n*)
bcd(double *n*)
bcd(double *n*, int *digits*)

The first two are self-explanatory. The last one creates a BCD number that uses *digits* number of digits after the decimal point.

In Turbo C++, BCD numbers have a range of 10^{-125} to 10^{125} with 17 digits of precision.

To convert a number from BCD format to normal binary floating-point format, use **real()**, whose prototype is shown here:

long double real(bcd *n*)

The **bcd** class overloads the arithmetic and relational operators as well as the functions shown in Table 7-2.

Here is a sample program that illustrates the advantage of BCD numbers when the prevention of round-off errors is important:

```
#include <iostream.h>
#include <bcd.h>

main()
{
  float f = 100.23, f1 = 101.337;
  bcd b(100.23), b1(101.337);
```

TABLE
7-2

The BCD Functions

Function	Purpose
bcd abs(bcd *n*)	Returns the absolute value of *n*
bcd acos(bcd *n*)	Returns the arc cosine of *n*
bcd asin(bcd *n*)	Returns the arc sine of *n*
bcd atan(bcd *n*)	Returns the arc tangent of *n*
bcd cos(bcd *n*)	Returns the cosine of *n*
bcd cosh(bcd *n*)	Returns the hyperbolic cosine of *n*
bcd exp(bcd *n*)	Returns e to the *n*th
bcd log(bcd *n*)	Returns the natural log of *n*
bcd log10(bcd *n*)	Returns the log base 10 of *n*
bcd pow(bcd *x*, bcd *y*)	Returns *x* to the *y* power
bcd sin(bcd *n*)	Returns the sine of *n*
bcd sinh(bcd *n*)	Returns the hyperbolic sine of *n*
bcd sqrt(bcd *n*)	Returns the square root of *n*
bcd tan(bcd *n*)	Returns the tangent of *n*
bcd tanh(bcd *n*)	Returns the hyperbolic tangent of *n*

```
  cout << f+f1 << " " << b+b1;

  return 0;
}
```

This program displays the following:

```
201.567001 201.567
```

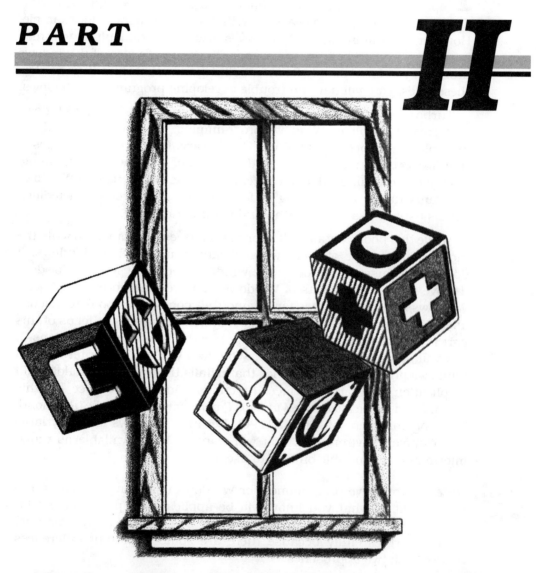

Windows Programming Using ObjectWindows

Part II of this book shows how to use Turbo C++ to create Windows applications using ObjectWindows. As you will see, writing a Windows application is not as easy as writing a DOS program, for example. However, programming for Windows is also not as difficult as you may have been lead to believe. In essence, to create a successful Windows program, you must simply follow a well-defined set of rules. If you follow these rules, you will have no trouble developing programs for Windows.

Turbo C++ for Windows provides a class library called ObjectWindows that greatly simplifies Windows programming. For this reason, all the examples described in Part II use this library. One of its advantages is that it effectively masks many of the details of Windows programming. Therefore, you will be able to concentrate on actually creating Windows programs rather than having to focus on the numerous and tedious details usually associated with Windows programming.

While this book contains all information necessary for you to write the most common type of Windows applications using ObjectWindows, it does not discuss all aspects of the Windows operating system. Nor does it delve into those aspects of Windows that are masked by the Object-Windows class library. It is far beyond the scope of this book to discuss all of Windows; it is simply too large a system. Instead, the focus of this part is on how to use ObjectWindows to write Windows applications. If you will be writing extensively for Windows, you will absolutely need a Windows programming reference that details the over 600 Windows API (application program interface) functions. One good source for this information is the *Microsoft Windows Programming Reference* (Redmond, Washington: Microsoft Press, 1990). Because Windows is a very large and complex environment, you will want to have available as much information as possible on how to use it.

 Note   If you have programmed for Windows using only the API functions, most of what you know will be applicable to programming for Windows using ObjectWindows. However, be sure to read the material in this part carefully because there are some important differences between the two approaches.

CHAPTER

ObjectWindows
Programming Overview

This chapter introduces ObjectWindows programming. The chapter has two main purposes. First, it discusses in a general way what Windows is, how a program must interact with it, and what rules must be followed by every Windows application. Second, it develops an application skeleton that will be used as a basis for all other Windows programs. As you will see, all Windows programs share a few common traits. It is these shared attributes that are contained in the application skeleton.

Note If you are familiar with Windows programming using the API interface, you will want to skip over the next few sections. However, be sure to read the material in this chapter that discusses the application skeleton. Since the examples use the ObjectWindows class library, there are some differences in the way you will create a Windows program.

What Is Windows?

To an extent, what Windows is depends upon whether you are an end user or a programmer. From the user's point of view, Windows is a shell with which he or she interacts in order to run applications. However, from the programmer's point of view, Windows is a graphics-oriented, multitasking operating system that is a collection of several hundred API functions. These functions support a specific application-designed philosophy. From the programmer's point of view, Windows is one giant toolbox of interrelated services that, when used correctly, allow the creation of application programs that all share a common interface.

The goal of Windows is to enable a person who has basic familiarity with the system to sit down and run virtually any application without prior training. In theory, if you can run one Windows program, you can run them all. Of course, in actuality, most useful programs will still require some sort of training in order to be used effectively, but at least this instruction can be restricted to what the program does, not how the user must interact with it. In fact, much of the code in a Windows application is there just to support the user interface.

At this point it is very important for you to understand that not every program that runs under Windows will necessarily present the user with a Windows-style interface. As you saw when running the examples in Part I, Turbo C++ can run any C++ program under Windows. However, only those programs written to take advantage of Windows will look and feel like Windows programs. While you can override the basic Windows design philosophy, you should have a good reason to do so because the users of your programs will, most often, be very disturbed. If you are writing application programs for Windows, they should conform to the accepted Windows programming philosophy.

As mentioned, Windows is graphics oriented, which means it provides a graphical user interface (GUI). While graphics hardware and video modes are quite diverse, many of the differences are handled by Windows. This means that, for the most part, your program does not need to worry about what type of graphics hardware or video mode is being used.

One important point: even though Windows runs on top of DOS, your Windows programs will not generally interact with DOS directly. Windows provides a complete set of its own services. If your program calls a DOS function, it may not be able to run as a Windows application. Therefore, your program will usually interact with the Windows API or with the ObjectWindows class library.

Let's look at a few of the more important features of Windows.

The Desktop Model

With few exceptions, the point of a window-based user interface is to provide on the screen the equivalent of a desktop. On a desk may be found several different pieces of paper, one on top of another, often with fragments of different pages visible beneath the top page. The equivalent of the desktop in Windows is the screen. The equivalents of pieces of paper are windows on the screen. On a desk you may move pieces of paper about, maybe changing which piece of paper is on top or how much of another is exposed to view. Windows allows the same type of operations on its windows. By selecting a window, you can make it *current*, which means putting it on top of all other windows. You can enlarge or shrink a window or move it about on the screen. In short, Windows lets you control the surface of the screen the way you control the surface of your desk.

The Mouse

Unlike DOS, Windows allows the use of the mouse for almost all control, selection, and drawing operations. Of course, to say that it *allows* the use of the mouse is an understatement. The fact is that the Windows interface was *designed* for the mouse; it *allows* the use of the keyboard! Although it is certainly possible for an application program to ignore the mouse, it does so only in violation of a basic Windows design principle.

Icons and Graphics Images

Windows allows (but does not require) the use of icons and bit-mapped graphics images. The theory behind the use of icons and graphics images is found in the old adage: A picture is worth a thousand words.

An *icon* is a small symbol that is used to represent some function or program that can be activated by moving the mouse to the icon and double-clicking. A graphics image is generally used to convey information quickly to the user.

Menus and Dialog Boxes

Aside from standard windows, Windows also provides special-purpose windows. The most common of these are the menu and dialog boxes. Briefly, a *menu* is, as you would expect, a special window that contains only a list of options from which the user makes a selection. However, instead of having to provide the menu selection functions in your program, you simply create a standard menu window using Windows functions.

A *dialog box* is a special window that allows more complex interaction with the application than that allowed by a menu. For example, your application might use a dialog box to input a file name. With few exceptions, nonmenu input is accomplished in Windows via a dialog box.

How Windows and Your Program Interact

When you write a program for many operating systems, it is your program that initiates interaction with the operating system. For example, in a DOS program, it is the program that requests such things as input and output. Put differently, programs written in the "traditional way" call the operating system. The operating system does not call your program. However, in large measure, Windows works in the opposite way. It is Windows that calls your program. The process works like this: A Windows program waits until it is sent a message by Windows. The message is passed to your program through a special function that is called by Windows. Once a message is received, your program is expected to take an appropriate action. While your program may call one or more Windows API functions when responding to a message, it is still Windows that initiates the activity. More than anything else, it is the message-based interaction with Windows that dictates the general form of all Windows programs.

There are many different types of messages that Windows may send your program. For example, each time the mouse is clicked on a window belonging to your program, a mouse-clicked message is sent to your program. Another type of message is sent each time a window belonging to your program must be redrawn. Still another message is sent each time the user presses a key when your program is the focus of input. Keep one fact firmly in mind: as far as your program is concerned, messages arrive randomly. This is why Windows programs resemble interrupt-driven programs. You can't know what message will be next.

It is the message-based nature of Windows that makes it especially compatible with C++ and object oriented programming in general. As you will see, each window you create is actually an object. All interactions with that object occur through special member functions that respond to messages sent by Windows.

Windows Is Multitasking

As mentioned, Windows is a multitasking operating system. As a multitasking operating system, it is somewhat unique in that it uses *nonpreemptive multitasking*. This means that each program executing in the system retains use of the processor until it relinquishes it. This differs radically from the type of multitasking done by other operating systems that employ preemptive task switches based upon time slices. In this scheme, the operating system simply stops executing one program and moves on to the next, in a round-robin fashion. Remember that this is not how Windows works. A Windows program must relinquish the CPU.

One of the most important rules a Windows program must follow is to return control to Windows when it is inactive. This allows Windows to grant the processor to another task. Fortunately, since you will be using the ObjectWindows library, the job of relenquishing control is automatically performed for you most of the time. Keep in mind, however, that it is possible for a program to monopolize the processor, effectively halting all other tasks.

ObjectWindows and the API

As stated, the Windows environment is accessed through a call-based interface called the application program interface. The approximately 600 API functions provide all the system services performed by Windows. ObjectWindows is a complex class hierarchy that encapsulates portions of the API to simplify the creation of Windows programs. However, ObjectWindows still eventually uses the API to actually perform its various operations.

There is a subsystem of the API called the GDI (graphics device interface); it is the part of Windows that provides device-independent graphics support. It is the GDI functions that make it possible for a Windows application to run on a variety of different hardware.

The Components of a Window

Before a discussion of specific aspects of Windows programming, a few important terms need to be defined. Figure 8-1 shows a standard window with each of its elements pointed out.

All windows have a *border* that defines the limits of the window and is used to move or resize the window. At the top of the window are several items. On the far left is the *system menu icon* (or *box,* as it is commonly called). Clicking on this box causes the system menu to be displayed. To the right of the system menu box is the window's *title bar.* At the far right

FIGURE
8-1

The elements of a standard window

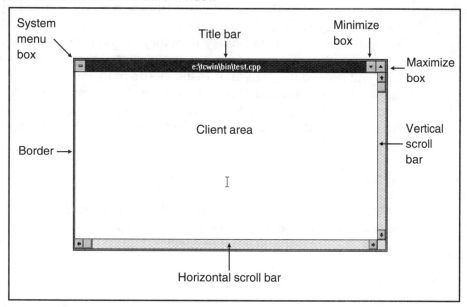

are the *minimize* and *maximize boxes*. The *client area* is the part of the window in which your program activity takes place. Most windows also have *horizontal* and *vertical scroll bars* that are used to move text through the window.

Preparing the Compiler for Windows Applications

Before you can compile a Windows application using Turbo C++ for Windows, you must set several options. First, all Windows applications, no matter how small, must be made into projects. To accomplish this, select the Project main menu entry and then select Open Project. Next, add the name of the source file that you want to compile to the project. (Since your first program is an ObjectWindows skeleton, use SKEL.CPP.)

Once you have created a project, you must tell Turbo C++ to include in its search path the **include** and **library** directories used by Object-Windows. By default, Turbo C++ does not search the ObjectWindows **include** directory or its **library** directory. To add these directories, first select the Options entry from the main menu. Next, select Directories. You will see a dialog box that displays the path Turbo C++ uses to find **include** directories and **library** directories. To the **include** directory path, add the following, if it is not already specified (be sure to keep all directories that are already specified and adjust the drive specifiers, if needed):

```
c:\tcwin\owl\include;c:\tcwin\classlib\include
```

To the **library** directories path, add the following if it is not already specified (again, be sure to keep all previously specified directories and adjust the drive specifiers, if needed):

```
c:\tcwin\owl\lib;c:\tcwin\classlib\lib
```

The **owl** directory contains the files that make up the ObjectWindows library. The **classlib** directory contains certain classes that are used by ObjectWindows.

Next, select the main menu Options entry and then select Application. To develop Windows applications, the linker output should be **Windows EXE**. If this is not the case, select Windows App at this time.

Once again select Options from the main menu. Then select Linker, followed by Libraries. Set all of the libraries to Static. By using static linking, the library routines will be statically linked when your program is compiled. (The other option is dynamic linking, which causes the ObjectWindows routines to be linked at run time using dynamic link libraries, or DLLs. However, using dynamic linking unnecessarily complicates things at this time.)

Some Windows Application Basics

Before the development of the ObjectWindows application skeleton, some basic information needs to be stated.

Two Important ObjectWindows Classes

There are two ObjectWindows classes that are fundamental to the development of a Windows application. These classes are **TApplication** and **TWindow**. The **TApplication** class creates an ObjectWindows application. The **TWindow** class creates an ObjectWindows window. These two classes are important because all ObjectWindows applications must define an application and at least one window.

Two Common Windows Data Types

In addition to the numerous classes defined by ObjectWindows, two data types are common to all types of Windows programming, and you will see them quite often in Windows programs. The first is **HANDLE**, which is a 16-bit value that identifies a window. All windows are referenced by their handles. The second data type is called **LPSTR**, which is a **far** pointer to a string.

All Windows Programs Begin at WinMain()

All windows programs, including those created by using Object-Windows, begin execution with a call to **WinMain()**. Windows programs do not have a **main()** function. Instead, they use **WinMain()**. **WinMain()** has some special properties that differentiate it from other functions in your application. First, it must be compiled as a Pascal function. As you may know, how functions are called varies among computer languages. The two most common calling conventions are those used by C and those used by Pascal. For various technical reasons, Windows begins executing your program by calling **WinMain()** using the Pascal calling convention. Further, **WinMain()** must be a **far** function. Turbo C++ (and most other Windows C compilers) define the type **PASCAL** to accommodate the needs of **WinMain()**. If you declare **WinMain()** as **PASCAL**, the function is automatically compiled using the correct conventions.

Using the API Functions

Although ObjectWindows provides an alternative method of accessing several Windows functions, it does not provide (nor was it intended to provide) an alternative to all of the over 600 API functions. Therefore, you may still call any API function directly. In fact, most ObjectWindows programs will contain several calls to API functions.

An ObjectWindows Skeleton

Now that the necessary background information has been covered, it is time to develop a minimal ObjectWindows application. As stated, all ObjectWindows programs have certain things in common. In this section, an ObjectWindows skeleton is developed that provides these necessary features. In the world of Windows programming, application skeletons are commonly used because there is a substantial "price of admission" when creating a Windows program. Unlike DOS programs that you may have written, in which a minimal program is about 5 lines long, a minimal Windows program is approximately 40 lines long. (In fact, if you are not using ObjectWindows, a minimal Windows program is even longer.) Therefore, application skeletons are commonly used when developing Windows applications.

The following program is a minimal Windows skeleton. It creates an application and a standard window. The window is capable of being minimized, maximized, moved, resized, and closed. Before continuing, enter this program and compile it. (Be sure you have configured Turbo C++ for Windows so that it will compile a Windows application.)

```
// ObjectWindows Windows application skeleton.

#include <owl.h>


// Define an application.
class AppName : public TApplication
{
public:
  AppName(LPSTR App_Name, HANDLE ThisInstance,
      HANDLE PrevInstance,LPSTR Args, int VidMode) :
      TApplication(App_Name, ThisInstance, PrevInstance, Args,
          VidMode) {};
```

```
  virtual void InitMainWindow();
};

// Define a window type.
class AppWindow : public TWindow
{
public:
  AppWindow(PTWindowsObject WType, LPSTR WTitle) :
        TWindow(WType, WTitle) {};
  // Additional window details go here.
};

// Creates and initializes an instance of the window.
void AppName::InitMainWindow()
{
  MainWindow = new AppWindow(NULL, Name);
}

// Entry point of windows program.
int PASCAL WinMain(HANDLE ThisInstance, HANDLE PrevInstance,
          LPSTR Args, int VidMode)
{
  AppName App("ObjectWindows Skeleton", ThisInstance,
              PrevInstance, Args, VidMode);

  App.Run(); // runs windows application

  return App.Status; // termination status
}
```

Let's go through this program step by step.

First, all ObjectWindows programs must include the header OWL.H. This file causes a number of other include files to be included. These files contain the prototypes and definitions used by the ObjectWindows library as well as the API system functions and type definitions.

The program creates two classes. The first is called **AppName**, which is simply a placeholder name. When you create your own applications, you will want to give this class a descriptive name. The purpose of **AppName** is to define a Windows application. Fortunately, this is especially easy using ObjectWindows because most of the work has been done for you by the class **TApplication**, which is inherited by **AppName**.

AppName's constructor takes several parameters, which are simply passed along to **TApplication**'s constructor. Here is what the parameters mean. The **App_name** parameter is a pointer to a string containing the application's name. **ThisInstance** and **PrevInstance** are handles that refer to the current instance and any previous instance of the application. (Remember, Windows is a multitasking system so it is possible that more than one instance of your program will be runnning at the same time.) **PrevInstance** will be zero if there are no previous instances. The **Args** parameter is a pointer to a string that holds any command-line arguments specified when the application began execution. The **VidMode** parameter contains a value that specifies how the window will be displayed.

Within **AppName**, the virtual function **InitMainWindow()** is declared. This function is declared within **TApplication** and is redefined by your application class. It initializes the application's main window. All applications require at least one window. This window is referred to as the *main window*, and it is **InitMainWindow()** that creates it.

After the application has been defined, its main window class must be constructed. This is done by inheriting the **TWindow** base class. In the skeleton program, the class that creates the main window is called **AppWindow**, but you will change this name to be appropriate for applications you create. In the skeleton, **AppWindow**'s only function is to pass its constructor's arguments along to **TWindow**'s constructor. The **WType** parameter describes the general type of window that will be created. If it is null, a standard window is created. The general type of window specified to **TWindow** is often referred to as the *parent window*. The second parameter is a pointer to the string that holds the window's title. The **Twindow** class defines several virtual functions that can be redefined by **AppWindow**. This allows the operation of the window to be customized. (You will see examples of this in Chapter 9.)

Once the application and main window classes have been defined, **InitMainWindow()** is created. In the skeleton, a new window is obtained using **new**. The variables **MainWindow** and **Name** are members of the **TApplication** class. **MainWindow** holds a pointer to the main window being created. **Name** is a pointer to a string containing the name of the application.

The final part of the skeleton is the **WinMain()** function. As stated, this is the function that begins execution of your Windows program. It is passed a handle to this instance and the previous instance (if any) of the application. It also is passed a pointer to any command-line arguments and the initial video mode. **WinMain()** first constructs an application. Next, it begins running that application by calling another member function of **TApplication**: **Run()**. Finally, when the application is terminated (by closing its main window) **WinMain()** returns the termination status as specified in **Status** to Windows. **Status** is a member variable of **TApplication**.

If you have programmed for windows before, you might be wondering where the message loop is. The *message loop* is a part of all Windows applications. Its purpose is to receive and process messages sent by Windows. The message loop still exists in an ObjectWindows program; it's just that it is automatically created by **TApplication** and the skeleton simply uses **TApplication**'s default message processing. In Chapter 9 you will see how to receive and process messages within your program.

Using a Definition File

When you compiled the skeleton, you probably received a warning message indicating that no definition file for the program was found. A *definition file* is simply a text file that specifies certain information and settings needed by your Windows program. However, Turbo C++ for Windows will automatically supply default settings, so you don't actually need to have a definition file.

If you want to prevent the warning message, you can provide a definition file. All definition files use the extension .DEF. For example, the definition file for the skeleton program could be called SKEL.DEF. Here is a definition file that you can use. Unless otherwise stated, this file is sufficient for the programs in this book.

```
NAME WinSkel
DESCRIPTION 'ObjectWindows Skeleton Program'
EXETYPE WINDOWS
CODE PRELOAD MOVEABLE DISCARDABLE
DATA PRELOAD MOVEABLE MULTIPLE
HEAPSIZE 8192
STACKSIZE 8192
```

Once you have created the definition file, remember to add its name to your project.

Naming Conventions

Before this chapter ends, a short comment on naming functions and variables needs to be made. For various reasons, Microsoft elected to use a special naming convention when it first developed Windows. For

TABLE 8-1

Variable Type Prefix Characters

Prefix	Data Type
b	Boolean (one byte)
c	Character (one byte)
dw	Long unsigned integer
f	16-bit bit-field
h	Handle
l	Long integer
lp	Long pointer
n	Short integer
p	Short pointer
pt	Long integer holding screen coordinates
w	Short unsigned integer
Less common:	
sz	Pointer to null-terminated string
lpsz	Long pointer to null-terminated string
rgb	Long integer holding RGB color values

functions, the name consists of a verb followed by a noun. The first character of the verb and noun are capitalized. This method was also adopted by ObjectWindows, and this book will continue to use this convention.

For variable names, Microsoft chose to use a rather complex system of imbedding the data type into a variable's name. To accomplish this, a lowercase type prefix is added to the start of the variable's name. The name itself is begun with a capital letter. The type prefixes are shown in Table 8-1. Frankly, the use of type prefixes is controversial and is not universally supported. Many Windows programmers use this method, but many do not. This book will, for the most part, not use this method when there seems to be little to gain from it. However, you will see examples of this approach when various ObjectWindows and API functions are discussed.

CHAPTER

Processing Messages

As explained in Chapter 8, Windows communicates with your application by sending it messages. For this reason, the processing of these messages is at the core of all Windows applications. In Chapter 8 you learned how to create a skeletal ObjectWindows application. In this chapter, that skeleton is expanded to receive and process the most common Windows messages.

What Are Windows Messages?

There are over 100 Windows messages. Each message is represented by a unique 16-bit integer value. In the header file WINDOW.H, included automatically by OWL.H, there are standard names for these messages. Generally, you will use the macro name, not the actual integer value, when referring to a message. Here are some common Windows message macros:

WM_CHAR
WM_PAINT
WM_MOVE
WM_LBUTTONUP
WM_LBUTTONDOWN

Two other values accompany each message and contain information related to the specific message. One of these values is an integer, the other is a long integer. Turbo C++ calls the parameters that receive these values **WParam** and **LParam**, respectively. They typically hold things like cursor or mouse coordinates; the value of a key press; or a system-related value, such as character size. As each message is discussed, the meaning of the values contained in **WParam** and **LParam** will be described.

Message Response Functions

For your program to receive and process messages, you must first create message-processing functions, commonly referred to as *message response functions*. All message response functions must be member functions of your window class. Although the **TWindow** base class provides default processing for a few messages, in general you will need to create response functions for any message that is important to your program. If you don't, that message will be ignored and, therefore, unavailable to your program. Since there are over 100 different Windows messages, it is common for your program to ignore many messages because they simply don't relate to any activity performed by the program. Just remember that if you want to process a message, you must create a response function for it.

When using ObjectWindows, message response functions are implemented in a special way. They are called by using a *dynamic dispatch virtual table*, or *DDVT*, for short. All DDVT functions have a unique index associated with them. The address of each DDVT function is put in a table at the location specified by the index. DDVT functions are executed by indexing the table and calling the function found at that index. All message response functions have as their index the message they will be responding to. Once you have declared a message reponse function, each time that message is received, your function is automatically called. The only thing you must supply is the message response functions. ObjectWindows automatically routes a message to the appropriate message response function using the DDVT.

Two ObjectWindows functions receive and route messages to their proper response functions. All messages are received by **MessageLoop()**, a function defined in **TApplication**. When a message is received, it is dispatched by **ProcessAppMsg()**, another function defined by **TApplication**, to your message response function.

To create a message function, you will use a Turbo C++-specific construct that specifies the index associated with the function. The general method of doing this is shown here:

virtual void *sample*(RTMessage *Msg*) = [*index*];

Here, *sample* is the name of the response function and *index* is the message that your function will respond to. For example, this declares **WMChar()** as a message response function that will have all **WM_CHAR** messages dispatched to it:

```
virtual void WMChar(RTMessage Msg) = [WM_CHAR];
```

Remember, **WM_CHAR** is a macro name for a message. This message is sent each time a key is pressed. (You will see how to use it shortly.) The function name **WMChar()** is completely arbitrary since Turbo C++ for Windows calls the message response function by using the index, not its name. However, Borland recommends a naming convention for message response functions. Using this convention, the names of message response functions will consist of the message name with the underscore removed and a mixture of upper- and lowercase letters applied. Of course, you are free to name your message reponse functions however you like.

While the preceding declaration is correct, Turbo C++ for Windows has included another macro, called **WM_FIRST**, which is defined as zero at the time of this writing. Borland suggests you add this value to the message. By doing this, you are ensuring that your code will be valid if the values of the message macros are ever transposed. The way you will normally see message response functions prototyped using this scheme is like this:

```
virtual void WMChar(RTMessage Msg) = [WM_FIRST + WM_CHAR];
```

RTMessage is a reference to a **TMessage** structure that contains, among other things, the two additional values that accompany every message. These two values are organized as shown here:

```
union {
  WORD WParam;
  struct tagWP {
    BYTE Lo;
    BYTE Hi;
  } WP;
};
union {
  DWORD LParam;
  struct tagLP {
    WORD Lo;
    WORD Hi;
  } LP;
};
```

These unions allow you to access these values either as 16- and 32-bit integers or by their byte and integer components. As you will see, often two or more pieces of information are compacted into each of these values.

Also contained in the **TMessage** structure is the integer **Result**. Occasionally, a Windows message will require some response. When this is the case, assign it to **Result**.

Responding to a Keypress

Now that you have seen, in theory, how to create a message response function, it is time to see one in practice. This section extends the skeletal application from Chapter 8 so that it processes keystrokes. It is easy to accomplish this. A response function is simply included as a member of **AppWindow**. Here is the enhanced **AppWindow** class and the definition of **WMChar()**. You will notice some unusual code in **WMChar()**. For the moment, don't worry about the calls to **GetDC()** and **ReleaseDC()**.

```
// Define a window type.
class AppWindow : public TWindow
{
public:
  AppWindow(PTWindowsObject WType, LPSTR WTitle) :
    TWindow(WType, WTitle) {};
  virtual void WMChar(RTMessage Msg) =
    [WM_FIRST + WM_CHAR]; // process a WM_CHAR message
  // Additional window details go here.
};

// Process a WM_CHAR message.
void AppWindow::WMChar(RTMessage Msg)
{
  HDC DC;
  ostrstream ostr(s, sizeof(s));

  DC = GetDC(HWindow); // get device context
  TextOut(DC, 1, 1, "    ", 3); // clear previous character
  ostr << (char) Msg.WParam << ends; // construct a string
  TextOut(DC, 1, 1, s, strlen(s)); // output the string
  ReleaseDC(HWindow, DC); // release device context
}
```

As you can see, **WMChar()** is a member function of **AppWindow()**, and it specifies as its dispatch index the **WM_CHAR** message. This is the message that Windows sends to your program each time a key is pressed on the keyboard. When this message is sent, **Msg.WParam** contains the ASCII value of the key pressed. **Msg.LP.Lo** contains the number of times the key has been repeated as a result of the key being held down. The bits of **Msg.LP.Hi** are encoded as shown here:

15	Set if the key is being pressed; cleared if the key has been released
14	Set if the key was pressed before the message was sent; cleared if it was not pressed
13	Set if the ALT key is also being pressed; cleared if ALT is not pressed
12	Used by Windows
11	Used by Windows
10	Not used
9	Not used
8	Set if the key pressed is a function key or an extended key; cleared otherwise
7-0	Manufacturer-dependent key code

At this time, the only value that is important is **WParam**, since it holds the key that was pressed. However, notice how much information Windows supplies about the state of the system. In general, Windows gives you more information than does DOS. Of course, you are free to use as much or as little of this information as you like.

The purpose of the code inside **WMChar()** is very simple: it simply echoes the key to the screen. You are probably surprised that it takes so many lines of code to accomplish this seemingly trivial feat. There are two reasons for this. First, Windows is multitasking, and you cannot output a character if your program is not the focus of output (for example, if another task has overlaid your window). The second reason is that another part of your program may have overlaid your window. In either situation, before performing output, your program must first acquire permission. This is done by calling **GetDC()**, which obtains a device context. (For now, don't worry about what this means. It is discussed in the next section.) Once you obtain a device context, you may write to the screen. At the end of the function, the device context is released using **ReleaseDC()**. Your program *must* release the device context when it is done with it. If it doesn't, the device context cannot be granted to another program or to your own program when requested again. Both **GetDC()** and **ReleaseDC()** are API functions. Their prototypes are shown here:

HDC GetDC(HWND *hWnd*);

int ReleaseDC(HWND *hWnd*, HDC *hDC*);

The type **HDC** specifies a handle to a device context. The type **HWND** is a handle to a window. These types are defined in the header files included automatically by OWL.H. **GetDC()** returns a device context. **ReleaseDC()** returns true if the device context was released, false otherwise.

The function that actually outputs the character is the API function **TextOut()**. Its prototype is shown here:

BOOL TextOut(HDC *DC*, int *x*, int *y*, LPSTR *str*, int *count*);

The type **BOOL** is a 16-bit integer that holds true/false values. The **TextOut()** function outputs the string pointed to by *str* at the screen coordinates specified by *x,y*. The length of the string is specified in *count*. The **TextOut()** function returns nonzero if successful, zero otherwise.

In the program, each character that is typed by the user is converted, using array-based I/O, into a string one character long and then displayed using **TextOut()** at location 1,1. In a window, the upper-left corner of the client area is location 1,1. Window coordinates are always relative to the window, not to the screen. Therefore, as characters are entered, they are displayed in the upper-left corner of the window no matter where the window is physically located on the screen.

The reason for the first call to **TextOut()** inside **WMChar()** is to erase whatever previous character was just displayed. Because Windows is a graphics-based system, characters are of different sizes, and the overwriting of one character by another does not necessarily cause all of the previous characters to be erased. For example, if you typed a "w" followed by an "l," part of the "w" would still be displayed if it wasn't manually erased. (Try commenting out the first call to **TextOut()** and observe what happens.)

It is important to understand that no Windows function will allow output beyond the borders. Output will automatically be clipped to prevent the window's boundaries from being crossed.

At first you might think that using **TextOut()** to output a character is not an efficient application of the function. The fact is that Windows does not contain a function that simply outputs a character. As you will see, Windows performs much of its user interaction through dialog and menu boxes. For this reason it contains only a few functions that output text to the client area.

Here is the entire skeleton that processes keystrokes:

```
/* ObjectWindows Windows application skeleton that processes
   WM_CHAR messages. */

#include <owl.h>
#include <string.h>
#include <strstream.h>

// Define an application.
class AppName : public TApplication
{
public:
  AppName(LPSTR App_Name, HANDLE ThisInstance,
      HANDLE PrevInstance, LPSTR Args, int VidMode) :
      TApplication(App_Name, ThisInstance, PrevInstance, Args,
              VidMode) {};
  void InitMainWindow();
};

// Define a window type.
class AppWindow : public TWindow
{
public:
  AppWindow(PTWindowsObject WType, LPSTR WTitle) :
      TWindow(WType, WTitle) {};
  virtual void WMChar(RTMessage Msg) =
    [WM_FIRST + WM_CHAR]; // process a WM_CHAR message
  // Additional window details go here.
};

// Creates and initializes an instance of the window.
```

```
void AppName::InitMainWindow()
{
  MainWindow = new AppWindow(NULL, Name);
}



// This is global because it will be used by other functions.
char s[20];

// Process a WM_CHAR message.
void AppWindow::WMChar(RTMessage Msg)
{
  HDC DC;
  ostrstream ostr(s, sizeof(s));

  DC = GetDC(HWindow); // get device context
  TextOut(DC, 1, 1, "    ", 3); // clear previous character
  ostr << (char) Msg.WParam << ends; // construct a string
  TextOut(DC, 1, 1, s, strlen(s)); // output the string
  ReleaseDC(HWindow, DC); // release device context
}

// Entry point of windows program.
int PASCAL WinMain(HANDLE ThisInstance, HANDLE PrevInstance,
          LPSTR Args, int VidMode)
{
  AppName App("ObjectWindows Skeleton", ThisInstance,
        PrevInstance, Args, VidMode);

  App.Run(); // runs windows application

  return App.Status; // termination status
}
```

Device Contexts

In the function **WMChar()** created in the previous section, it was necessary to obtain a device context prior to outputting to the window. Also, that device context had to be released prior to the termination of that function. It is now time to understand what a device context is. A *device context* is an output path from your Windows application, through the appropriate device driver, to the client area of your window. The device context also fully defines the state of the device driver.

Before your application can output information to the client area of the window, a device context must be obtained. Until this is done, there is no linkage between your program and the window relative to output. As mentioned earlier, several things can occur that will temporarily prevent a device context from being obtained. For example, if another application has obscured your window, it must be brought to the forefront again. In any event, remember that it is necessary to obtain a device context prior to performing any output to a window. Since **TextOut()** and other output functions require a handle to a device context, this is a self-enforcing rule.

Processing the WM_PAINT Message

Before continuing, run the second skeleton program and enter a few characters. Next, resize the window. As you will see, the last character typed is not displayed after the window is resized. Also, if the window is overwritten by another window and then redisplayed, the character is not redisplayed. The reason for this is simple: in general, Windows does not keep a record of what a window contains. Instead, it is your program's job to maintain the contents of a window. To help your program accomplish this, each time the contents of a window must be redisplayed, your program will be sent a **WM_PAINT** message. Each time your program receives this message, it must redisplay the contents of the window. In this section, you will add a message response function that processes the **WM_PAINT** message.

 Note   For various technical reasons, when the window is moved without being resized, its contents are redisplayed. However, this will not occur when the window is resized or overwritten and then redisplayed.

Before giving you an explanation of how to create a **WM_PAINT** message response function, it might be useful to explain why Windows does not automatically rewrite your window. The answer is short and to the point. In many situations, it is easier for your program, which has intimate knowledge of the contents of the window, to rewrite the window than it would be for Windows to do so. While the merits of this approach have been much debated by programmers, you should simply accept it because it is unlikely to change.

When you use ObjectWindows, it is not necessary to create a function that responds directly to a **WM_PAINT** message. Instead, it is easier to let ObjectWindows intercept the **WM_PAINT** message, using **WMPaint()**, a member function of **TWindow**. This function performs all the necessary startup and shutdown actions, such as obtaining and releasing a device context. To redraw the window, it calls the virtual function **Paint()**, which your program must redefine.

The first step in processing a paint request is to add the prototype to the redefined **Paint()** function to **AppWindow**, as shown here:

```
// Define a window type.
class AppWindow : public TWindow
{
public:
 AppWindow(PTWindowsObject Parent, LPSTR Title) :
      TWindow(Parent, Title) {};
  virtual void WMChar(RTMessage Msg) =
    [WM_FIRST + WM_CHAR]; // process a WM_CHAR message
  virtual void Paint(HDC DC, PAINTSTRUCT &PI);
  // Additional window details go here.
};
```

As you can see, this function has two parameters. The first is a device context handle that is automatically obtained by ObjectWindows when it intercepts the **WM_PAINT** message. The second is a reference to a structure that contains information related to painting the window. This structure is shown here:

```
typedef struct tagPAINTSTRUCT {
  HDC hdc; // handle to device context
  BOOL fErase; // true if background has been redrawn
  RECT rcPaint; // coordinates of region to redraw
  BOOL fRestore; // reserved
  BOOL fIncUpdate; // reserved
  BYTE rgbReserved[16]; // reserved
} PAINTSTRUCT;
```

The type **RECT** is a structure that specifies the upper-left and lower-right coordinates of the rectangular region that must be redrawn. This structure is shown here:

```
typedef tagRECT {
  int left, top; // upper left
  int right, bottom; // lower right
} RECT;
```

For now, you will not need to use the contents of **PAINTSTRUCT** or **RECT** because you can assume that the background has been redrawn and that the entire window must be redisplayed.

Paint() can be redefined for the skeleton application as shown here:

```
// Process a WM_PAINT message.
void AppWindow::Paint(HDC DC, PAINTSTRUCT &)
{
  TextOut(DC, 1, 1, s, strlen(s));  // redisplay s
}
```

As you can see, since ObjectWindows provides all the startup and shutdown services, all that **Paint()** must do is redisplay the information in the window. The details are left to ObjectWindows.

Here is the entire skeleton program that processes the **WM_CHAR** and **WM_PAINT** messages:

```
/* ObjectWindows Windows application skeleton that responds
   to WM_CHAR and WM_PAINT. */

#include <owl.h>
#include <string.h>
#include <strstream.h>

// Define an application.
class AppName : public TApplication
{
public:
  AppName(LPSTR AppName, HANDLE ThisInstance,
       HANDLE PrevInstance, LPSTR Args, int VidMode) :
       TApplication(AppName, ThisInstance, PrevInstance, Args,
              VidMode) {};
```

```
  virtual void InitMainWindow();
};

// Define a window type.
class AppWindow : public TWindow
{
public:
  AppWindow(PTWindowsObject Parent, LPSTR Title) :
       TWindow(Parent, Title) {};
  virtual void WMChar(RTMessage Msg) =
    [WM_FIRST + WM_CHAR]; // process a WM_CHAR message
  virtual void Paint(HDC DC, PAINTSTRUCT &PI);
  // Additional window details go here.
};

// Creates and initializes an instance of the window.
void AppName::InitMainWindow()
{
  MainWindow = new AppWindow(NULL, Name);
}

// Make s global so it can be accessed by other functions.
char s[20] = "hello";

// Process a WM_CHAR message.
void AppWindow::WMChar(RTMessage Msg)
{
  HDC DC;
  ostrstream ostr(s, sizeof(s));

  DC = GetDC(HWindow); // get device context
  TextOut(DC, 1, 1, "        ", 8); // clear old string
  ostr << (char) Msg.WParam << ends; // construct string
  TextOut(DC, 1, 1, s, strlen(s)); // display the character
  ReleaseDC(HWindow, DC); // release device context
}

// Process a WM_PAINT message.
void AppWindow::Paint(HDC DC, PAINTSTRUCT &)
{
  TextOut(DC, 1, 1, s, strlen(s));  // redisplay s
}
```

```
// Entry point of windows program.
int PASCAL WinMain(HANDLE ThisInstance, HANDLE PrevInstance,
          LPSTR Args, int VidMode)
{
  AppName App("ObjectWindows Skeleton", ThisInstance,
          PrevInstance, Args, VidMode);

  App.Run(); // runs windows application

  return App.Status; // termination status
}
```

Before continuing, enter, compile, and run this program. Try typing a few characters and then resizing the window. As you will see, each time the window is redisplayed, the last character you typed is automatically redrawn.

Notice that the global array **s** is initialized to **hello** and that this is displayed when the program begins execution. The reason for this is that when a window is created, a **WM_PAINT** message is automatically generated.

While the **Paint()** function in the skeleton is quite simple, it must be emphasized that most real-world versions of this function are more complex because most windows contain considerably more output.

Since it is your program's responsibility to restore the window if it is resized or overwritten, you must always provide some mechanism to accomplish this. In real-world programs, this is usually accomplished one of three ways. First, your program can simply regenerate the output by computational means. This is most feasible when no user input is used. Second, your program can maintain a virtual screen that you simply copy to the window each time it must be redrawn. Finally, in some instances, you can keep a record of events and replay the events when the window needs to be redrawn. Which approach is best depends completely upon the application. Most of the examples in this book won't bother to redraw the window because doing so typically involves substantial additional code that often just muddies the point of the example. However, your programs will need to restore their windows in order to be conforming Windows applications.

Although all the examples in this book will respond to the **WM_PAINT** message by redefining the **Paint()** function, your program can respond manually, if you want. To do this you will need to add a message response function to **AppWindow** that has a dispatch index of **WM_PAINT**, and you will need to define the function. The changes are shown here:

```
// Define a window type.
class AppWindow : public TWindow
{
public:
  AppWindow(PTWindowsObject WType, LPSTR WTitle) :
        TWindow(WType, WTitle) {};
  virtual void WMChar(RTMessage Msg) =
    [WM_FIRST + WM_CHAR]; // process a WM_CHAR message

  virtual void WMPaint(RTMessage Msg) =
    [WM_FIRST + WM_PAINT]; // process WM_PAINT manually;

  // Additional window details go here.
};


// Process a WM_PAINT message manually.
void AppWindow::WMPaint(RTMessage Msg)
{
  HDC DC;
  PAINTSTRUCT PI;

  DC = BeginPaint(HWindow, &PI); // get paint DC
  TextOut(DC, 1, 1, s, strlen(s));  // redisplay s
  EndPaint(HWindow, &PI); // release paint DC
}
```

Notice that in the definition of **WMPaint()**, the device context is obtained using **BeginPaint()** and not **GetDC()**. When your program responds to a **WM_PAINT** message, it must obtain the device context by using **BeginPaint()**. For various reasons, it cannot use **GetDC()**. (Essentially, the act of completely redrawing the contents of a window is different from simply outputting to that window.) Correspondingly, when your function is done, it must release the device context by calling **EndPaint()**. Both of these functions take a handle to the window as their first parameter and a pointer to **PAINTSTRUCT** as their second. Both **BeginPaint()** and **EndPaint()** are API, not ObjectWindows, functions.

Responding to Mouse Messages

Since Windows is, to a great extent, a mouse-based operating system, all Windows programs should respond to mouse input. Because the mouse is so important, there are several different types of mouse messages. This section examines the two most common. These are **WM_LBUTTONDOWN** and **WM_RBUTTONDOWN**, which are generated when the left button and right button are pressed, respectively.

To begin, you must add the two mouse message response functions to the **AppWindow** class, as shown here:

```
// Define a window type.
class AppWindow : public TWindow
{
public:
  AppWindow(PTWindowsObject WType, LPSTR WTitle) :
      TWindow(WType, WTitle) {};
  virtual void WMChar(RTMessage Msg) =
    [WM_FIRST + WM_CHAR]; // process a WM_CHAR message
  virtual void Paint(HDC DC, PAINTSTRUCT &PI);

  virtual void WMLButtonDown(RTMessage Msg) =
    [WM_FIRST + WM_LBUTTONDOWN]; // respond to left button
  virtual void WMRButtonDown(RTMessage Msg) =
    [WM_FIRST + WM_RBUTTONDOWN]; // respond to right button
  // Additional window details go here.
};
```

For this example, the two mouse response functions are defined as shown here:

```
// Process left mouse button.
void AppWindow::WMLButtonDown(RTMessage Msg)
{
  HDC DC;
  ostrstream ostr(s, sizeof(s));
```

```
  DC = GetDC(HWindow);
  ostr << "Left Button" << ends;
  TextOut(DC, Msg.LP.Lo, Msg.LP.Hi, s, strlen(s));
  ReleaseDC(HWindow, DC);
}

// Process right mouse button.
void AppWindow::WMRButtonDown(RTMessage Msg)
{
  HDC DC;
  ostrstream ostr(s, sizeof(s));

  DC = GetDC(HWindow);
  ostr << "Right Button" << ends;
  TextOut(DC, Msg.LP.Lo, Msg.LP.Hi, s, strlen(s));
  ReleaseDC(HWindow, DC);
}
```

When either button is pressed, the mouse's current X,Y location is specified in **Msg.LP.Lo** and **Msg.LP.Hi**, respectively. The mouse message response functions use these coordinates as the location to display their output. That is, each time you press a mouse button, a message will be displayed at the location of the mouse pointer.

Here is the complete skeleton that responds to the mouse messages:

```
/* ObjectWindows Windows application skeleton that responds
   to WM_CHAR, WM_PAINT, and mouse messages. */

#include <owl.h>
#include <string.h>
#include <strstream.h>

// Define an application.
class AppName : public TApplication
{
public:
  AppName(LPSTR App_Name, HANDLE ThisInstance,
      HANDLE PrevInstance, LPSTR Args, int VidMode) :
      TApplication(App_Name, ThisInstance, PrevInstance, Args,
              VidMode) {};
  virtual void InitMainWindow();
```

```
};

// Define a window type.
class AppWindow : public TWindow
{
public:
  AppWindow(PTWindowsObject WType, LPSTR WTitle) :
        TWindow(WType, WTitle) {};
  virtual void WMChar(RTMessage Msg) =
    [WM_FIRST + WM_CHAR]; // process a WM_CHAR message
  virtual void Paint(HDC DC, PAINTSTRUCT &PI);

  virtual void WMLButtonDown(RTMessage Msg) =
    [WM_FIRST + WM_LBUTTONDOWN]; // respond to left button
  virtual void WMRButtonDown(RTMessage Msg) =
    [WM_FIRST + WM_RBUTTONDOWN]; // respond to right button
  // Additional window details go here.
};

// Creates and initializes an instance of the window.
void AppName::InitMainWindow()
{
  MainWindow = new AppWindow(NULL, Name);
}

// This is global because it will be used by other functions.
char s[20] = "hello";

// Process a WM_CHAR message.
void AppWindow::WMChar(RTMessage Msg)
{
  HDC DC;
  ostrstream ostr(s, sizeof(s));

  DC = GetDC(HWindow); // get device context
  TextOut(DC, 1, 1, "         ", 8); // clear previous character
  ostr << (char) Msg.WParam << ends; // construct a string
  TextOut(DC, 1, 1, s, strlen(s)); // output the string
  ReleaseDC(HWindow, DC); // release device context
}

// Process a WM_PAINT message.
```

```
void AppWindow::Paint(HDC DC, PAINTSTRUCT &)
{
  TextOut(DC, 1, 1, s, strlen(s));
}

// Process left mouse button.
void AppWindow::WMLButtonDown(RTMessage Msg)
{
  HDC DC;
  ostrstream ostr(s, sizeof(s));

  DC = GetDC(HWindow);
  ostr << "Left Button" << ends;
  TextOut(DC, Msg.LP.Lo, Msg.LP.Hi, s, strlen(s));
  ReleaseDC(HWindow, DC);
}

// Process right mouse button.
void AppWindow::WMRButtonDown(RTMessage Msg)
{
  HDC DC;
  ostrstream ostr(s, sizeof(s));

  DC = GetDC(HWindow);
  ostr << "Right Button" << ends;
  TextOut(DC, Msg.LP.Lo, Msg.LP.Hi, s, strlen(s));
  ReleaseDC(HWindow, DC);
}


// Entry point of windows program.
int PASCAL WinMain(HANDLE ThisInstance, HANDLE PrevInstance,
          LPSTR Args, int VidMode)
{
  AppName App("ObjectWindows Skeleton", ThisInstance,
          PrevInstance, Args, VidMode);

  App.Run(); // runs windows application

  return App.Status; // termination status
}
```

Figure 9-1 shows sample output from this program.

A Closer Look at the Mouse Messages

Each time a **WM_LBUTTONDOWN** or a **WM_RBUTTONDOWN** message is generated, several pieces of information are also supplied in the **WParam** parameter. It may contain any combination of the following values:

MK_CONTROL
MK_SHIFT
MK_LBUTTON
MK_RBUTTON

If the CTRL key is pressed when a mouse button is pressed, **WParam** will contain **MK_CONTROL**. If the SHIFT key is pressed when a mouse button is pressed, **WParam** will contain **MK_SHIFT.** If the right button is down when the left button is pressed, **WParam** will contain

Sample output from the application skeleton

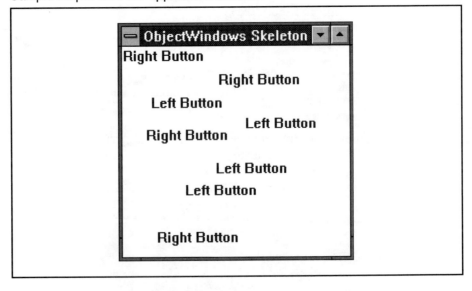

MK_RBUTTON. If the left button is down when the right button is pressed, **WParam** will contain **MK_LBUTTON.**

To see how this extra information can be used, substitute these mouse functions in the preceding program. Now, the status of the CTRL and SHIFT keys are also reported.

```
// Process left mouse button.
void AppWindow::WMLButtonDown(RTMessage Msg)
{
  HDC DC;
  ostrstream ostr(s, sizeof(s));

  DC = GetDC(HWindow);
  ostr << "Left Button" << ends;
  TextOut(DC, Msg.LP.Lo, Msg.LP.Hi, s, strlen(s));
  ostr.seekp(0, ios::beg);
  if(Msg.WParam & MK_CONTROL) {
    ostr << "LB + Control Down" << ends;
    TextOut(DC, Msg.LP.Lo, Msg.LP.Hi, s, strlen(s));
    ostr.seekp(0, ios::beg);
  }
  if(Msg.WParam & MK_SHIFT) {
    ostr << "LB + Shift Down" << ends;
    TextOut(DC, Msg.LP.Lo, Msg.LP.Hi, s, strlen(s));
    ostr.seekp(0, ios::beg);
  }
  ReleaseDC(HWindow, DC);
}

// Process right mouse button.
void AppWindow::WMRButtonDown(RTMessage Msg)
{
  HDC DC;
  ostrstream ostr(s, sizeof(s));

  DC = GetDC(HWindow);
  ostr << "Right Button" << ends;
  TextOut(DC, Msg.LP.Lo, Msg.LP.Hi, s, strlen(s));
  ostr.seekp(0, ios::beg);
  if(Msg.WParam & MK_CONTROL) {
    ostr << "RB + Control Down" << ends;
    TextOut(DC, Msg.LP.Lo, Msg.LP.Hi, s, strlen(s));
```

```
    ostr.seekp(0, ios::beg);
  }
  if(Msg.WParam & MK_SHIFT) {
    ostr << "RB + Shift Down" << ends;
    TextOut(DC, Msg.LP.Lo, Msg.LP.Hi, s, strlen(s));
    ostr.seekp(0, ios::beg);
  }
  ReleaseDC(HWindow, DC);
}
```

Generating a WM_PAINT Message

Before this chapter concludes, it is necessary to explain how your program can generate a **WM_PAINT** message and why this is important. At first, you might wonder why your program would need to generate a **WM_PAINT** message since it seems that it can repaint its window whenever it wants. However, this is a false assumption. Because Windows is a nonpreemptive multitasking system, it is best that your program return control back to Windows as soon as possible, letting Windows decide when it is best to perform output to your window by sending a **WM_PAINT** message. This allows Windows to better manage the system. When you use this approach, your program simply holds all output until this message is received and then updates the window.

In the previous skeleton applications, the **WM_PAINT** message was received only when the window was resized or uncovered. However, if all output is held until a **WM_PAINT** message is received, then to achieve interactive I/O, there must be some way to tell Windows that it needs to send a **WM_PAINT** message to your window whenever output is pending. As expected, Windows includes such a feature. Thus, when your program has information to output, it simply requests that a **WM_PAINT** message be sent when Windows is ready to do so.

To cause Windows to send a **WM_PAINT** message, your program will call the **InvalidateRect()** API function. Its prototype is shown here:

void InvalidateRect(HWND *hWnd*, LPRECT *lpRect*, BOOL *bErase*);

Here, *hWnd* is the handle of the window you want to send the
WM_PAINT message to. The type **LPRECT** is a pointer to a **RECT**
structure. This structure specifies the coordinates within the window
that must be redrawn. If this value is null, the entire window will be
specified. If *bErase* is true, the background will be erased. If it is zero,
then the background is left unchanged.

When **InvalidateRect()** is called, it tells Windows that the window is
invalid and must be redrawn. This, in turn, causes Windows to send a
WM_PAINT message to the window.

Here is a reworked version of the application skeleton that routes all
output through **Paint()**. The other message response functions simply
prepare the information to be displayed and then call **InvalidateRect()**.

```
/* ObjectWindows Windows application skeleton that responds
   to WM_CHAR, WM_PAINT, and mouse messages. This version routes
   all output through the Paint() function by generating a
   WM_CHAR message using InvalidateRect(). */

#include <owl.h>
#include <string.h>
#include <strstream.h>

// Define an application.
class AppName : public TApplication
{
public:
  AppName(LPSTR App_Name, HANDLE ThisInstance,
      HANDLE PrevInstance, LPSTR Args, int VidMode) :
      TApplication(App_Name, ThisInstance, PrevInstance, Args,
              VidMode) {};
  virtual void InitMainWindow();
};

// Define a window type.
class AppWindow : public TWindow
{
public:
  AppWindow(PTWindowsObject WType, LPSTR WTitle) :
```

```
        TWindow(WType, WTitle) {};
  virtual void WMChar(RTMessage Msg) =
    [WM_FIRST + WM_CHAR]; // process a WM_CHAR message
  virtual void Paint(HDC DC, PAINTSTRUCT &PI);

  virtual void WMLButtonDown(RTMessage Msg) =
    [WM_FIRST + WM_LBUTTONDOWN]; // respond to left button
  virtual void WMRButtonDown(RTMessage Msg) =
    [WM_FIRST + WM_RBUTTONDOWN]; // respond to right button
  // Additional window details go here.
};

// Creates and initializes an instance of the window.
void AppName::InitMainWindow()
{
  MainWindow = new AppWindow(NULL, Name);
}

// These are global because they are used by other functions.
char s[20] = "hello";
int x=1, y=1;

// Process a WM_CHAR message.
void AppWindow::WMChar(RTMessage Msg)
{
  HDC DC;
  ostrstream ostr(s, sizeof(s));

  ostr << (char) Msg.WParam << ends;
  x = 1; y = 1;
  InvalidateRect(HWindow, NULL, 1); // repaint
}

// Process a WM_PAINT message.
void AppWindow::Paint(HDC DC, PAINTSTRUCT &)
{
  TextOut(DC, x, y, s, strlen(s)); // redisplay string
}
```

```
// Process left mouse button.
void AppWindow::WMLButtonDown(RTMessage Msg)
{
    ostrstream ostr(s, sizeof(s));

    ostr << "Left Button" << ends;
    x = Msg.LP.Lo;
    y = Msg.LP.Hi;
    InvalidateRect(HWindow, NULL, 1); // repaint
}

// Process right mouse button.
void AppWindow::WMRButtonDown(RTMessage Msg)
{
    ostrstream ostr(s, sizeof(s));

    ostr << "Right Button" << ends;
    x = Msg.LP.Lo;
    y = Msg.LP.Hi;
    InvalidateRect(HWindow, NULL, 1); // repaint
}



// Entry point of windows program.
int PASCAL WinMain(HANDLE ThisInstance, HANDLE PrevInstance,
           LPSTR Args, int VidMode)
{
    AppName App("ObjectWindows Skeleton", ThisInstance,
             PrevInstance, Args, VidMode);

    App.Run(); // runs windows application

    return App.Status; // termination status
}
```

Notice that the program adds two new global variables called **x** and **y** that hold the location at which the text will be displayed when a **WM_PAINT** message is received.

As you can see, by channeling all output through **Paint()**, the program has actually become smaller and, in some ways, easier to understand. Also, as stated at the start of this section, the program allows Windows to decide when it is most appropriate to update the window.

Note   Many Windows applications route all (or most) output through the **Paint()** function, for the reasons already stated. However, the previous programs are not techinically wrong by outputting text within their message response functions. It is just that this approach may not be the best for all purposes.

CHAPTER

Message Boxes and Menus

ow that you know how to construct a basic ObjectWindows skeleton and receive and process messages, it is time to begin exploration of Windows' user interface components. Although you can write a Windows application that appears just like a DOS application, doing so is not in the spirit of Windows programming. In order for your Windows applications to conform to Windows' general design principles, you will need to communicate with the user using several different types of special windows. There are three basic types of user-interface windows: message boxes, menus, and dialog boxes. This chapter discusses message boxes and menus. (Chapter 11 examines dialog boxes.) As you will see, the basic style of each of these windows is predefined by Windows. You need only supply the specific information that relates to your application.

Keep in mind that message boxes and menus are *child windows* of your original application windows. This means they are owned by your application and are dependent upon it. They cannot exist by themselves. Your application must always create a main window.

Message Boxes

By far the simplest interface window is the *message box*. A message box simply displays a message to the user and waits for an acknowledgment. It is possible to construct message boxes that allow the user to select among a few basic alternatives, but in general, the purpose of a message box is simply to inform the user that some event has taken place.

To create a message box, use the **MessageBox()** API function. Its prototype is shown here:

int MessageBox(HWND *HWindow*, LPSTR *lpText*, LPSTR *lpCaption*,
                    WORD *wMBType*);

Here, *HWindow* is the handle to the parent window. The *lpText* parameter is a pointer to a string that will appear inside the message box. The string pointed to by *lpCaption* is used as the caption for the box. The value of *wMBType* determines the exact nature of the message box, including what type of buttons will be present. Some of its most common values are shown in Table 10-1. These macros are defined in WINDOWS.H, and

TABLE 10-1 Some Common Values for wMBType

Value	Effect
MB_ABORTRETRYIGNORE	Displays Abort, Retry, and Ignore push buttons
MB_ICONEXCLAMATION	Displays exclamation-point icon
MB_ICONHAND	Displays a stop sign icon
MB_ICONINFORMATION	Displays an information icon
MB_ICONQUESTION	Displays a question mark icon
MB_ICONSTOP	Same as MB_ICONHAND
MB_OKCANCEL	Displays OK and Cancel push buttons
MB_RETRYCANCEL	Displays Retry and Cancel push buttons
MB_YESNO	Displays Yes and No push buttons
MB_YESNOCANCEL	Displays Yes, No, and Cancel push buttons

you can OR together two or more of these macros as long as they are not mutually exclusive. (Remember, WINDOWS.H is automatically included in your ObjectWindows program when you include OWL.H.)

MessageBox() returns the user's response to the box. The possible return values are shown here:

Button Pressed	Return Value
Abort	IDABORT
Retry	IDRETRY
Ignore	IDIGNORE
Cancel	IDCANCEL

No   IDNO

Yes   IDYES

OK   IDOK

These macros are defined in WINDOWS.H. Remember, depending upon the value of *wMBType*, only certain buttons will be present.

To display a message box, simply call the **MessageBox()** function. Windows will display it at its first opportunity. You do not need to obtain a device context or generate a **WM_PAINT** message. **MessageBox()** handles all of these details for you.

Here is a simple example that displays a message box when you press a mouse button:

```
// Demonstrate message boxes.

#include <owl.h>
#include <string.h>
#include <strstream.h>

// Define an application.
class AppName : public TApplication
{
public:
  AppName(LPSTR App_Name, HANDLE ThisInstance,
      HANDLE PrevInstance, LPSTR Args, int VidMode) :
      TApplication(App_Name, ThisInstance, PrevInstance, Args,
            VidMode) {};
  virtual void InitMainWindow();
};

// Define a window type.
class AppWindow : public TWindow
{
public:
  AppWindow(PTWindowsObject WType, LPSTR WTitle) :
      TWindow(WType, WTitle) {};
  virtual void WMChar(RTMessage Msg) =
    [WM_FIRST + WM_CHAR]; // process a WM_CHAR message
  virtual void Paint(HDC DC, PAINTSTRUCT &PI);
```

```
  virtual void WMLButtonDown(RTMessage Msg) =
    [WM_FIRST + WM_LBUTTONDOWN]; // respond to left button
  virtual void WMRButtonDown(RTMessage Msg) =
    [WM_FIRST + WM_RBUTTONDOWN]; // respond to right button
  // Additional window details go here.
};

// Creates and initializes an instance of the window.
void AppName::InitMainWindow()
{
  MainWindow = new AppWindow(NULL, Name);
}

// These will be used by other functions.
char s[20] = "hello";
int x=1, y=1;

// Process a WM_CHAR message.
void AppWindow::WMChar(RTMessage Msg)
{
  HDC DC;
  ostrstream ostr(s, sizeof(s));

  ostr << (char) Msg.WParam << ends;
  x = 1; y = 1;
  InvalidateRect(HWindow, NULL, 1); // repaint
}

// Process a WM_PAINT message.
void AppWindow::Paint(HDC DC, PAINTSTRUCT &)
{
  TextOut(DC, x, y, s, strlen(s)); // redisplay string
}

// Process left mouse button.
void AppWindow::WMLButtonDown(RTMessage Msg)
{
  MessageBox(HWindow, "Left Button", "Left",
            MB_OK | MB_ICONHAND);
}

// Process right mouse button.
```

```
void AppWindow::WMRButtonDown(RTMessage Msg)
{
  MessageBox(HWindow, "Right Button", "Right",
            MB_OK | MB_ICONHAND);
}


// Entry point of windows program.
int PASCAL WinMain(HANDLE ThisInstance, HANDLE PrevInstance,
          LPSTR Args, int VidMode)
{
  AppName App("Demonstrate Message Boxes", ThisInstance,
            PrevInstance, Args, VidMode);

  App.Run(); // runs windows application

  return App.Status; // termination status
}
```

Each time a button is pressed, a message box is displayed. For example, pressing the left button displays the message box shown in Figure 10-1.

A sample message box

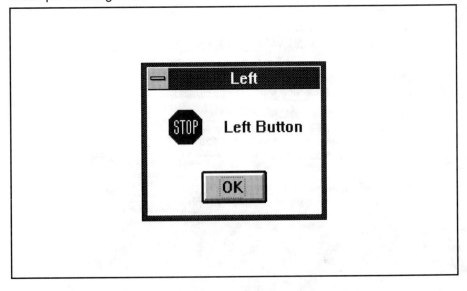

In this example, the program does not use the value returned by **MessageBox()**. However, try substituting this mouse response function into the program:

```
// Process left mouse button.
void AppWindow::WMLButtonDown(RTMessage Msg)
{
  int response;

  response = MessageBox(HWindow, "Select One", "Left Button",
                    MB_ABORTRETRYIGNORE);
  switch(response) {
    case IDABORT : MessageBox(HWindow, "", "Abort", MB_OK);
      break;
    case IDRETRY : MessageBox(HWindow, "", "Retry", MB_OK);
      break;
    case IDIGNORE : MessageBox(HWindow, "", "Ignore", MB_OK);
      break;
  }
}
```

As you will see, when you press the left button, a message box displays the buttons Abort, Retry, and Ignore. Depending upon your response, a second message box will be displayed that indicates which button you pressed.

Before continuing, experiment with message boxes, trying different types. Just for fun, you might also want to add one to the **Paint()** function that tells you what character was pressed.

Introducing Menus

As you know, in Windows the most common element of control is the menu. Virtually all main windows have some type of menu associated with them. Because menus are so common and important in Windows applications, Windows provides substantial built-in support for them. Adding a menu to a window involves these relatively few steps:

1. Define the form of the menu in a resource file.

2. Load the menu when your program creates its main window.

3. Process menu selections.

In Windows, the top level of a menu is displayed across the top of the window. Submenus are displayed as pop-up menus. (You should be accustomed to this approach because it is used by virtually all Windows programs.)

Before a discussion of menus, it is necessary to explain what Windows resources and resource files are.

Using Resources

Windows defines several common types of objects as *resources*. Resources include items such as menus, icons, dialog boxes, and bit-mapped graphics. Since a menu is a resource, you need to understand resources before you can add a menu to your program.

A resource is created separately from your program but is added to the .EXE file when your program is linked. Resources are contained in *resource files*, which have the extension .RC. Resource files are source files you create using a standard text editor, such as the Turbo C++ for Windows IDE editor. (You usually generate certain resources, such as icons, by using the Turbo C++ Resource Workshop, but they still must be included in the .RC file that is associated with your application.) However, instead of being compiled by Turbo C++, they must be compiled by using a *resource compiler*. The resource compiler converts an .RC file into an .RES file, which may be linked with your program.

 Note You can embed comments into resource files on a line-by-line basis by beginning the comments with a semicolon. You cannot use C- or C++-like comments.

Compiling .RC Files

Once you have created an .RC file (and saved it to disk), you compile it into an .RES file by using the Turbo C++ for Windows Resource

Workshop. To do this, first activate the Resource Workshop. Next, activate the File menu and select the Open Project option. Next, enter the name of your .RC file. Once the file is read in, the Resource Workshop automatically compiles your .RC file. If it encounters an error, it is displayed and you are given a chance to fix it.

Once your resource file compiles without error, you need to save it so it can be linked with your application. By default, the Resource Workshop does not save the compiled version of your .RC file (which is what you need to link to your Windows application.) To cause the Resource Workshop to save the compiled version of your resource file, you need to set two options. First, select the File menu, and then select Preferences. Next, in the Multi-save box, check the .RES and Executable options. By selecting these options, when you save your resource project, you will also create the .RES file that will be linked to your program. Also, if your program already exists in an .EXE form, the updated resources will automatically be added to it. Remember, neither of these options is on by default.

To create or update the .RES or .EXE file, you must explicitly save your project before leaving the Resource Workshop. To do so, select File and then Save Project. If you don't do this, no changes will be made to the .RES or .EXE files on disk. (Remember, you must have already turned on the options described in the preceding paragraph.)

Once you have compiled the .RC file, return to Turbo C++ for Windows and compile, link, and run your application. Your resources will automatically be added to your program.

Creating a Simple Menu

Before a menu can be included, you must define its content in a resource file. All menu definitions have this general form:

MenuName MENU [*options*]
{
    menu items
}

Here, *MenuName* is the name of the menu. (It may also be an integer value identifying the menu, but all examples in this book will use the name when referring to the menu.) The keyword **MENU** tells the resource compiler that a menu is being created. There are several options you can specify when creating the menu. They are shown here:

Option	Meaning
DISCARDABLE	Menu may be removed from memory when no longer needed
FIXED	Menu is fixed in memory
LOADONCALL	Menu is loaded when used (default)
MOVEABLE	Menu may be moved in memory (default)
PRELOAD	Menu is loaded when your program begins execution

(Again, these macros are defined in WINDOWS.H.) You may use any nonconflicting combination. The examples in this book simply use the default settings.

There are two types of items you can use to define the menu: **MENUITEM**s and **POPUP**s. A **MENUITEM** specifies a final selection. A **POPUP** specifies a pop-up submenu, which may, in itself, contain other **MENUITEM**s or **POPUP**s. The general form of each of these two statements is shown here:

MENUITEM "*ItemName*", *MenuID* [,*Options*]
POPUP "*PopupName*" [,*Options*]

Here, *ItemName* is the name of the menu selection, such as Help or File. *MenuID* is a unique integer associated with a menu item that will be sent to your Windows application when a selection is made. Typically, these values are defined as macros inside a header file that is included both in your application code and in the .RC resource file. *PopupName* is the name of the pop-up menu. For both cases, the values for *Options* (defined in WINDOWS.H) are shown in Table 10-2.

Here is an example of a simple menu that you should enter into your computer at this time. Call the file MENU.RC.

```
; Sample menu resource file.
#include "menu.h"
```

```
MYMENU MENU
{
  POPUP "&One"
  {
    MENUITEM "&Alpha", IDM_ALPHA
    MENUITEM "&Beta", IDM_BETA
  }
  POPUP "&Two"
  {
    MENUITEM "&Gamma", IDM_GAMMA
    POPUP "&Delta"
    {
      MENUITEM "&Epsilon", IDM_EPSILON
      MENUITEM "&Zeta", IDM_ZETA
    }
    MENUITEM "&Eta", IDM_ETA
    MENUITEM "&Theta", IDM_THETA
  }
  MENUITEM "&Help", IDM_HELP, HELP
}
```

TABLE 10-2

The MENUITEM and POPUP Options

Option	Meaning
CHECKED	A check mark is displayed next to the name (not applicable to top-level menus)
GRAYED	The name is shown in gray and may not be selected
HELP	The name, usually "Help," is displayed at the far right of the menu bar
INACTIVE	The option may not be selected
MENUBARBREAK	For menu bars, causes a vertical bar to separate this item from the previous. For pop-up menus, causes the item to be put in a different column.
MENUBREAK	Same as MENUBARBREAK except no separator bar is used

This menu, called MYMENU, contains three top-level menu bar options: One, Two, and Help. The One and Two options contain pop-up submenus. In the Two submenu, the Delta option activates a pop-up submenu of its own. Notice that options that activate submenus do not have menu ID values associated with them; only actual menu items have ID numbers. In this menu, all menu ID values are specified as macros beginning with **IDM**. (These macros are defined in the header file MENU.H.) The names you give these values are arbitrary.

The & causes the key it precedes to become the shortcut key associated with that option. That is, once that menu is active, pressing that key causes that menu item to be selected. It doesn't have to be the first key in the name, but it should be unless a conflict with another name exists.

The MENU.H header file contains the macro definitions of the menu ID values. It is shown here. Enter it at this time.

```
#define IDM_ALPHA    100
#define IDM_BETA     101
#define IDM_GAMMA    102
#define IDM_DELTA    103
#define IDM_EPSILON  104
#define IDM_ZETA     105
#define IDM_ETA      106
#define IDM_THETA    107
#define IDM_HELP     108
```

This file defines the menu ID values that will be returned when the various menu items are selected. This file will also be included in the program that uses the menu. Remember, the actual names and values you give the menu items are arbitrary, but each value must be unique.

Including a Menu in Your Program

Once you have created a menu, you include that menu in an ObjectWindows program by calling the **AssignMenu()** function when the main window is constructed. **AssignMenu()** is a member of the **TWindow** class. It has this prototype:

BOOL AssignMenu(LPSTR *MenuName*);

where *MenuName* is the name of the menu you want to use. It returns false if the menu cannot be loaded and true otherwise.

For example, to load the menu MYMENU, use this constructor function when you create your main application window:

```
// call AssignMenu here
AppWindow(PTWindowsObject WType, LPSTR WTitle) :
      TWindow(WType, WTitle) {AssignMenu("MYMENU");}
```

Responding to Menu Selections

Each time the user selects a menu item, your program is sent a command message that corresponds to the menu item ID plus a constant. This message is used by ObjectWindows to call the DDVT function you have defined for this item.

You define a menu response function just the same way you define any other message response function, inside the application window class declaration. The only exception is that you need to add to the item ID value the constant **CM_FIRST** rather than **WM_FIRST**. For example, here are the menu response functions that correspond to the menu defined in the previous section:

```
// Define a window type.
class AppWindow : public TWindow
{
public:
  // call AssignMenu here
  AppWindow(PTWindowsObject WType, LPSTR WTitle) :
        TWindow(WType, WTitle) {AssignMenu("MYMENU");}

  virtual void WMChar(RTMessage Msg) =
    [WM_FIRST + WM_CHAR]; // process a WM_CHAR message
```

```
virtual void Paint(HDC DC, PAINTSTRUCT &PI);

virtual void WMLButtonDown(RTMessage Msg) =
  [WM_FIRST + WM_LBUTTONDOWN]; // respond to left button
virtual void WMRButtonDown(RTMessage Msg) =
  [WM_FIRST + WM_RBUTTONDOWN]; // respond to right button

virtual void IDMAlpha(RTMessage Msg) = [CM_FIRST + IDM_ALPHA];
virtual void IDMBeta(RTMessage Msg) = [CM_FIRST + IDM_BETA];
virtual void IDMGamma(RTMessage Msg) = [CM_FIRST + IDM_GAMMA];
virtual void IDMEpsilon(RTMessage Msg)=[CM_FIRST+IDM_EPSILON];
virtual void IDMZeta(RTMessage Msg) = [CM_FIRST + IDM_ZETA];
virtual void IDMEta(RTMessage Msg) = [CM_FIRST + IDM_ETA];
virtual void IDMTheta(RTMessage Msg) = [CM_FIRST + IDM_THETA];
virtual void IDMHelp(RTMessage Msg) = [CM_FIRST + IDM_HELP];

// Additional window details go here.
};
```

As with other message response functions, the names of the functions are arbitrary. ObjectWindows executes each by using its index, not its name. For the most part, the **Msg** parameter is not needed when using ObjectWindows. However, for your information, **Msg.WParam** contains the value associated with the item selected. **Msg.LP.Hi** is 1 if the item was selected using an accelerator key (discussed later) and zero otherwise.

A Sample Menu Program

Here is a program that demonstrates the menu created in the previous section. Enter it at this time. When you run the program, your screen will look like that shown in Figure 10-2.

```
// Demonstrate menus.

#include <owl.h>
#include <string.h>
#include <strstream.h>
```

```
#include "menu.h"

// Define an application.
class AppName : public TApplication
{
public:
  AppName(LPSTR App_Name, HANDLE ThisInstance,
      HANDLE PrevInstance, LPSTR Args, int VidMode) :
      TApplication(App_Name, ThisInstance, PrevInstance, Args,
             VidMode) {}
  virtual void InitMainWindow();
};

// Define a window type.
class AppWindow : public TWindow
{
public:
  // call AssignMenu here
  AppWindow(PTWindowsObject WType, LPSTR WTitle) :
        TWindow(WType, WTitle) {AssignMenu("MYMENU");}

  virtual void WMChar(RTMessage Msg) =
    [WM_FIRST + WM_CHAR]; // process a WM_CHAR message
  virtual void Paint(HDC DC, PAINTSTRUCT &PI);

  virtual void WMLButtonDown(RTMessage Msg) =
    [WM_FIRST + WM_LBUTTONDOWN]; // respond to left button
  virtual void WMRButtonDown(RTMessage Msg) =
    [WM_FIRST + WM_RBUTTONDOWN]; // respond to right button

  virtual void IDMAlpha(RTMessage Msg) = [CM_FIRST + IDM_ALPHA];
  virtual void IDMBeta(RTMessage Msg) = [CM_FIRST + IDM_BETA];
  virtual void IDMGamma(RTMessage Msg) = [CM_FIRST + IDM_GAMMA];
  virtual void IDMEpsilon(RTMessage Msg)=[CM_FIRST+IDM_EPSILON];
  virtual void IDMZeta(RTMessage Msg) = [CM_FIRST + IDM_ZETA];
  virtual void IDMEta(RTMessage Msg) = [CM_FIRST + IDM_ETA];
  virtual void IDMTheta(RTMessage Msg) = [CM_FIRST + IDM_THETA];
  virtual void IDMHelp(RTMessage Msg) = [CM_FIRST + IDM_HELP];

  // Additional window details go here.
};
```

```
// Creates and initializes an instance of the window.
void AppName::InitMainWindow()
{
  MainWindow = new AppWindow(NULL, Name);
}


// These will be used by other functions.
char s[20] = "hello";
int x=1, y=1;


// Process a WM_CHAR message.
void AppWindow::WMChar(RTMessage Msg)
{
  HDC DC;
  ostrstream ostr(s, sizeof(s));

  ostr << (char) Msg.WParam << ends;
  x = 1; y = 1;
  InvalidateRect(HWindow, NULL, 1); // repaint
}


// Process a WM_PAINT message.
void AppWindow::Paint(HDC DC, PAINTSTRUCT &)
{
  TextOut(DC, x, y, s, strlen(s)); // redisplay string
}


// Process left mouse button.
void AppWindow::WMLButtonDown(RTMessage Msg)
{
  int response;

  response = MessageBox(HWindow, "Select One", "Left Button",
                        MB_ABORTRETRYIGNORE);
  switch(response) {
    case IDABORT : MessageBox(HWindow, "", "Abort", MB_OK);
      break;
    case IDRETRY : MessageBox(HWindow, "", "Retry", MB_OK);
      break;
    case IDIGNORE : MessageBox(HWindow, "", "Ignore", MB_OK);
      break;
  }
```

```
    }

// Process right mouse button.
void AppWindow::WMRButtonDown(RTMessage Msg)
{
  MessageBox(HWindow, "Did you press the Right Button?",
          "Right Button", MB_OK | MB_ICONQUESTION);
}

// Process the IDM_ALPHA selection.
void AppWindow::IDMAlpha(RTMessage Msg)
{
  ostrstream ostr(s, sizeof(s));

  ostr << "ALPHA ALPHA" << ends;
  MessageBox(HWindow, "--Alpha--", "Alpha Selected", MB_OK);
  InvalidateRect(HWindow, NULL, 1);
}

// Process the IDM_BETA selection.
void AppWindow::IDMBeta(RTMessage Msg)
{
  ostrstream ostr(s, sizeof(s));

  ostr << "BETA BETA" << ends;
  InvalidateRect(HWindow, NULL, 1);
}

// Process the IDM_GAMMA selection.
void AppWindow::IDMGamma(RTMessage Msg)
{
  ostrstream ostr(s, sizeof(s));

  ostr << "GAMMA GAMMA" << ends;
  InvalidateRect(HWindow, NULL, 1);
}

// Process the IDM_EPSILON selection.
void AppWindow::IDMEpsilon(RTMessage Msg)
{
  ostrstream ostr(s, sizeof(s));
```

```
  ostr << "EPSILON EPSILON" << ends;
  InvalidateRect(HWindow, NULL, 1);
}


// Process the IDM_ZETA selection.
void AppWindow::IDMZeta(RTMessage Msg)
{
  ostrstream ostr(s, sizeof(s));

  ostr << "ZETA ZETA" << ends;
  InvalidateRect(HWindow, NULL, 1);
}


// Process the IDM_ETA selection.
void AppWindow::IDMEta(RTMessage Msg)
{
  ostrstream ostr(s, sizeof(s));

  ostr << "ETA ETA" << ends;
  InvalidateRect(HWindow, NULL, 1);
}


// Process the IDM_THETA selection.
void AppWindow::IDMTheta(RTMessage Msg)
{
  ostrstream ostr(s, sizeof(s));

  ostr << "THETA THETA" << ends;
  InvalidateRect(HWindow, NULL, 1);
}


// Process the IDM_HELP selection.
void AppWindow::IDMHelp(RTMessage Msg)
{
  MessageBox(HWindow, "Demonstrate Menus", "Help", MB_OK);
}


// Entry point of windows program.
int PASCAL WinMain(HANDLE ThisInstance, HANDLE PrevInstance,
          LPSTR Args, int VidMode)
{
  AppName App("Demonstrate Menus", ThisInstance,
```

```
                PrevInstance, Args, VidMode);

    App.Run();  // runs windows application

    return App.Status; // termination status
}
```

Adding Menu Accelerator Keys

There is one more feature to discuss that relates to menus. This feature is the accelerator key. *Accelerator keys* are special keystrokes you define that, when pressed, automatically select a menu option even though the menu in which that option resides is not displayed. Put differently, you can select an item directly by pressing an accelerator key, bypassing the menu entirely. The term "acclerator keys" is an accurate description because pressing one is generally a faster way to select a menu item than first activating its menu and then selecting the item.

Sample output from the menu example

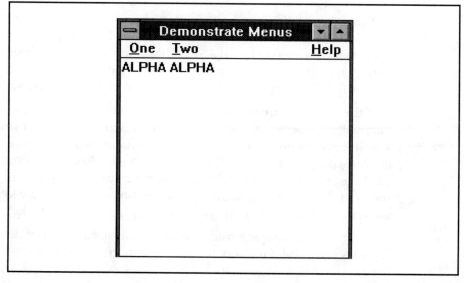

To define accelerator keys relative to a menu, you must add an accelerator key table to your resource file. All accelerator table definitions have this general form:

MenuName ACCELERATORS
{
    Key1, *MenuID1* [,*type*] [*option*]
    Key2, *MenuID2* [,*type*] [*option*]
    Key3, *MenuID3* [,*type*] [*option*]
    .
    .
    .
    Keyn, *MenuIDn* [,*type*] [*option*]
}

Here, *MenuName* is the name of the menu that the accelerators will be applied to and is also the name of the accelerator table. *Key* is the keystroke that selects the item and *MenuID* is the ID value associated with the desired item. The *type* specifies whether the key is a standard key (the default) or a virtual key (discussed shortly). The options may be one of the following macros: **NOINVERT**, **ALT**, **SHIFT**, or **CONTROL**. **NOINVERT** causes no top level menu to be displayed when an item is selected. With one exception noted shortly, the other three apply only to virtual keys.

The value of *Key* can be a quoted character, an ASCII integer value corresponding to a key, or a virtual key code. If a quoted character is used, it is assumed to be an ASCII character. If it is an integer value, you must tell the resource compiler explicitly that this is an ASCII character by specifying *type* as **ASCII**. If it is a virtual key, *type* must be **VIRTKEY**.

If the key is an uppercase quoted character, its corresponding menu item will be selected if the user presses it while holding down the SHIFT key. If it is a lowercase character, its menu item will be selected if the key is pressed by itself. If the key is specified as a lowercase character and **ALT** is specified as an option, pressing ALT and the character will select the item. Finally, if you want the user to press CTRL and the key to select an item, specify the key in uppercase and precede it with a ^.

A *virtual key* is a system-independent code for a variety of keys. Virtual keys include the function keys F1 through F12, the arrow keys, and various non-ASCII keys. They are defined by macros in the header file WINDOWS.H. All virtual key macros begin with **VK_**. The function keys are **VK_F1** through **VK_F12**, for example. You should refer to WINDOWS.H for the other virtual key code macros. To use a virtual key as an accelerator, simply specify its macro for the *key* and specify **VIRTKEY** for its *type*. You may also specify **ALT**, **SHIFT**, or **CONTROL** to achieve the desired key combination.

Here are some examples:

```
"A", IDM_x              ; select by pressing SHIFT-A
"a", IDM_x              ; select by pressing a
"^A", IDM_x             ; select by pressing CTRL-A
"a", IDM_x, ALT         ; select by pressing ALT-A
VK_F2, IDM_x            ; select by pressing F2
VK_F2, IDM_x, SHIFT     ; select by pressing SHIFT-F2
```

Here is the MENU.RC resource file that also contains accelerator key definitions for the menu specified in the previous section:

```
; Sample menu resource file
#include "menu.h"

MYMENU MENU
{
  POPUP "&One"
  {
    MENUITEM "&Alpha\tF2", IDM_ALPHA
    MENUITEM "&Beta\tF3", IDM_BETA
  }
  POPUP "&Two"
  {
    MENUITEM "&Gamma\tSHIFT-G", IDM_GAMMA
    POPUP "&Delta"
    {
      MENUITEM "&Epsilon\tCntl-E", IDM_EPSILON
      MENUITEM "&Zeta\tCntl-Z", IDM_ZETA
    }
    MENUITEM "&Eta\tCntl-F4", IDM_ETA
    MENUITEM "&Theta\tF5", IDM_THETA
  }
  MENUITEM "&Help", IDM_HELP, HELP
```

```
}

; Define menu accelerators
MYMENU ACCELERATORS
{
  VK_F2, IDM_ALPHA, VIRTKEY
  VK_F3, IDM_BETA, VIRTKEY
  "G", IDM_GAMMA
  "^E", IDM_EPSILON
  "^Z", IDM_ZETA
  VK_F4, IDM_ETA, VIRTKEY, CONTROL
  VK_F5, IDM_THETA, VIRTKEY
  VK_F1, IDM_HELP, VIRTKEY
}
```

Loading the Accelerator Table

Even though the accelerators are contained in the same resource file as the menu, you must load them separately by using another API function called **LoadAccelerators()**, whose prototype is shown here:

HANDLE LoadAccelerators(HANDLE *ThisInstance*, LPSTR *Name*);

where *ThisInstance* is the handle of the application and *Name* is the name of the accelerator table.

You must call **LoadAccelerators()** inside the **InitMainWindow()** ObjectWindows function, after you have constructed the main window. For example, this shows how to load the MYMENU accelerator table:

```
// Creates and initializes an instance of the window.
void AppName::InitMainWindow()
{
  MainWindow = new AppWindow(NULL, Name);

  HAccTable = LoadAccelerators(hInstance, "MYMENU");
}
```

HAccTable is a handle to the accelerator table that is defined by the **TApplication** base class.

To try using accelerators, substitute this function into the preceding application and add the accelerator table to your resource file.

Before moving on to the next chapter, experiment on your own using message boxes, menus, and accelerators. Try the various options and see what they do.

CHAPTER

Using Dialog Boxes

$\mathbf{A}$fter menus, there is no more important Windows interface element than the dialog box. A *dialog box* is a type of window that provides a more flexible means by which the user can interact with your Windows application. In general, dialog boxes allow the user to select or enter information that would be difficult or impossible using a menu.

A dialog box is another resource that is contained in your program's resource file. Although it is possible to specify the contents of a dialog box by using a text editor and entering its specifications, the much better (and easier) way is to use Turbo C++'s Resource Workshop. Since the complete .RC files for the examples in this chapter are supplied, you should simply enter them as text. However, when creating your own dialog boxes, you will want to use the Resource Workshop.

How Dialog Boxes Interact with the User

A dialog box interacts with the user through one or more controls. A *control* is a specific type of input or output window. A control is owned by its parent window, which, for the examples presented in this chapter, is the dialog box. Windows supports the following controls: push buttons, check boxes, radio buttons, list boxes, edit boxes, combination boxes, scroll bars, and static controls. Each is briefly described here.

❏ A *push button* is a control that the user "pushes on" (by clicking the mouse or tabbing to it and then pressing ENTER) to activate some response. You have already been using push buttons in message boxes. For example, the OK button that you have been using in most message boxes is a push button. There can be one or more push buttons in a dialog box.

❏ A *check box* contains one or more items that are either checked or not checked. If the item is checked, it means it is selected. In a check box, more than one item may be selected.

❏ A *radio button* is essentially a check box in which one and only one item may be selected.

❏ A *list box* displays a list of items from which the user selects one or more. List boxes are commonly used to display things such as file names.

❏   An *edit box* allows the user to enter a string. Edit boxes provide all necessary text editing features required by the user. Therefore, to input a string, your program simply displays an edit box and waits until the user has finished typing in the string.

❏   A *combination box* is a combination of a list box and an edit box.

❏   As you know, a *scroll bar* is used to scroll text in a window.

❏   A *static* control is used to output text (or graphics) that provides information to the user but accepts no input.

In the course of explaining how to use dialog boxes with Object-Windows, the examples in this chapter illustrate three of these controls: push buttons, the list box, and the edit box.

It is important to understand that controls both generate messages when accessed by the user, and receive messages from your application. A message generated by a control indicates what type of interaction the user has had with the control. A message sent to the control is essentially an instruction to which the control must respond. You will see examples of this type of message passing later in this chapter.

Using TDialog

To add a dialog box to your application, you will need to define one by using the ObjectWindows base class **TDialog**. **TDialog** serves as a base class that your dialog boxes use. One of its constructor functions has this prototype:

TDialog (PTWindowsObject *Owner*, LPSTR *DName*);

Here, *Owner* receives a pointer to the dialog box's parent, and *DName* is the name of the dialog box as specified in the resource file.

Each dialog box you create will be a new class derived from **TDialog**. For example, this skeleton derives the dialog class **MyDialog**:

```
// Define a dialog box type.
class MyDialog : public TDialog
```

```
{
public:
  MyDialog(PTWindowsObject Owner, LPSTR DName) :
    TDialog(Owner, DName) {}

  // process dialog box messages here
};
```

Receiving Dialog Box Messages

Since a dialog box is a window (albeit a special kind of window), events that occur within it are sent to your program using the same message-passing mechanism the main window uses. Thus, to receive messages from the dialog box, you need to define its own set of message response functions. To do this, you will again use DDVT functions. The index of each function will be the combination of the macro **ID_FIRST**, which specifies the starting point for all dialog box messages, and the specific resource identifier of the control within the dialog box that generates the message.

In general, each control within a dialog box will be given its own resource ID. Each time that control is accessed by the user, a message will be sent, indicating the type of action the user has taken. ObjectWindows uses the resource ID to index the DDVT dispatch table to call the function associated with that control. That function will then decode the message and take appropriate actions.

Activating a Dialog Box

Before a dialog box can be accessed, it must be displayed. To do this you must call the **ExecDialog()** ObjectWindows member function. (**ExecDialog()** is a member of **TModule**, which is a base class of **TApplication**.) Its prototype is shown here:

int ExecDialog(PTWindowsObject *DBox*);

Here, **PTWindowsObject** is a pointer to a windows object. Since **ExecDialog()** is a member function (indirectly) of **TApplication**, its call must be linked to the currently executing application. To obtain the current application, use the **GetApplication()** member function. It returns a pointer to the application. It has this prototype:

PTApplication GetApplication();

Finally, to create the dialog box, use **new**. Therefore, to create a dialog box, use this statement:

GetApplication()–>ExecDialog(new *D-type*(this, "*D-name*"));

Here, *D-type* is the name of dialog box class you create and *D-name* is the name of the dialog box specification in the resource file.

Creating a Simple Dialog Box

For a first dialog box, a simple example will be created. This dialog box will contain three push buttons called Red, Green, and Cancel. When either the Red or Green button is pressed, it will activate a message box indicating the choice selected. The box will be removed from the screen when the Cancel button is pressed.

The program will have a top-level menu containing three options: Dialog 1, Dialog 2, and Help. Only Dialog 1 will have a dialog box associated with it. The Dialog 2 entry is a placeholder so you can define your own dialog box as you work through the examples.

While this and other examples in this chapter don't do much with the information provided by the dialog box, they illustrate the central features you will use in your own applications.

The Dialog Box Example Resource File

Before developing a program that uses a dialog box, you need a resource file that specifies one. The following file defines a menu that is used to activate the dialog box, accelerator keys, and then the dialog box itself. You should enter it into your computer at this time, calling it MYDIALOG.RC.

```
; Sample dialog box and menu resource file.
#include "mydialog.h"

MYMENU MENU
{
  MENUITEM "Dialog &1", IDM_DIALOG1
  MENUITEM "Dialog &2", IDM_DIALOG2
  MENUITEM "&Help", IDM_HELP, HELP
}


MYMENU ACCELERATORS
{
  VK_F2, IDM_DIALOG1, VIRTKEY
  VK_F3, IDM_DIALOG2, VIRTKEY
  VK_F1, IDM_HELP, VIRTKEY
}


MYDB DIALOG 18, 18, 142, 92
CAPTION "Test Dialog Box"
STYLE DS_MODALFRAME | WS_POPUP | WS_CAPTION | WS_SYSMENU
{
    DEFPUSHBUTTON "Red", IDD_RED, 32, 36, 28, 13,
                  WS_CHILD | WS_VISIBLE | WS_TABSTOP
    PUSHBUTTON "Green", IDD_GREEN, 74, 36, 30, 13,
              WS_CHILD | WS_VISIBLE | WS_TABSTOP
    PUSHBUTTON "Cancel", IDCANCEL, 52, 65, 37, 14,
              WS_CHILD | WS_VISIBLE | WS_TABSTOP
}
```

The dialog box definition in this file was created using the Resource Workshop. However, you can simply type in the information and use the Resource Workshop to compile it.

The header file MYDIALOG.H, which is also used by the example program, is shown here:

```
#define IDM_DIALOG1   100
#define IDM_DIALOG2   101
#define IDM_HELP      102

#define IDD_RED       103
#define IDD_GREEN     104
```

Enter this file now.

The Dialog Box Response Functions

At this point, the dialog box will need to respond to two buttons: Red and Green. It doesn't need to respond to the Cancel button because ObjectWindows does this automatically for you. Therefore, inside the dialog class definition, you need to add two response functions, as shown here:

```
// Define a dialog box type.
class MyDialog : public TDialog
{
public:
  MyDialog(PTWindowsObject Owner, LPSTR DName) :
    TDialog(Owner, DName) {}

  // respond to push buttons
  virtual void PBRed(RTMessage Msg) = [ID_FIRST + IDD_RED];
  virtual void PBGreen(RTMessage Msg) = [ID_FIRST + IDD_GREEN];
};
```

The response functions are defined as shown here:

```
// Process an IDD_RED message.
void MyDialog::PBRed(RTMessage Msg)
{
  MessageBox(HWindow, "You pushed Red.", "R E D", MB_OK);
}
```

```
// Process an IDD_Green message.
void MyDialog::PBGreen(RTMessage Msg)
{
  MessageBox(HWindow, "You pushed Green.", "G R E E N", MB_OK);
}
```

Each time the user clicks on a push button, the message associated with it is sent to the dialog box. Therefore, pressing the Red button causes **PBRed()** to be executed. In general, push buttons ignore the contents of **Msg**.

The First Dialog Box Sample Program

Following is the entire dialog box example. When the program begins execution, only the top-level menu is displayed on the menu bar. By selecting Dialog 1, the user causes the dialog box to be displayed. Once the dialog box is displayed, selecting a push button causes the appropriate response. A sample screen is shown in Figure 11-1.

```
// Demonstrate dialog boxes.

#include <owl.h>
#include <string.h>
#include <strstream.h>

#include "mydialog.h"

// Define an application.
class AppName : public TApplication
{
public:
  AppName(LPSTR App_Name, HANDLE ThisInstance, HANDLE PrevInstance,
      LPSTR Args, int VidMode) :
      TApplication(App_Name, ThisInstance, PrevInstance, Args,
            VidMode) {};
  virtual void InitMainWindow();
};

// Define a window type.
```

```
class AppWindow : public TWindow
{
public:

  AppWindow(PTWindowsObject WType, LPSTR WTitle) :
        TWindow(WType, WTitle) {AssignMenu("MYMENU"); }
  virtual void Paint(HDC DC, PAINTSTRUCT &PI);

  virtual void IDMDIALOG1(RTMessage Msg) = [CM_FIRST + IDM_DIALOG1];
  virtual void IDMDIALOG2(RTMessage Msg) = [CM_FIRST + IDM_DIALOG2];
  virtual void IDMHelp(RTMessage Msg) = [CM_FIRST + IDM_HELP];

  // Additional window details go here.
};

// Define a dialog box type.
class MyDialog : public TDialog
{
public:
  MyDialog(PTWindowsObject Owner, LPSTR DName) :
    TDialog(Owner, DName) {}

  // respond to button messages
  virtual void PBRed(RTMessage Msg) = [ID_FIRST + IDD_RED];
  virtual void PBGreen(RTMessage Msg) = [ID_FIRST + IDD_GREEN];
};

// Creates and initializes an instance of the window.
void AppName::InitMainWindow()
{
  MainWindow = new AppWindow(NULL, Name);

  HAccTable = LoadAccelerators(hInstance, "MYMENU");
}

char s[20] = "hello";
int x=1, y=1;

// Process a WM_PAINT message.
void AppWindow::Paint(HDC DC, PAINTSTRUCT &)
```

```
{
  TextOut(DC, x, y, s, strlen(s)); // redisplay string
}


// Process the IDM_DIALOG1 selection.
void AppWindow::IDMDIALOG1(RTMessage Msg)
{
  GetApplication()->ExecDialog(new MyDialog(this, "MYDB"));
}


// Process the IDM_DIALOG2 selection.
void AppWindow::IDMDIALOG2(RTMessage Msg)
{
  MessageBox(HWindow, "2nd Dialog not yet defined",
            "Fill in your own details", MB_OK);
}


// Process the IDM_HELP selection.
void AppWindow::IDMHelp(RTMessage Msg)
{
  MessageBox(HWindow, "Demonstrate A Dialog Box", "Help", MB_OK);
}


// Process an IDD_RED message.
void MyDialog::PBRed(RTMessage Msg)
{
  MessageBox(HWindow, "You pushed Red.", "R E D", MB_OK);
}


// Process an IDD_Green message.
void MyDialog::PBGreen(RTMessage Msg)
{
  MessageBox(HWindow, "You pushed Green.", "G R E E N", MB_OK);
}


// Entry point of windows program.
int PASCAL WinMain(HANDLE ThisInstance, HANDLE PrevInstance,
           LPSTR Args, int VidMode)
{
  AppName App("Demonstrate a Dialog Box", ThisInstance,
          PrevInstance, Args, VidMode);
```

```
    App.Run(); // runs windows application

    return App.Status; // termination status
}
```

Adding a List Box

To continue exploring dialog boxes, let's add another control to the dialog box defined in the previous program. One of the most common controls after the push button is the list box.

First, add this list box description to the dialog definition in the MYDIALOG.RC resource file:

```
CONTROL "Listbox Tester", ID_LB1,
        "LISTBOX", LBS_NOTIFY | WS_CHILD | WS_VISIBLE |
        WS_BORDER | WS_VSCROLL, 4, 12, 49, 30
```

Sample output from the first dialog box

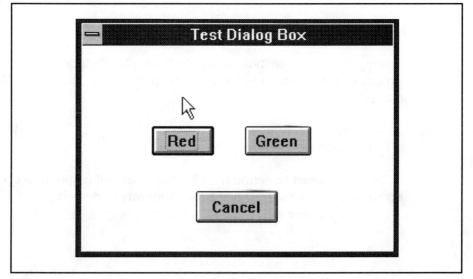

That is, your dialog box definition should now look like this:

```
MYDB DIALOG 18, 22, 142, 102
CAPTION "Test Dialog Box"
STYLE DS_MODALFRAME | WS_POPUP | WS_CAPTION | WS_SYSMENU
{
    DEFPUSHBUTTON "Red", IDD_RED, 32, 46, 28, 13,
                  WS_CHILD | WS_VISIBLE | WS_TABSTOP
    PUSHBUTTON "Green", IDD_GREEN, 74, 46, 30, 13,
                  WS_CHILD | WS_VISIBLE | WS_TABSTOP
    PUSHBUTTON "Cancel", IDCANCEL, 52, 75, 37, 14,
              WS_CHILD | WS_VISIBLE | WS_TABSTOP
    CONTROL "Listbox Tester", ID_LB1,
            "LISTBOX", LBS_NOTIFY | WS_CHILD | WS_VISIBLE |
            WS_BORDER | WS_VSCROLL, 4, 12, 49, 30
}
```

You also need to add this macro to MYDIALOG.H:

```
#define ID_LB1          105
```

ID_LB1 identifies the list box specified in the dialog box definition in the resource file. It is used as an index to the message response function that responds to activity inside the list box.

Responding to a List Box

Responding to list box events is a simple addition to the preceding program. First, add this message response function to the **MyDialog** class declaration:

```
// Respond to list box
virtual void LB1(RTMessage Msg) = [ID_FIRST + ID_LB1];
```

Next, you need to define the function that will respond to events that occur inside this list box. List boxes generate various types of messages. The two used here are

Macro	Event
LBN_DBLCLK	The user has double-clicked an entry in the list or selected it using a keyboard command
LBN_SETFOCUS	The list box has just acquired input focus

These messages are contained in **Msg.LP.Hi.**

The meaning of **LBN_DBLCLK** is self evident. **LBN_SETFOCUS** is more subtle. This message is generated each time the list box gains input focus. This message occurs only when the input focus was elsewhere, perhaps on a push button or edit box, and then moved to the list box. This message is not generated during the normal activity of using a list box.

Unlike a push button, a list box is a control that receives messages as well as generating them. You can send a list box any of 26 different messages. However, the example sends only these three:

Macro	Purpose
LB_ADDSTRING	Adds a string (selection) to the list box
LB_GETCURSEL	Requests the index of the item selected
LB_RESETCONTENT	Clears all items from the list box

LB_ADDSTRING is a message that tells the list box to add a specified string to the list. That is, the specified string becomes another selection within the box. You will see how to use this message shortly. **LB_GETCURSEL** causes the list box to return the index of the item within the list box that the user selects. All list box indexes begin with zero. To clear all items from the list box, your application sends it the **LB_RESETCONTENT** message.

To send a message to the list box (or any other control), use the **SendDlgItemMsg()** ObjectWindows function. Its prototype is shown here:

DWORD SendDlgItemMsg(int *ID*, WORD *ID_Msg*, WORD *WParam*,
DWORD *LParam*);

SendDlgItemMsg() sends to the control (within the dialog box) whose ID is specified by *ID* the message specified by *ID_Msg*. Any additional information required by the message is specified in *WParam* and *LParam*. The additional information, if any, varies from message to message. If there is no additional information to pass to a control, the *WParam* and the *LParam* arguments should be zero.

Here is the list box response function:

```
// Process the first list box.
void MyDialog::LB1(RTMessage Msg)
{
  DWORD i;
  char str[80];
  ostrstream ostr(str, sizeof(str));

  // list box is acquiring input focus
  if(Msg.LP.Hi==LBN_SETFOCUS) {
    SendDlgItemMsg(ID_LB1, LB_RESETCONTENT, 0, 0L);

    SendDlgItemMsg(ID_LB1, LB_ADDSTRING, 0, (LONG)"Apple");
    SendDlgItemMsg(ID_LB1, LB_ADDSTRING, 0, (LONG)"Orange");
    SendDlgItemMsg(ID_LB1, LB_ADDSTRING, 0, (LONG)"Pear");
    SendDlgItemMsg(ID_LB1, LB_ADDSTRING, 0, (LONG)"Grape");
  }

  // user made a selection
  if(Msg.LP.Hi==LBN_DBLCLK) {
    i = SendDlgItemMsg(ID_LB1, LB_GETCURSEL, 0, 0L);  // get index
    ostr << "Index in list is: " << i << ends;
    MessageBox(HWindow, str, "Selection Made", MB_OK);
  }
}
```

This function works like this. Whenever user activity occurs in the list box, the **LB1** message is sent by the dialog box, causing the **LB1()** function to be called. When the list box becomes the focus of input (for example, when the user first clicks on it), **Msg.LP.Hi** contains the **LBN_SETFOCUS** message. Each time this message is received, **LB1()** first clears any existing contents of the list box by sending the **LB_RESETCONTENT** message, which requires no additional information. Once the box is clear, it loads the list box with a set of strings that become the items from which the user will choose. (By default, the list box is empty.) Each string is added to the list box by calling **SendDlgItemMsg()** with the **LB_ADDSTRING** message. The string to add is pointed to by the *LParam* parameter. (The type cast to **LONG** is necessary.) In this case, each string is added to the list box in the order it is sent. (However, depending upon how you construct the list box, it is possible to have the items displayed in alphabetical order.) If the number of items you send to a list box exceeds what it can display in its window, vertical scroll bars will be added automatically.

Each time the user selects an item in the list box either by double-clicking or by positioning the highlight using the arrow keys and then pressing ENTER, the **LBN_DBLCLK** message is generated. To determine which selection was made, the function sends the **LB_GETCURSEL** message to the list box. The list box returns the index of the item.

For your convenience, the entire expanded dialog box program is shown here. (Be sure to update MYDIALOG.H and MYDIALOG.RC before compiling this program.)

```
// Demonstrate list boxes.

#include <owl.h>
#include <dialog.h>
#include <string.h>
#include <strstream.h>

#include "mydialog.h"

// Define an application.
class AppName : public TApplication
{
public:
  AppName(LPSTR App_Name, HANDLE ThisInstance, HANDLE PrevInstance,
      LPSTR Args, int VidMode) :
      TApplication(App_Name, ThisInstance, PrevInstance, Args,
            VidMode) {};
  virtual void InitMainWindow();
};
```

```
// Define a window type.
class AppWindow : public TWindow
{
public:

  AppWindow(PTWindowsObject WType, LPSTR WTitle) :
        TWindow(WType, WTitle) {AssignMenu("MYMENU"); }
  virtual void Paint(HDC DC, PAINTSTRUCT &PI);

  virtual void IDMDIALOG1(RTMessage Msg) = [CM_FIRST + IDM_DIALOG1];
  virtual void IDMDIALOG2(RTMessage Msg) = [CM_FIRST + IDM_DIALOG2];
  virtual void IDMHelp(RTMessage Msg) = [CM_FIRST + IDM_HELP];

  // Additional window details go here.
};

// Define a dialog box.
class MyDialog : public TDialog
{
public:
  MyDialog(PTWindowsObject Owner, LPSTR DName) :
    TDialog(Owner, DName) {}

  // Respond to button messages
  virtual void PBRed(RTMessage Msg) = [ID_FIRST + IDD_RED];
  virtual void PBGreen(RTMessage Msg) = [ID_FIRST + IDD_GREEN];

  // Respond to list box
  virtual void LB1(RTMessage Msg) = [ID_FIRST + ID_LB1];
};

// Creates and initializes an instance of the window.
void AppName::InitMainWindow()
{
  MainWindow = new AppWindow(NULL, Name);

  HAccTable = LoadAccelerators(hInstance, "MYMENU");
}

char s[20] = "hello";
```

```
int x=1, y=1;

// Process a WM_PAINT message.
void AppWindow::Paint(HDC DC, PAINTSTRUCT &)
{
  TextOut(DC, x, y, s, strlen(s)); // redisplay string
}

// Process the IDM_DIALOG1 selection.
void AppWindow::IDMDIALOG1(RTMessage Msg)
{
  GetApplication()->ExecDialog(new MyDialog(this, "MYDB"));
}

// Process the IDM_DIALOG2 selection.
void AppWindow::IDMDIALOG2(RTMessage Msg)
{
  MessageBox(HWindow, "2nd Dialog Box not yet defined",
         "Fill in your own details", MB_OK);
}

// Process the IDM_HELP selection.
void AppWindow::IDMHelp(RTMessage Msg)
{
  MessageBox(HWindow, "Demonstrate Menus", "Help", MB_OK);
}

// Process an IDD_RED message.
void MyDialog::PBRed(RTMessage Msg)
{
  MessageBox(HWindow, "You pushed Red.", "R E D", MB_OK);
}

// Process an IDD_Green message.
void MyDialog::PBGreen(RTMessage Msg)
{
  MessageBox(HWindow, "You pushed Green.", "G R E E N", MB_OK);
}

// Process the first list box.
void MyDialog::LB1(RTMessage Msg)
{
```

```
    DWORD i;
    char str[80];
    ostrstream ostr(str, sizeof(str));

    // list box is acquiring input focus
    if(Msg.LP.Hi==LBN_SETFOCUS) {
      SendDlgItemMsg(ID_LB1, LB_RESETCONTENT, 0, 0L);

      SendDlgItemMsg(ID_LB1, LB_ADDSTRING, 0, (LONG)"Apple");
      SendDlgItemMsg(ID_LB1, LB_ADDSTRING, 0, (LONG)"Orange");
      SendDlgItemMsg(ID_LB1, LB_ADDSTRING, 0, (LONG)"Pear");
      SendDlgItemMsg(ID_LB1, LB_ADDSTRING, 0, (LONG)"Grape");
    }

    // user made a selection
    if(Msg.LP.Hi==LBN_DBLCLK) {
      i = SendDlgItemMsg(ID_LB1, LB_GETCURSEL, 0, 0L);  // get index
      ostr << "Index in list is: " << i << ends;
      MessageBox(HWindow, str, "Selection Made", MB_OK);
    }
}

// Entry point of windows program.
int PASCAL WinMain(HANDLE ThisInstance, HANDLE PrevInstance,
          LPSTR Args, int VidMode)
{
  AppName App("Demonstrate a Dialog with a List Box", ThisInstance,
         PrevInstance, Args, VidMode);

//  if(App.HAccTable)
  App.Run(); // runs windows application

  return App.Status; // termination status
}
```

Sample output from this program is shown in Figure 11-2.

Sample output that includes a list box

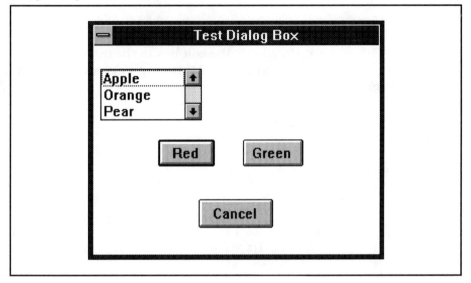

Adding an Edit Box

The last control you will add to the sample dialog box is the edit box. Edit boxes are particularly useful because they allow the user to enter a string of his or her own choosing. Before you can use an edit box, you must define one in your resource file. For this example, add this line to the definition of your dialog box in the MYDIALOG.RC file:

```
CONTROL "Default", ID_EB1, "EDIT", ES_LEFT | ES_AUTOHSCROLL |
        WS_CHILD | WS_VISIBLE | WS_BORDER | WS_HSCROLL |
        WS_TABSTOP, 61, 8, 56, 19
```

This definition causes a standard edit box to be created that contains the default text "Default". It also contains a horizontal scroll bar.

Next, add this macro definition to MYDIALOG.H:

```
#define ID_EB1          106
```

The next step in adding the edit box to the dialog box is to include its message response function in **MyDialog**'s class declaration, as shown here:

```
// Define a dialog box.
class MyDialog : public TDialog
{
public:
  MyDialog(PTWindowsObject Owner, LPSTR DName) :
    TDialog(Owner, DName) {}

  // Respond to button messages
  virtual void PBRed(RTMessage Msg) = [ID_FIRST + IDD_RED];
  virtual void PBGreen(RTMessage Msg) = [ID_FIRST + IDD_GREEN];

  // Respond to list box
  virtual void LB1(RTMessage Msg) = [ID_FIRST + ID_LB1];

  // Respond to edit box
  virtual void EB1(RTMessage Msg) = [ID_FIRST + ID_EB1];
};
```

Edit boxes recognize many messages and generate several of their own. However, for the purpose of this example, the edit box response function will respond to only one message: **EN_KILLFOCUS**. This message is generated when the edit box loses input focus. When this message is received, the function sends the message **EM_GETLINE** to the edit box. This causes the edit box to copy the current contents of the box to the string pointed to by the *LParam* parameter. It also returns the length of the string. The string is not null terminated, so a null terminator is added manually by the function. Finally, the function displays the string. The **EB1()** function is shown here:

```
// Respond to EB1 message.
void MyDialog::EB1(RTMessage Msg)
{
  char str[80];
```

```
if(Msg.LP.Hi==EN_KILLFOCUS) {
  str[SendDlgItemMsg(ID_EB1, EM_GETLINE, 0, (LONG) str)] = '\0';
  MessageBox(HWindow, str, str, MB_OK);
}
}
```

Try adding these additions to the previous program.

As stated, an edit box responds to many messages and generates several of its own. While it is beyond the scope of this book to discuss them all, one other message you might want to try having **EB1()** respond to is **EN_CHANGE**. This message is sent when (and if) the contents of the box are altered.

Some Things to Try

Before continuing, you might want to try adding other controls to the dialog box or defining your own. Dialog boxes are the principal way your applications interact with Windows, and you should master their use.

CHAPTER

Using Icons, Cursors, and Bitmaps

This final chapter explains how to control the appearance of two important items linked with all Windows applications: the design of the icon that is displayed when an application is minimized and the shape of the mouse cursor. How to display a bitmapped image is also discussed.

Icons, cursors, and bitmaps are resources that must be defined within an application's resource definition file. The easiest way to create these resources is to use the Resource Workshop. However, the definitions for these items as they are used in the examples in this chapter are given in text form, and you can simply type them in.

Changing the Icon and the Cursor

Although masked by ObjectWindows, all Windows applications first create a window class that defines the attributes of the window, including the shape of the application's icon and cursor. (Here, the word "class" is used in a non-C++ sense.) This window class is then registered with Windows. Only after these steps have been performed can you actually create a window. When you use ObjectWindows, these steps are automatically performed for you. In the process, default icon and cursor shapes are defined. Since the shapes of the icon and cursor are defined when a window class is created, you must actively intervene in the window-class-creation process to alter these items. To do this, you need to redefine another virtual function defined by **TWindow**, called **GetWindowClass()**. This function obtains the window class definition before it is registered and allows you to change certain attributes.

The prototype for **GetWindowClass()** is shown here:

void GetWindowClass(WNDCLASS _FAR & *WClass*);

The structure WNDCLASS is defined in WINDOWS.H, and it contains the attributes that define the window class. In addition to several other pieces of information, the structure contains these two elements:

HICON hIcon;   Handle of minimized icon

HCURSOR hCursor;   Handle of cursor

As stated, these values are given defaults by ObjectWindows. The icon is a blank box and the mouse cursor is the arrow.

To change the shape of the minimized icon and cursor, you must first obtain the window class structure and then change their handles to the objects you want. To do this, you must redefine **GetWindowClass()** inside your main window class definition. Inside this function, first call **TWindow**'s base class version of **GetWindowClass()** to obtain the default window attributes provided by ObjectWindows. Next, load the new icon and the new cursor. For example, this redefinition of **GetWindowClass()** loads the icon identified as MYICON and the cursor called MYCURSOR:

```
// change window defaults .
virtual void GetWindowClass(WNDCLASS _FAR &WClass) {
  TWindow::GetWindowClass(WClass);
  WClass.hIcon = LoadIcon(hInst, "MYICON");
  WClass.hCursor = LoadCursor(hInst, "MYCURSOR");
}
```

Here, **hInst** is the handle of the current instance of the program that is obtained from the **TApplication** class. (You will see how, shortly.)

Before developing a complete program to demonstrate changing the minimized icon and cursor, it is necessary to discuss the operation of the **LoadIcon()** and **LoadCursor()** API functions.

LoadIcon()

The **LoadIcon()** function has this prototype:

HICON LoadIcon(HANDLE *hInst*, LPSTR *IName*);

Here, HICON is a type that holds an icon handle. The handle to the current instance of the application is passed in *hInst* and the name of the icon as defined in the application's resource file is passed in the string pointed to by *IName*. The function returns **NULL** if it cannot load the icon. It returns the handle of the icon, otherwise.

In addition to using icons that you create, you can specify one of Windows' five built-in icons. To use a built-in icon, set the *hInst* argument to **NULL** and then use one of these macros for the *IName* argument:

Macro	Icon Style
IDI_APPLICATION	Standard default icon
IDI_ASTERISK	Information symbol
IDI_EXCLAMATION	Exclamation point
IDI_HAND	Stop sign
IDI_QUESTION	Question mark

For example, to change the icon to a stop sign, use this statement:

```
WClass.hIcon = LoadIcon(NULL, IDI_HAND);
```

LoadCursor()

The **LoadCursor()** function works much like **LoadIcon()**. Its prototype is shown here:

HCURSOR LoadCursor(HANDLE *hInst*, LPSTR *CName*);

Here, **HCURSOR** is a type that holds handles to cursors. The *hInst* parameter holds the handle of the current instance of the application. The name of the cursor as defined inside your application's resource file is pointed to by *CName*. The function returns the handle to the cursor if successful. It returns **NULL** otherwise.

In addition to using the cursors you define, you can use any of the 11 built-in cursors. Some of the most common are shown here:

Macro	Cursor Type
IDC_ARROW	Default arrow cursor
IDC_CROSS	Crosshair
IDC_IBEAM	I-beam
IDC_WAIT	Hourglass

To use a built-in cursor, set *hInst* to **NULL** and use one of the built-in cursor macros for the *CName*.

Defining an Icon and a Cursor

As stated, when you create your own icons or cursors, you will need to use the Resource Workshop. The Workshop contains a paint editor that allows you to draw the icon or cursor. When you save your project, your resource file is automatically updated with the icon or cursor. For the examples that follow, you will need both an icon and a cursor definition. Either create these by using the Resource Workshop or enter the following into your resource file. Call the file IC.RC. (If you use the definitions given here, your program will display output similar to that shown in Figure 12-1.)

```
; Define an icon.
MYICON ICON
{
    '00 00 01 00 01 00 20 20 10 00 00 00 00 00 E8 02'
    '00 00 16 00 00 00 28 00 00 00 20 00 00 00 40 00'
    '00 00 01 00 04 00 00 00 00 00 80 02 00 00 00 00'
    '00 00 00 00 00 00 00 00 00 00 00 00 00 00 00 00'
    '00 00 00 00 80 00 00 80 00 00 00 80 80 00 80 00'
    '00 00 80 00 80 00 80 80 00 00 80 80 80 00 C0 C0'
    'C0 00 00 00 FF 00 00 FF 00 00 00 FF FF 00 FF 00'
    '00 00 FF 00 FF 00 FF FF 00 00 FF FF FF 00 AA AA'
    'AA AA AA AA AA AA AA AA AA AA AA AA AA AA AA AA'
    'AA AA AA AA AA AA AA AA AA AA AA AA AA AA AA AA'
    'AA AA AA AA AA AA AA AA AA AA AA AA AA AA AA AA'
    'CA AA CC CA AA CC CA AC AA AC AA AA CA AA AA AA'
```

```
'CA AC AA AC AC AA AC AC AA AC AA AA AA AA AA AA'
'CA AC AA AA AC AA AC AC AA AC AA AA CA AA AA AA'
'CA AC AA AA AC AA AC AC AA AC AA AA CA AA AA AA'
'CA AC AA AC AC AA AC AC CA AC AA AA CA AA AA AA'
'CA AA CC CA AA CC CA AC AC CA AA AA CA AA AA AA'
'CA AA AA AA AA AA AA AA AA AA AA AA CA AA AA AA'
'CA AA AA AA AA AA AA AA AA AA AA AA CA AA AA AA'
'CA AA AA AA AA AA AA AA AA AA AA AA CA AA AA AA'
'AA AA AA AA AA AA AA AA AA AA AA AA AA AA AA AA'
'AA AA AA AA AA AA AA AA AA AA AA AA AA AA AA AA'
'AA AA AA AA AA AA AA AA AA AA AA AA AA AA AA AA'
'AA AA AA AA AA AA AA AA AA AA AA AA AA AA AA AA'
'AA AA AA AA AA AC CA AA AA AA AA AA AA AA AA AA'
'AA AA AA AA AA AA AC AA AA AA AA AA AA AA AA AA'
'AA AC AA AA AC AA AC AA AA AA AA AA AA AA AA AA'
'AA AC AA CA AC AA AC CA AA AA AA AA AA AA AA AA'
'AA AC AA CA AC AA CA AC AA AA AA AA AA AA AA AA'
'AA AC AC AC AC AA CA AC AA AA AA AA AA AA AA AA'
'AA AC AC AC AC AA CA AC AA AA AA AA AA AA AA AA'
'AA AC CA AA CC AA CA AC AA AA AA AA AA AA AA AA'
'AA AC CA AA CC AA AA AA AA AA AA AA AA AA AA AA'
'AA AC AA AA AC AA AA AA AA AA AA AA AA AA AA AA'
'AA AC AA AA AC AA AA AA AA AA AA AA AA AA AA AA'
'AA AA AA AA AA AA AA AA AA AA AA AA AA AA AA AA'
'AA AA AA AA AA AA AA AA AA AA AA AA AA AA AA AA'
'AA AA AA AA AA AA AA AA AA AA AA AA AA AA AA AA'
'AA AA AA AA AA AA AA AA AA AA AA AA AA AA AA AA'
'AA AA AA AA AA AA AA AA AA AA AA AA AA AA 00 00'
'00 00 00 00 00 00 00 00 00 00 00 00 00 00 00 00'
'00 00 00 00 00 00 00 00 00 00 00 00 00 00 00 00'
'00 00 00 00 00 00 00 00 00 00 00 00 00 00 00 00'
'00 00 00 00 00 00 00 00 00 00 00 00 00 00 00 00'
'00 00 00 00 00 00 00 00 00 00 00 00 00 00 00 00'
'00 00 00 00 00 00 00 00 00 00 00 00 00 00 00 00'
'00 00 00 00 00 00 00 00 00 00 00 00 00 00 00 00'
'00 00 00 00 00 00 00 00 00 00 00 00 00 00 00'
}

MYCURSOR CURSOR
{
    '00 00 02 00 01 00 20 20 02 00 00 00 00 00 30 01'
    '00 00 16 00 00 00 28 00 00 00 20 00 00 00 40 00'
```

```
'00 00 01 00 01 00 00 00 00 00 00 02 00 00 00 00'
'00 00 00 00 00 00 00 00 00 00 00 00 00 00 00 00'
'00 00 FF FF FF 00 00 00 00 00 00 00 00 00 00 00'
'00 00 00 00 00 00 00 00 00 00 00 00 00 00 00 00'
'00 00 00 00 00 00 00 00 00 00 00 00 00 00 00 00'
'00 00 00 00 00 00 00 00 00 00 00 00 00 00 00 00'
'00 00 00 00 00 00 00 00 00 00 00 00 00 00 00 00'
'00 00 00 00 00 00 00 00 00 00 00 00 00 00 00 00'
'00 00 00 00 00 00 00 00 00 00 00 00 00 00 00 00'
'00 00 00 00 00 00 00 00 00 00 00 00 00 00 00 00'
'00 00 00 00 00 00 00 00 00 00 5F FF FF FC 6F FF'
'FF FA 77 FF FF F6 7B FF FF EE 7D FF FF DE 7E FF'
'FF BE 7F 7F FF 7E 7F B8 1E FE 7F D7 ED FE 7F EF'
'F3 FE 7F D7 F3 FE 7F DB EB FE 7F BD DD FE 7F BE'
'BD FE 7F BE 7D FE 7F BE BD FE 7F BD DD FE 7F DB'
'EB FE 7F D7 F3 FE 7F EF F3 FE 7F D7 ED FE 7F B8'
'1E FE 7F 7F FF 7E 7E FF FF BE 7D FF FF DE 7B FF'
'FF EE 77 FF FF F6 6F FF FF FA 5F FF FF FC 3F FF'
'FF FE 00 00 00 00'
}
```

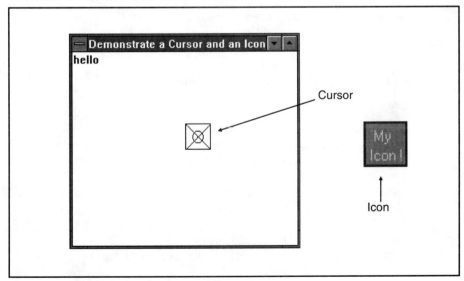

FIGURE
12-1

The customized icon and mouse cursor

A Sample Program That Demonstrates an Icon and a Cursor

The following program uses the icon and cursor defined in the preceding resource file. The icon is displayed when the window is minimized. The cursor will be used when the mouse pointer is over the window.

```
// Demonstrate a cursor and an icon.

#include <owl.h>
#include <string.h>
#include <strstream.h>

HANDLE hInst; // holds handle of current instance

// Define an application.
class AppName : public TApplication
{
public:
  AppName(LPSTR App_Name, HANDLE ThisInstance, HANDLE PrevInstance,
      LPSTR Args, int VidMode) :
      TApplication(App_Name, ThisInstance, PrevInstance, Args,
            VidMode) {};
  virtual void InitMainWindow();
};

// Define a window type.
class AppWindow : public TWindow
{
public:

  AppWindow(PTWindowsObject WType, LPSTR WTitle) :
        TWindow(WType, WTitle) {}
  virtual void Paint(HDC DC, PAINTSTRUCT &PI);

  // change window defaults
  virtual void GetWindowClass(WNDCLASS _FAR &WClass) {
    TWindow::GetWindowClass(WClass);
    WClass.hIcon = LoadIcon(hInst, "MYICON");
```

```
   WClass.hCursor = LoadCursor(hInst, "MYCURSOR");
  }
  // Additional window details go here.
};

// Creates and initializes an instance of the window.
void AppName::InitMainWindow()
{
  MainWindow = new AppWindow(NULL, Name);

  hInst = hInstance;
}

char s[20] = "hello";
int x=1, y=1;

// Process a WM_PAINT message.
void AppWindow::Paint(HDC DC, PAINTSTRUCT &)
{
  TextOut(DC, x, y, s, strlen(s)); // redisplay string
}

// Entry point of windows program.
int PASCAL WinMain(HANDLE ThisInstance, HANDLE PrevInstance,
          LPSTR Args, int VidMode)
{
  AppName App("Demonstrate a Cursor and an Icon", ThisInstance,
        PrevInstance, Args, VidMode);

  App.Run(); // runs windows application

  return App.Status; // termination status
}
```

Notice that both **LoadIcon()** and **LoadCursor()** require the instance handle of the application. In ObjectWindows, this handle is kept in a member variable, called **hInstance,** defined by **TApplication.** However, **GetWindowClass()** is a member of **TWindow,** which is not related to **TApplication** and cannot directly access **hInstance**. One way to solve this problem is to make a global copy of **hInstance** that can be used by **GetWindowClass()** when it calls **LoadIcon()** and **LoadCursor().** The reason this works is that ObjectWindows initializes the application before it initializes the main window. This is why **hInst** is global and why it is assigned the **hInstance** handle inside the **InitMainWindow()** function. The icon and cursor are shown in Figure 12-1.

Using a Bitmap

A *bitmap* is a graphics image. Since Windows is a graphics-based operating system, it makes sense that you can include graphics images in your applications. It is important to understand that you can draw graphics images, such as lines, circles, and boxes, inside the client area of a window by using the rich set of graphics functions contained in the Windows API. However, a bitmap, and the mechanism used to display one, are separate from those types of graphics. A bitmap is a self-contained graphical resource that your program utilizes as a single entity. Put differently, a bitmap generally contains a complete image that your program displays in its totality.

Creating a Bitmap

Before continuing, you must create a bitmap resource. As with other graphical resources, the best way to create your own bitmaps is to use the Resource Workshop's paint editor. However, if you want, you can add the following bitmap definition to your IC.RC resource file. Doing so will cause your bitmap to look like the one shown in Figure 12-2.

```
MYBITMAP BITMAP
{
    '42 4D 76 08 00 00 00 00 00 00 76 00 00 00 28 00'
    '00 00 40 00 00 00 40 00 00 00 01 00 04 00 00 00'
    '00 00 00 08 00 00 00 00 00 00 00 00 00 00 00 00'
    '00 00 10 00 00 00 00 00 00 00 00 00 80 00 00 80'
    '00 00 00 80 80 00 80 00 00 00 80 00 80 00 80 80'
    '00 00 80 80 80 00 C0 C0 C0 00 00 00 FF 00 00 FF'
    '00 00 00 FF FF 00 FF 00 00 00 FF 00 FF 00 FF FF'
    '00 00 FF FF FF 00 BB BB BB BB BB BB BB BB BB BB'
    'BA BB BB BB BB BB BB BB BB BB BB BB BB BB BB BB'
    'BB BB AB BB BB BB BB BB BB BB BB BB BB BB BB BB'
    'BB BB BB BB BB BB BB BB BB BB BA BA BB BB AB AB'
```

```
'BB BB BB BB BB BB BB BB BB BB BB BB BB BB BB BB'
'BA BA BB BB BB BB BB BB BB BB BB BB BB BB BB BB'
'BB BB AB AB BB BB BB BB BB BB BB BB BB BB BB BB'
'BB BB BB BB BB BB BB BB BB BB BB BB BB BB BB BB'
'BB BB BB BB BB BB BB BB BB BB BA BE BB BB BB BB'
'BB BB BB BB BB BB BB BB BB BB BB BB BB BB BB BB'
'BB BB BB BB BB BB BB BB BB BB BB BE EE BB BB BB'
'BB BB BB BB BB BB BB BB BB BB BB BB BB BB BB AB'
'BB BB BB BB BB BB BB BB BB BB BA BA BB EB BB BB'
'BB BB BB BB BB BB BB BB BB BB BB BB BB BB BB BB'
'BB BB BB BB BB BB BB BB BB BB BB BE BB BE BB BB'
'BB BB BB BB BB BB BB 9B BB BB BB BB BB BB BB AA'
'AB BB BB BB BB BB BB BB BB BB BB BE BB BB EE BB'
'BB BB BB BB BB BB BB 9B BB BB BB BB BB BB BB BB'
'BB BB BB BB BB BB BB BB BB BB BB BE BB BB BB EB'
'BB BB BB BB BB BB B9 9B BB BB BB BB BB BB BB BA'
'BA BB BB BB BB BB BB BB BB BB BB BE BB BB BB BE'
'BB BB BB BB BB BB 9C 9B BB BB BB BB BB BB BB AB'
'BB BB BB BB BB BB 9C 9B BB BB BB BE BB BB BB BB'
'EE BB BB BB BB BB 9C 9B BB BB BB BB BB BB BB BB'
'BB BB BB BB BB BB BB BB BB BB BB BE BB BB BB BB'
'BB EB BB BB BB B9 CC 9B BB BB BB BB BB BB 9B AB'
'AB BB BB BB BB BB BB BB BB BA BB BE BB BB BB BB'
'BB BE EB BB BB 9C CC 9B BB BB BB BB BB B9 AA 9B'
'BB BB BB BB BB BB BB BB BB BB BB BE BB BB B9 BB'
'BB BB BE BB B9 CC CC 9B BB BB BB BB B9 9C 9C 9B'
'BB BB BB BB BB BB BB BB BB BA BA BE BB BB B9 BB'
'BB BB BB EB B9 CC CC 9B BB BB BB 99 9C CC AA AA'
'BB BB BB BB BB BB BB BB BB BB BB BE BB BB B9 BB'
'BB BB BB BE EC CC CC 9B BB B9 99 CC CC CC 99 BB'
'BB BB BB BB BB BB BB BB BB BB BB BE BB BB B9 9B'
'BB BB BB B9 CE CC CC 9B B9 9C CC CC CC CC 9B BB'
'BB BB BB BB BB BB BB BB BB BB BB BE BB BB BB 9B'
'BB BB BB 9C CC CC CC 99 9C CC CC CC CC CC 9B BB'
'BB BB BE BB BB BB BB BB BB BB BB BE BB BB BB 9B'
'BB BB BB 9C CC CC 99 9C CC CC CC CC CC CC 9B BB'
'BB BB BE BB BB BB BB AB BB BB BB BE BB BB BB 9B'
'BB BB B9 CC C9 99 CC 9C CC CC CC CC CC CC 9B BB'
'BB BB BE BB BB BB BB BB BB DD DB BE BB BB BB 99'
'9B BB 9C 99 9C CC CC 9C CC CC CC CC CC CC 9B BB'
'BB BB BE EB BB BB BB AB AB BB BB BE BB BB BB BB'
'B9 99 99 CC CC CC CC 9C CC CC CC CC CC CC 9B BB'
```

```
'BB BB BE EB BB BB BB BB BB BB BB BE BB BB BB BB'
'BB 99 99 99 99 CC CC 9C CC CC CC CC CC CC 9B BB'
'BB BB BE EB BB BB BB BB BB BB BB BE BB BB BB BB'
'BB 9B B9 9B BB 99 9C 9C CC CC CC CC CC CC 9B BB'
'BB BB BE EB BB BB BB BB BB BB BB BE BB BB BB BB'
'BB BB BB 9B BB BB 99 CC CC CC CC CC CC CC 9B BB'
'BB BB BE EB BB BB BB BB BB BB BB BE BB BB BB BB'
'BB BB BB 9B BB BB 99 CC CC CC CC CC CC CC 9B BB'
'BB BB BE CE BB BB BB BB BB BB BB BE BB BB BB BB'
'BB BB BB 9B BB BB B9 CC CC CC CC CC CC CC 9B BB'
'BB BB EC CE BB BB BB BB BB BB BB BE BB 9B BB BB'
'BB BB B9 9B BB BB B9 CC CC CC CC CC CC CC 9B BB'
'BB BB EC CE BB BB BB BB BB BB BB BE B9 B9 9B BB'
'BB BB BB BB BB BB B9 CC CC CC CC CC CC CC 99 9B'
'BB BB EC CE BB BB BB BB BB BB BB BE BB BB B9 BB'
'BB BB BB BB BB BB B9 CC CC CC CC CC CC CC 9B BB'
'BB BB EC CE BB BB BB BB BB BB BB BE BB BB BB 9B'
'BB BB B9 99 99 99 99 99 99 9C CC CC CC CC 9B BB'
'BB BB EC CC EB BB BB BB BB BB BB BE BB BB BB B9'
'9B BB B9 BB BB BB B9 BB BB B9 99 99 99 99 99 99'
'99 99 EC CC EB BB BB BB BB BB BB BE BB BB BB BB'
'B9 BB BB 9B BB BB BB BB BB BB BB BB BB BB BB BB'
'BB 99 E9 99 EB BB BB BB BB BB BB BE BB BB BB BB'
'BB 99 BB BB BB BB BB BB BB BB BB BB BB BB BB BB'
'BB BB EB BB E9 9B BB BB BB BB BB BE BB BB BB BB'
'BB BB 9B BB BB BB BB BB BB BB BB BB BB BB BB BB'
'BB BB EB BB EB BB BB BB BB BB BB BE BB BB BB BB'
'BB BB B9 BB BB BB BB BB BB BB BB BE BB BB BB BB'
'BB BB EB BB BE BB BB BB BB BB BB BE BB BB BB BB'
'BB BB BB 99 BB BB BB BB BB BB BB BE EB BB BB BB'
'BB BB EB BB BE BB BB BB BB BB BB BE BB BB BB BB'
'BB BB BB BB 99 BB BB BB BB BB BB BE EB BB BB BB'
'BB BB EB BB BE BB BB BB BB BB BB BE BB BB BB BB'
'BB BB BB BB BB 99 BB BB BB BB BB BE EE BB BB BB'
'BB BB EB BB BE BB BB BB BB BB BB BE BB BB BB BB'
'BB BB BB BB BB BB 99 BB BB BB BB BB EE BB BB BB'
'BB BB EB BB BE BB BB BB BB BB BB BE BB BB BB BB'
'BB AB BA AB B9 BB BB 99 9B BB BB BB BB EE BB BB'
'BB BB EB BB BB EB BB BB BB BB BB BE BB BB BB BB'
'BB BB BB BB B9 BB BB BB B9 9B BB BB BB EC EB BB'
'BB BE BB BB BB EB BB BB BB BB BB BE BE BB BB BB'
'BB AB AA AA A9 BB BB BB BB B9 9B BB BB BE EB BB'
```

```
'BB BE BB BB BB EB BB BB BB BB BB EE BB BB BB BB'
'BB BB BB BB BB 9B BB BB BB BB B9 9B BB BE EB BB'
'BB BE BB BB BB BB BB BB BB BB BB BB BB BB BB BB'
'BB AB AB BB BB 99 99 BB BB BB BB B9 99 BE EB BB'
'BB BE BB BB BB BB BB BB BB BB BB BB BB BB BB BB'
'BB BB BB BB BB BB BB 99 99 99 BB BB BB 9E CE BB'
'BB BE BB BB BB BB BB BB BB BB BB BB BB BB BB BB'
'BB BB BB BB BB BB BB BB BB BB 99 99 99 9C EE EE'
'BB BE BB BB BB BB BB BB BB BB BB BB BB B9 99 99'
'99 99 99 99 99 BB BB BB BB BB BB BB BB B9 E9 99'
'BE BE BB BB BB BB BB BB BB BB BB BB BB 99 BB BB'
'B9 BB BB BB B9 BB BB BB BB BB BB BB BB BB EB BB'
'BE EB BB BB BB BB BB BB BB BB BB B9 BB BB BB BB'
'BB BB BB BB B9 BB BB BB BB BB BB BB BB BB BE BB'
'BB BA BB BB BB BB BB BB BB BB BB BB B9 BB BB BB'
'BB BB BB BB B9 BE EE EE EE EE EE EE EE EE EE BB'
'BB BB BB BB BB BB BB BB BB BB BB BB B9 BB BB BB'
'AB BB BE AE EE EB BB BB BB BB BB BB BB BB BB BB'
'BB BA BA BB BB BB BB BB BB BB BB BB B9 BB BB BB'
'AB BB BB BB BE EE EB BB BB BB BB BB BB BB BB BB'
'BB BB BB BB BB BB BB BB BB BB BB BB B9 BB BB BB'
'AB AB BB AB A9 BB BB BB BB BB BB BB BB BB BB BA'
'BB BB BB BB BB BB BB BB BB BB BB BB B9 BB BB BB'
'AB AB BB BB B9 BB BB BB BB BB BB BB AB AB BB BB'
'BB BB BB BB BB BB BB BB BB BB BB BB B9 BB BB BA'
'AB BB BB BB B9 BB BB BB BB BB BB BB AB BB BB BA'
'BA BB BB BB BB BB BB BB BB BB BB BB B9 BB BB BB'
'BB BB BB BB B9 BB BB BB BB BB BB BB AB AB AB BB'
'BB BA BB BB BB BB BB BB BB BB BB BB BB BB BB BA'
'AA AB BB BB B9 BB BB BB BB BB BB BB AB AB BB BB'
'BB BB BB BB BB BB BB BB BB BB BB BB B9 99 99 99'
'99 99 99 99 99 BB BB BB BB BB BB BB BB BB BB BB'
'BB BA BA BB BB BB BB BB BB BB BB BB BB BB BB BB'
'BB BB BB BB BB BB BB BB BB BB BB BB BB BB BB BB'
'BB BB BB BB BB BB BB BB BB BB BB BB BB BB BB BB'
'BB BB BB BB BB BB BB BB BB BB BB BB BB BB BB BB'
'BB BB BB BB BB BB BB BB BB BB BB BB BB BB BB BB'
'BB BB BB BB BB BB BB BB BB BB BB BB BB BB BB BB'
'BB BB BB BB BB BB BB BB BB BB BB BB DD BB BB BB'
'BB BB BB BB BB BB BB BB BB BB BB BB BB BB BB BB'
'BB BB BB BB BB BB'
}
```

Sample output from the bitmap program

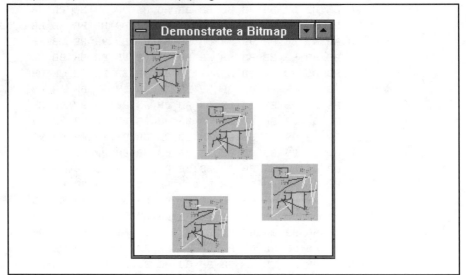

Displaying a Bitmap

Once you have created a bitmap and included it in your application's resource file, you can display it as many times as you want. In the example that follows, the bitmap will be displayed each time the left mouse button is pressed, at the current location of the mouse pointer.

Displaying a bitmap requires that you perform a number of steps. Here is the general procedure. First, you must obtain the device context. Then you must load the bitmap and store its handle. You must obtain an equivalent memory device context that will hold the bitmap until it is displayed; that is, a bitmap is held in memory until it is copied to your window. To actually display the bitmap, you first select it and then call the **BitBlt()** function, which finally displays the image.

Here is the code that implements the steps just described. It loads a bitmap and displays it on the screen each time the left mouse button is pressed.

```
// Display a bitmap.
void AppWindow::WMLButtonDown(RTMessage Msg)
```

```
{

    HBITMAP hBit;
    HDC DC, memDC;

    DC = GetDC(HWindow);
    hBit = LoadBitmap(hInst, "MYBITMAP");
    memDC = CreateCompatibleDC(DC);
    SelectObject(memDC, hBit);
    BitBlt(DC, Msg.LP.Lo, Msg.LP.Hi, 64, 64, memDC, 0, 0,SRCCOPY);
    ReleaseDC(HWindow, DC);
    DeleteDC(memDC);
}
```

Let's examine this function step by step.

First, the function declares a bitmap handle called **hBit**, of handle type
HBITMAP. This will hold the handle to the bitmap when it is loaded.
Next, two device context handles are declared. **DC** holds the current
device context as obtained by **GetDC()**. The other, called **memDC**, holds
the device context of the memory that stores the bitmap until it is drawn
in the window.

The first action the function takes is to obtain a device context. This
is necessary because the bitmap will be displayed in the client area of
the window. Next, the bitmap is loaded and its handle is stored in **hBit**,
using the **LoadBitmap()** API function, whose prototype is shown here:

HBITMAP LoadBitmap(HANDLE *hInst*, LPSTR *BName*)

As stated, HBITMAP is a type that holds a handle to a bitmap. The
current instance is specified in *hInst*, and a pointer to the name of the
bitmap as specified in the resource file is passed in *BName*. (Windows
also defines several built-in bitmaps, which you may want to explore on
your own.) The function returns the handle to the bitmap, or null if an
error occurs.

Next, a memory context is created that will hold the bitmap using the
CreateCompatibleDC() API function. Its prototype is shown here:

HDC CreateCompatible(HDC *dc*)

This function returns a handle to a region of memory that is compatible with the device context of the window, specified by *dc*. This memory will be used to construct an image before it is actually displayed.

Before a bitmap can be displayed, it must be selected, using the **SelectObject()** API function. Since there can be several bitmaps associated with an application, you must select the one you want to display before it can actually be output to the window. The **SelectObject()** prototype is shown here:

HANDLE SelectObject(HDC *mdc*, HANDLE *object*)

Here, *mdc* is the memory device context that holds the object, and *object* is the handle of that object.

To actually display the object once it has been selected, use the **BitBlt()** API function. Its prototype is shown here:

BOOL BitBlt(HDC *dest*, int *x*, int *y*, int *width*, int *height*,
            HDC *source*, int *sourcex*, int *sourcey*,
            DWORD *raster*);

Here, *dest* is the handle of the target device context, and *x* and *y* are the upper-left coordinates, at which point the bitmap will be drawn. The width and height of the bitmap are specified in *width* and *height*. The *source* parameter contains the handle of the source device context, which in this case will be the memory context obtained using **GetCompatibleDC()**. The *sourcex* and *sourcey* specify the upper-left coordinates in the bitmap. These values are usually zero. The value of *raster* determines how the bit-by-bit contents of the bitmap will actually be drawn on the screen. Some of its most common values are shown here:

Raster Macro	Effect
SRCCOPY	Copies bitmap as is, overwriting existing information
SRCAND	ANDs bitmap with current destination
SRCPAINT	ORs bitmap with current destination
SRCINVERT	XORs bitmap with current destination

In the program, the call to **BitBlt()** displays the entire bitmap at the destination location at which the left mouse button was pressed, simply copying the bitmap to the window.

After the bitmap is displayed, both device contexts are released. Only a device context obtained through a call to **GetDC()** can be released using a call to **ReleaseDC()**. To release the memory device context, use **DeleteDC()**, which takes as its parameter the handle of the device context to release.

The Complete Bitmap Example Program

Here is the complete program that displays a bitmap. Sample output is shown in Figure 12-2.

```
// Demonstrate a bitmap.

#include <owl.h>
#include <string.h>
#include <strstream.h>

HANDLE hInst; // holds the current instance

// Define an application.
class AppName : public TApplication
{
public:
  AppName(LPSTR App_Name, HANDLE ThisInstance, HANDLE PrevInstance,
      LPSTR Args, int VidMode) :
      TApplication(App_Name, ThisInstance, PrevInstance, Args,
            VidMode) {};
  virtual void InitMainWindow();
};

// Define a window type.
class AppWindow : public TWindow
{
public:

  AppWindow(PTWindowsObject WType, LPSTR WTitle) :
```

```
        TWindow(WType, WTitle) {}
  virtual void Paint(HDC DC, PAINTSTRUCT &PI);

  virtual void WMLButtonDown(RTMessage Msg) =
    [WM_FIRST + WM_LBUTTONDOWN]; // respond to left button

  // change defaults
  virtual void GetWindowClass(WNDCLASS _FAR &WClass) {
    TWindow::GetWindowClass(WClass);
    WClass.hIcon = LoadIcon(hInst, "MYICON");
    WClass.hCursor = LoadCursor(hInst, "MYCURSOR");
  }
  // Additional window details go here.
};


// Creates and initializes an instance of the window.
void AppName::InitMainWindow()
{
  MainWindow = new AppWindow(NULL, Name);

  hInst = hInstance; // save the current instance
}

char s[20] = "hello";
int x=1, y=1;

// Process a WM_PAINT message.
void AppWindow::Paint(HDC DC, PAINTSTRUCT &)
{
  TextOut(DC, x, y, s, strlen(s)); // redisplay string
}

// Display a bitmap.
void AppWindow::WMLButtonDown(RTMessage Msg)
{

  HBITMAP hBit;
  HDC DC, memDC;

  DC = GetDC(HWindow);
  hBit = LoadBitmap(hInst, "MYBITMAP");
```

```
   memDC = CreateCompatibleDC(DC);
   SelectObject(memDC, hBit);
   BitBlt(DC, Msg.LP.Lo, Msg.LP.Hi, 64, 64, memDC, 0, 0,SRCCOPY);
   ReleaseDC(HWindow, DC);
   DeleteDC(memDC);
}


// Entry point of windows program.
int PASCAL WinMain(HANDLE ThisInstance, HANDLE PrevInstance,
          LPSTR Args, int VidMode)
{
  AppName App("Demonstrate a Bitmap", ThisInstance,
         PrevInstance, Args, VidMode);

  App.Run(); // runs windows application

  return App.Status; // termination status
}
```

Learning More about ObjectWindows

While the material in Part II of this book is sufficient to get you started with ObjectWindows programming, you will want to continue to learn about it by thoroughly studying the Borland reference manuals. Also, if you are new to Windows programming in general, you must thoroughly study a Windows programming reference. Windows is a very complex operating system, and the more you know about it, the better you will be at writing applications for it.

Index